# History of the Episcopal Church of Liberia Since 1980

## WORKS BY
## D. ELWOOD DUNN

*The Foreign Policy of Liberia During the Tubman Era* (1979)

*Historical Dictionary of Liberia*, 1st ed. (with Svend Holsoe, 1985)

*Liberia: A National Polity in Transition* (with Byron Tarr, 1988)

*A History of the Episcopal Church in Liberia, 1821–1980* (1992)

*Historical Dictionary of Liberia*, 2nd ed. (with A.Beyan & C.P. Burrowes, 2001)

"Constitutional Documents of Liberia, 1820–1861," in *Constitutional Documents of the United States of America 1776–1869,Supplement: Hawaii and Liberia*, edited with Robert Stauffer and Miriam Leitner (2008)

*Liberia and the United States During the Cold War: Limits of Reciprocity* (2009)

*The Annual Messages of the Presidents of Liberia, 1848–2010* (editor, 2011)

*Liberia and Independent Africa, 1940s to 2012: A Brief Political Profile* (2012)

# History of the Episcopal Church of Liberia Since 1980

## A Sequel

D. Elwood Dunn

HAMILTON BOOKS
*Lanham • Boulder • New York • Toronto • London*

Published by Hamilton Books
An imprint of The Rowman & Littlefield Publishing Group, Inc.
4501 Forbes Boulevard, Suite 200, Lanham, Maryland 20706
www.rowman.com

6 Tinworth Street, London SE11 5AL, United Kingdom

Copyright © 2020 by The Rowman & Littlefield Publishing Group, Inc.

*All rights reserved.* No part of this book may be reproduced in any form or by any electronic or mechanical means, including information storage and retrieval systems, without written permission from the publisher, except by a reviewer who may quote passages in a review.

British Library Cataloguing in Publication Information Available

**Library of Congress Control Number: 2020902791**
ISBN: 978-0-7618-7098-2 (pbk. : alk. paper)
ISBN: 978-0-7618-7099-9 (electronic)

∞™ The paper used in this publication meets the minimum requirements of American National Standard for Information Sciences—Permanence of Paper for Printed Library Materials, ANSI/NISO Z39.48-1992.

*St. John's Episcopal Church, present day*
Photograph courtesy of St. John's Episcopal Church, Lower Buchanan, Grand Bassa County, Liberia.

St. John's Episcopal Church
Lower Buchanan, Grand Bassa County, Liberia (author's home Church)
Established 1908, first edifice consecrated by
Bishop Samuel David Ferguson, February 25, 1912
Present edifice consecrated by Bishop Coadjutor Dillard Houston Brown,
March 22, 1964

# Contents

List of Illustrations and Tables ... ix

Foreword ... xi
  *Bishop Jonathan B. B. Hart*

Prologue ... xiii

Acknowledgments ... xv

List of Abbreviations ... xvii

Introduction ... 1

1 Episcopate of Bishop George Daniel Browne (1970–1993) ... 7
  A Measure of the Man, George Daniel Browne ... 9
  Domestic and International Contexts of Browne's Ministry ... 10
  Stewardship and Self-Support ... 10
  Evangelism ... 18
  Education ... 26
  Social Issues, Civil War, and the Church to 1993 ... 42
  Identity with Church of the Province of West Africa as Covenant
    Redefines Relations with American Church ... 47
  Browne's Ministry Assessed ... 52

2 Interim Between Bishop Browne and Bishop Neufville
  (1993–1996) ... 61
  Browne's Health Condition and Ad Hoc Administrative
    Arrangements ... 61
  State of the Church on Browne's Sudden Death:
    Leadership Controversy ... 67

|   |   |   |
|---|---|---|
|   | Church of the Province of West Africa Oversight Amid Uneasy Relations Between Neufville and Team Ministry | 69 |
|   | Election of Successor Diocesan Bishop | 72 |
|   | Assessing the Interim Period | 75 |
| 3 | Episcopate of Bishop Edward Wea Neufville II (1996–2007) | 79 |
|   | Another Challenging Beginning | 79 |
|   | Journey to the Episcopacy | 80 |
|   | Vision and Thrust of Leadership | 86 |
|   | Stewardship Ministry | 88 |
|   | Evangelism Ministry | 93 |
|   | Education Ministry | 99 |
|   | External Ties: Church of the Province of West Africa and The Episcopal Church (USA) | 107 |
|   | Neufville's Episcopacy Assessed | 110 |
| 4 | Episcopate of Bishop Jonathan Bau-Bau Bonaparte Hart (2008–) | 117 |
|   | Election of Bishop Coadjutor | 120 |
|   | Events Leading to Consecration of Twelfth Diocesan Bishop | 122 |
|   | Highlights of First Twelve Years | 126 |
|   | Re-Launching Sustainability Efforts: Episcopal Church of Liberia Strategic Plan of 2019 | 129 |
|   | Tentative Assessment | 136 |

| | |
|---|---|
| Conclusion | 139 |
| Epilogue: Church That Was, Church That Is, Church of the Future | 143 |
| Appendix 1  Bishops of the Episcopal Church of Liberia | 151 |
| Appendix 2  Biographical Data of Episcopal Church of Liberia and Diaspora Clergy | 153 |
| Appendix 3  Chancellors of the Diocese Since 1976 | 163 |
| Appendix 4  Presidents of Cuttington College/University, 1949–2019 | 165 |
| Appendix 5  Brief Historical Sketch of St. John's Episcopal Church, Lower Buchanan, Grand Bassa County | 167 |
| List of Interviews | 173 |
| Bibliography | 175 |
|    Primary Archives | 175 |
|    Sources | 176 |
| Index | 181 |
| About the Author | 189 |

# Illustrations and Tables

Frontispiece. St. John's Episcopal Church, present day.
Photograph courtesy of St. John's Episcopal Church,
Lower Buchanan, Grand Bassa County, Liberia.     v

Figure A.1.   Dr. D. Elwood Dunn, author.
Courtesy of D. Elwood Dunn Archives.     183

Table 1.   A Review of the Assessment, Rally, and
Endowment Balances for 1981–1990.     17

Table 2.   A Review of Transfers from the TEC to the ECL.
1995–2006.     92

**Photo spread**

George Daniel Browne, Diocesan Bishop, 1970–1993.
Courtesy of the Bishop's family.

Edward Wea Neufville, II, Diocesan Bishop, 1996–2007.
Courtesy of the Bishop's family.

Jonathan B. B. Hart, Diocesan Bishop, 2008.
Courtesy of Bishop Hart.

Joseph K, Dadson, CPWA/Interim Bishop, 1993–1996.
Courtesy of the CPWA.

Bishop and Mrs. Clavender Railey Browne.
Courtesy of Bishop Browne's family.

Bishop and Mrs. Louise Morais Neufville.
Courtesy of Bishop Neufville's family.

The Rev. Emmanuel Hodges (1952–2006).
Courtesy of D. Elwood Dunn Archives.

The Rev. Theodora N. Brooks.
Courtesy of Rev. Brooks.

Bishop Neufville exits Cavalla River after Baptism.
Courtesy of Bishop Neufville.'s family

The Rev. Samuel Lloyd (left) (Chaplain, Sewanee: The University of the South), Bishop Browne (center), and author D. Elwood Dunn (right).
Courtesy of D. Elwood Dunn Archives.

The Rev. Seth C. Edwards, President, CU, 1949–1960.
Courtesy of D. Elwood Dunn Archives.

Dr. Christian E. Baker, President, CU, 1960–1972.
Courtesy of Dr. Yede Baker Dennis.

The Rev. E. Bolling Robertson, Interim President, 1972–1973.
Courtesy of D. Elwood Dunn Archives.

The Rev. Emmanuel W. Johnson, President, CU, 1974–1980.
Courtesy of Rev. Johnson's family.

Dr. Stephen M. Yekeson, President, CU, 1981–1986.
Courtesy of Mrs. Janet Yekeson.

The Rev. Samuel Y. Reed, Interim President. 1987.
Courtesy of D. Elwood Dunn Archives.

Dr. Melvin J. Mason, President, CU, 1988–2002,
Courtesy of Dr. Mason.

Dr. Henrique F. Tokpa, President, CU, 2002–2015.
Courtesy of Dr. Tokpa.

Dr. D. Evelyn Kandakai, Interim President, 2015–2016.
Courtesy of Dr. Kandakai.

The Rev. Dr. Herman B. Browne, President, CU, 2016–.
Courtesy of Dr. Browne.

# Foreword

The Episcopal Church of today is heir to a history that now spans almost 200 years. From the seeds planted in today's Maryland County, the Church has expanded and now has a presence in fourteen counties of the Republic, impacting the lives of our people through its ministries of evangelism, education, and healing. Though that impact has been uneven over time and space, testimonies to that presence dot our landscape.

Dr. D. Elwood Dunn first undertook to tell the Church's story in the 1980s as he published in 1992, the first book titled *A History of the Episcopal Church in Liberia, 1821–1980*. In this present iteration of his continuing effort, he has updated the story of the Church in his new book titled *History of the Episcopal Church of Liberia Since 1980: A Sequel*. The new book seeks to relate the history of the Church to the developments in the country since 1980, as it explores the leadership of those of us who have overseen the spiritual and material development of the Church.

To clearly appreciate where we are and where we wish to go, we must know where we are coming from as a Church people. Dunn has helped to remind us about our past, and he has done this with passion and clarity. It pleases me to present this new book about the history of our Church to the Diocese, to the people of Liberia, and to the global Anglican Communion.

The Most Rev. Dr. Jonathan B. B. Hart
Bishop of the Episcopal Church of Liberia, Monrovia, Liberia
October 2019

# Prologue

More than three decades ago, I was inspired by circumstances of exile from my Liberian homeland to undertake research into the history of the Missionary District of the Episcopal Church of the United States in Liberia. Given the urgings and encouragement of the then Diocesan Bishop of Liberia, The Most Rev. George Daniel Browne, it was for me personally rewarding that I was able to complete and publish the study, as well as deliver copies of the book to the Bishop before his death on February 14, 1993. *A History of the Episcopal Church in Liberia, 1821–1980* was released mid-1992 and copies reached Bishop Browne October 1992.

The first volume ended largely with highlighting the episcopacy of Bishop Browne. We could do no more since he was the incumbent Bishop and only beginning the second decade of what came to be a twenty-two-year episcopacy. I was fully aware of the extraordinary character of the Bishop's leadership and ministry and longed even then for the opportunity to cover in some subsequent book the entirety of his episcopacy. The circumstances of his death and burial and the crisis in the Church that ensued heightened my passion to tell this part of the story of my beloved Church.

In retirement from the faculty of that citadel of American Episcopalianism, Sewanee: The University of the South, since 2012, I soon began preparing for the task. As the Liberian civil war came to an end following a comprehensive peace agreement in 2003, I developed an avid interest in things archival. I soon teamed up with colleagues at Indiana University in the enhancement of its already important Liberia collections as we approached the family of former President William V. S. Tubman with regard to what remained of his presidential papers at his estate in Totota, Bong County. While we were working on that project, we visited Bishop Browne's own estate in Virginia, Montserrado County where his widow and children decided to have the badly damaged but rich Browne collection deposited with the Archives of the Episcopal Church in Austin, Texas, USA for safe keeping and for posterity. Knowing that the Browne papers were in Austin, I began my research for the contents of this present volume with several visits to Texas. And then the hunt for primary source material continued, first with Mrs. Louise Morais Neufville, the widow of Browne's successor, The Right Rev. Edward W. Neufville II, and subsequently with a number of largely Liberian makers of church history, including the present Diocesan Bishop, The Most Rev. Jonathan B. B. Hart. We availed ourselves as well of documents related to the Liberian church at headquarters of the Episcopal Church (TEC) in New York City, as we did the papers of the Order of the Holy Cross (OHC) at its West Park, New York headquarters.

As was the case with the first book, this sequel book is not an "official" account of the history of the Episcopal Church of Liberia (ECL). Nor is it about theoretical and conceptual issues of conversion, or in the genre of defending faith and mission such that no line separates "research from sermons" or "scholars from parishioners." Rather, the study is an analytical historical account of the ECL since 1980. It focuses the episcopacies of the three diocesan bishops who have led the church and their times. As such, it seeks to understand the ministry of the church in the contexts of the society within which it is embedded and of the external environment with which it interacts.

# Acknowledgments

Projects of this nature happen because many are inspired to lend a helping hand. Those that have provided modest grants include: the Historical Society of the Episcopal Church, Bishop Mark Beckwith of the Episcopal Diocese of Newark, and individuals within the Liberian Episcopal Community in the United States (LECUSA). These resources supplemented my own and enabled me to access the Archives of the Episcopal Church in Austin, Texas, the Order of the Holy Cross in West Park, New York, and trips to Liberia from my Silver Spring, Maryland base. I gratefully acknowledge these institutions and individuals, as I do Sam Brawand of Brawand Consulting for professional formatting services rendered.

A relatively large number of individuals responded to my requests for research material and other information. Foremost among the individuals are Mrs. Louise Morais Neufville, widow of Bishop Neufville and their son, Attorney Edward W. Neufville III, who welcomed me into their homes in Sumter, South Carolina and Paynesville (Liberia), respectively, sharing many of the Bishop's church papers and documents, and responding to innumerable questions. The incumbent Bishop of the Episcopal Church of Liberia (ECL), The Most Rev. Jonathan B. B. Hart was most generous with his time when I showed up at his office in Liberia between 2016 and 2019. I thank Bishop Hart as well for honoring the effort by writing the Foreword to this book. Others who liberally shared ECL-related documents include Alpha Simpson (papers of the late Chancellor C. L. Simpson Jr.), Taylor Neal (papers of the late Trustee chair, Juanita Neal), and Wilbert Clarke (a former Trustee chair as well). The Treasurer's office of the American church was also helpful in sharing information regarding ECL endowment and related matters.

There is yet another category of individuals, this one the largest, who consented to be my interviewees. They responded to questionnaires, informal email requests, phone calls, as well as face-to-face interviews. The Rev. Canon J. Jellico Bright provided the most extensive and detailed responses, and then patiently answered my many follow-up questions. The Rev. Suzanne A. Fageol's phone interview was critical to the research as she is the American female priest who helped pave the way for the ECL's decision to admit women to ordained ministry. And Dr. Herman Browne's gift of his late father's diaries and log books, in addition to an interview, remains deeply appreciated. Then there is The Rev. Fr. A-Too Williams, rector of St. Stephen's Episcopal Church, Monrovia, who was the critical *on the ground* resource person for me, digging up and sending me information right up to the concluding stages of the project. Thank you, Fr. A-Too! The full list of my interviewees can be found in the List of Interviews.

Three persons read drafts of the manuscript and offered valuable critical comments—Dr. C. William Allen, Ms. Marlene Smith (MDiv, Union Theological Seminary, New York), and my college professor, Dr. John Gay. My sincere thanks to all of them! Gay's interest in the project was particularly stimulating and encouraging. He went beyond providing critical comments as he repeatedly probed and challenged, often sending me back to the drawing board on sections of the manuscript. And when he finally endorsed the manuscript with these words—"You have done well. . . . I have very few if any substantive text changes, mostly because you are a professional historian and writer!"—I felt rewarded to receive such words as though I was in a college course, which I had given my best efforts. Thank you, John!

In the course of things, families endure such undertakings. Matilda and the adult kids have been no exception. I thank them all, including the two grandsons, Abram Elwood Dunn and Lucas Thomas Dunn, who arrived while the study was in progress. For errors of fact and judgment, the responsibility can only be mine.

D. Elwood Dunn<br>
Silver Spring, Maryland, USA<br>
October 2019

# List of Abbreviations

| | |
|---|---|
| AACC | All African Conference of Churches |
| ASHA | American Schools and Hospitals Abroad |
| ATR | African Traditional Religions |
| BAFFA | Bolahun Alumni Family and Friends Association |
| BD | Bachelor of Divinity |
| CIE | Cuttington In Exile |
| CLJ | The Community of the Love of Jesus Christ |
| CORAT | Christian Organizations Research and Advisory Trust |
| CPWA | Church of the Province of West Africa |
| CU | Cuttington University |
| CUC | Cuttington University College |
| DFMS | Domestic and Foreign Missionary Society |
| ECL | Episcopal Church of Liberia |
| ECOMOG | Economic Community Monitoring Group |
| ECOWAS | Economic Community of West African States |
| ECUSA | Episcopal Church USA |
| GOL | Government of Liberia |
| GST | Gbarnga School of Theology |
| IGNU | Interim Government of National Unity |
| IMC | Interfaith Mediation Committee |
| IPWA | Internal Province of West Africa |
| LAP | Liberia Action Party |
| LCC | Liberian Council of Churches |

| | |
|---|---|
| LECUSA | Liberian Episcopal Community in the United States |
| LISGIS | Liberia Institute of Statistics and Geo-Information Services |
| MDiv | Masters of Divinity |
| MLRP | Mbalotahun Leprosy Rehabilitation Program |
| MOU | Memorandum of Understanding |
| MRU | Mano River Union |
| NDPL | National Democratic Party of Liberia |
| NPFL | National Patriotic Front of Liberia |
| NPRAG | National Patriotic Reconstruction Assembly Government |
| OAU | Organization of African Unity |
| OHC | Order of the Holy Cross |
| RDI | Rural Development Institute |
| STM | Masters of Sacred Theology |
| TEC | The Episcopal Church (USA) |
| UL | University of Liberia |
| UNESCO | United Nations Educational, Scientific and Cultural Organization |
| USAID | United States Agency for International Development |
| UTO | United Thank Offering |
| VTS | Virginia Theological Seminary |

# Introduction

The first volume adopted as a framing tool or model Roland Oliver's 1952 *The Missionary Factor In East Africa*.[1] Oliver underscoring of the role of Christian missions in the making of modern Africa became a refrain in the study of mid-twentieth-century Africa. It was this refrain or investigative trend that was pursued in my first foray into the writing of the church's history, though my study was confined to Liberia and the work largely of a single Christian mainline denomination.

This sequel volume posits a church challenged with a paradigm shift, perhaps an identity crisis more complex than the nineteenth-century church-planting ethos. That ethos would evolve to a transplanted American church in Liberia as opposed to the struggle to make real the Episcopal Church of Liberia (ECL). Though the ECL has since 1982 expanded its vision with the formal severance of ecclesiastical ties with the American church, The Episcopal Church (USA) (TEC), and by joining the Anglican Church of the Province of West Africa (CPWA), there is an ongoing transition with the making and remaking of new relationships. It is this ongoing transition, punctuated by moments of hesitancy, that points to the identity crisis the church currently faces. The current Covenant arrangement between the Liberian and American Episcopal Churches underscores a dilemma of acceptance and rejection.

The identity crisis also finds expression in two other ways. The first is a theological mindset of the Liberian society as set forth by Bishop George Daniel Browne in a 1980 Commencement address at the Liberia Baptist Theological Seminary. He contended that this mindset predisposes toward religious syncretism. The second way in which the identity crisis finds expression is a national social character that has Liberia, according to a Christian Organizations Research and Advisory Trust (CORAT) study, "hanging between the U.S. and Africa" where it has seemingly "copied the cultural patterns of the former at the expense of forging its own identity," a strong wind of change, notwithstanding. In like manner as Liberia seems to be in search of a national identity, many Liberian Episcopalians and perhaps communicants of other mainline Christian denominations as well, also seem to be in search of a new religious identity. This situation has prompted one observer to characterize Liberian Episcopalians as being of a divided spiritual personality dubbed "spiritual schizophrenia" or "theological schizophrenia." The identity crisis, in evidence in the 1970s, remained unresolved as sorting it out was arrested with the intervention of a national crisis and civil war between 1980 and 2003. How has the church related to this unresolved issue since the 2003 end of the civil war?[2]

Bishop Browne was expansive regarding the theological mindset. He held that the mindset of Liberian society is derived from a way of life characterized by concepts, opinions, and a variety of approaches to religion. One group, African Traditional Religions (ATR), views God as a force indifferent to his creation, "so they have to rely on natural forces and the spirits of their ancestors as intermediaries between them and God."[3] For them God is too far away for direct contact. They thus resort to spirit-possessed rocks, rivers, and other such objects. It is suggested that one can extract potency from any of these objects and infuse them into an amulet through ritual. Considered a religion of fear by ethicists, it teaches that people inherently are suspicious of one another and thus the need for protective gears. Though some observers think there is more tolerance than implied here, approximately 70% of Liberians adhered to this religion prior to the civil war of 1989–2003.

The remaining groups of Liberians are Muslims and Christians. For Muslims, salvation comes by walking in a straight and narrow path in accordance with certain practices and principles. About 15% of Liberians followed this faith, again before the war. So, between followers of the African Traditional Religions and Islam we had the adherence of some 85% of the national population.[4]

For the Christian population with mainline denominations in the lead in terms of influence in society, many confused religious "syncretism" with Christianity. Syncretism is a mixture of ATR, Islam. and some elements of Christianity combined, as well as basic human secularism. Against this backdrop, most Christians moved freely between mainline Churches and Pentecostal groups claiming to be serving "the same God." It is this syncretist religion that held sway over many in pre-war Liberia and thus was a powerful context for genuine Christian ministry. As the Church in community sought to serve the economic, social, and spiritual needs of people and to provide them a sense of belonging and dignity, a people with this mindset posed a serious challenge to the traditional church.

Fast-forward to the post-civil war era and the national census tells us a different story—not of theological mindset (that is left to us to discover), but of fundamental reversals in percentages of religious adherents. If we are to believe the 2008 National Census we now have 85.6% of Liberians claiming to be Christians, 12.2% Muslim, and a 0.6% of adherents to the ATR. These percentages are largely borne out by the Pew survey of religions in Africa in their 2010 Pew-Templeton Global Religions Futures.[5] Add to this the Pentecostal surge in Liberia, or that "movement within evangelical Christianity that places special emphasis on the direct personal experience of God through the baptism of the Holy Spirit, as shown in the biblical account of the Day of Pentecost." And a healthy reversal such that one begins to think of "congregational diversification" rather than a process of endless fragmentation that saps the energy of the church and its organizational unity. The Liberian version of this movement has seemingly overtaken in Liberia the mainline Christian denominations, for it is reported that in 2005, the Pentecostals counted 3,000 denominations with upwards of 200,000 people in Liberia as adherents. The challenge to mainline denominations such as the ECL is unambiguous. With the dramatic reversal in numbers, are we looking at a fundamental reversal in mindset?[6]

The other way in which the identity crisis finds expression is a problematic national character that has Liberia "hanging between the U.S. and Africa." A 1977 study commissioned by the ECL, executed by the CORAT of Africa, and written by a group of East African churchmen, offers some interesting insights into a Diocese then seeking autonomy from TEC toward joining CPWA. Writing about the contextual framework or the Liberian setting of the church and estimating the Liberian character, the study observed, "Liberians are in a sense people in search of their own national identity. The Liberian nation is historically unique in that it is the only African Republic never under European domination. Yet it is also unique in its close ties to the United States." It continues: "In truth Liberia has always been hanging between the U.S. and Africa. It has copied the cultural patterns of the former at the expense of forging its own identity. The absence of identity is manifested in the lack of creativity within the arts and sciences. The field of literature provides a prime example. Almost all of the serious literature within the country has been imported from the United States." While Liberia excessively emulates America, there is serious Liberian literature, though it has not been adequately absorbed into the way of life of the people. And there is more Liberian literature being produced but among Diaspora Liberians with the challenge of remaining outside and not transferring to the motherland.[7]

The study acknowledges that a wind of change was evident in Liberia of the 1970s such that while Liberians struggled with a national identity issue, many Liberian Christians were also searching for a new "religious identity," and many people looked to "independent churches" for personal and cultural fulfillment. "The tremendous impact of these churches cannot be doubted." As one Episcopalian churchman stated, 'they attend my church in the morning with their minds, but in the afternoon and evening they attend the independent churches with their heart and money.' Furthermore, the study continued: "The fact that so many Liberians attend a traditional church out of social obligation and another church out of spiritual needs suggests the presence of a divided spiritual personality (spiritual schizophrenia), with an ultimate destruction of an integrated spiritual life and witness. Here is a major spiritual problem within the church which calls for much deeper study and renewal in the life of the church so that it relates far more closely to the cultural needs and spiritual problem of life today in Liberia."[8]

All told, and while flagging, not necessarily pursuing these framing ideas, it is imperative that we bear in mind both Browne's "theological mindset" and the CORAT report's articulation of a national identity problem for a church struggling to minister to a rapidly changing population of rural and urban dwellers. The convergence then of the theological mindset with the national identity problem has the propensity to lead to a "divided spiritual personality" and slow genuine church growth. In actuality, the move from TEC to CPWA entails serious reflection on establishing "a new self-identity" which is "rooted in African and more especially Liberian culture." The challenge remains to think, teach; indeed to preach at all levels in a truly Liberian context "as well as drawing on the worldwide and historical riches of the church universal."[9]

This book begins with a prologue aimed at setting forth the purpose of the undertaking, its context and framing ideas for the historical narrative. Put otherwise, why am I doing this study, what do I hope to achieve, and how do I intend to proceed? Taking my cue from the first volume of the history of the Episcopal Church *in* Liberia, which focused on the episcopates of the various Missionary or Diocesan Bishops of the church, this sequel volume will focus the episcopates of Bishop George Daniel Browne (1970–1993), Bishop Edward Wea Neufville II (1996–2007), and the current Bishop Jonathan Bau-Bau Bonaparte Hart who has been in office since 2008. I impose no uniform rubric of development and assessment given the differences in time frames, the peculiar dispositions of each bishop, and the changing character of the societal issues each was challenged to address.

Chapter 1 will introduce Browne's episcopate, take a measure of the man, and then narrate his ministry under the rubrics of stewardship, evangelism, education, social issues, and the church's external relations. This chapter will climax with an assessment of the Browne episcopacy.

Chapter 2 takes up the interregnum occasioned by the civil war in Liberia, Browne's illness and subsequent death, and the high tensions in the church consequent on these developments. The chapter will also feature an assessment of this interim period between Browne and Neufville and how it shaped the church going forward.

Chapter 3 is the episcopate of Bishop Neufville, which begins with an introduction that contextualizes his journey and accession to the leadership of the church. Then in succession, his ministry will be examined under the rubrics of stewardship, evangelism, education, and external ties or the dual relationship with the American church (TEC) and the CPWA. An assessment will then follow of the ministry of the 11th Diocesan Bishop of the church.

Chapter 4 will largely initiate the episcopate of the incumbent Bishop Hart, as well as his rapid rise in the CPWA, first as Dean, then Archbishop of the Internal Province, and finally as Primate of the Province. It will begin with introducing the circumstances that brought him to the high office of Diocesan Bishop—his candidacy, his election as the 12th Diocesan Bishop of the church, and his consecration and installation. His rapid rise in the CPWA will be chronicled, culminating with his accession as the 11th Primate of the Province. Highlights of his first dozen years will be followed by a tentative assessment on his ministry.

A general conclusion and assessment of the work of the ECL will then follow. This will be an attempt to capture the state of Christianity in Liberia and the place of the Episcopal Church in Christian witness. It will climax with an epilogue or reflections on the Episcopal Church *that was*, the Episcopal Church *that is*, and the Episcopal Church *of the future*.

## NOTES

1. Roland Oliver, *The Missionary Factor In East Africa* (London: Longmans Green, 1952).

2. George D. Browne, "The Theological Mindset of The Liberian Society," Commencement Address, Baptist Theological Seminary, Schieffelin, Liberia, Class of 1980, 7 pages, (DFMS Papers), in which he sought to warn the graduates of "the theological snares that await then" as they embark upon their ministries. The DFMS Papers are located in Archives of the Episcopal Church, Austin, Texas, Domestic and Foreign Missionary Society, boxes 2–18 (hereafter cited DFMS Papers).

See also Episcopal Church of Liberia (ECL), "A Survey of the Administrative Organization of the Episcopal Church of Liberia, by CORAT (Africa)," at invitation of Bishop Browne, Nairobi, Kenya, July 1977, 48 pages (DFMS Papers). CORAT is the Christian Organizations Research and Advisory Trust of Africa. Its mission is "to enable Churches and Church-related organizations in Africa improve their management capability."

3. African Traditional Religions (ATR) (Dunn Archives).

4. Religious affiliation of Liberia's population can be gleaned from Liberian National Censuses, including those of 1984 and 2008. See Liberia Institute of Statistics and Geo-Information Services (LISGIS), "Census," 2019, https://www.lisgis.net/ (accessed October 8, 2019).

5. See also Pew 2010 survey of religions in Africa which has 85% of Liberians as Christians, 12% as Muslims, and 1% as ATR/ folk religions. See Pew-Templeton, "Global Religious Futures Project," 2016, http://www.globalreligiousfutures.org/ (accessed October 8, 2019).

6. Herman B. Browne, *Appreciating Pentecostalism*, Monrovia, National Printers, September 2011. See also LISGIS, "Census," and note that the next census which is now due could reveal even greater shifts as the overwhelming Christian numbers is causing stirs within Muslim communities.

7. ECL, "Survey of the Administrative . . . CORAT" (1977).

8. ECL, "Survey of the Administrative . . . CORAT" (1977), 3, 5.

9. ECL, "Survey of the Administrative . . . CORAT" (1977), 16. Note also Bishop Browne's search for a model in East African Church as he undertook a study trip to Uganda in the beginning years of his episcopate.

*Chapter One*

# Episcopate of Bishop George Daniel Browne (1970–1993)

After thirty-one years of clerical ministry, twenty-two years of Episcopal ministry, and ten years of archiepiscopal ministry, Bishop Browne died on February 14, 1993 at the Milwaukee Regional Medical Center at age fifty-nine years, from complications of Isoniazid (INH) Hepatitis. Rites were said over his remains in New York City at the Cathedral Church of St. John the Divine and at a State funeral at Trinity Cathedral in Monrovia on March 9, 1993. He was interred at his estate in Virginia, Montserrado County, Liberia. Thus ended thirty-one years of prodigious ministry having been consecrated the 10th Bishop of the Diocese of Liberia on August 6, 1970 at age thirty-seven years, and enthroned the 6th Archbishop of the Anglican Church of the Province of West Africa on November 22, 1982 at age forty-nine years.

He focused the first decade of his Episcopal ministry on the general themes of self-support, self-governance, and self- propagation, and thought his effort successful regarding self-governance, and while the path to self-support was clear, self-propagation was to be the focus of his ministry in the decade ahead. What actually transpired in the decade of the 1980s and early 1990s will be fleshed out in the pages that follow.

The first volume of the history of Episcopal Church of Liberia (ECL) predicted, that given the dynamism of Browne's leadership to 1980, it would be difficult to imagine anything likely to be of greater import in the remainder of his episcopacy. And yet there was more coming, as we will see going forward given the vicissitudes of the State within which the Church is embedded. Political instability and war changed the calculus.

The decade started with a bloody military coup d'état that toppled the government of President William R. Tolbert Jr. (1971–1980) and with it a True Whig Party hegemony that was in place in excess of a century. Many leading Liberians who were Episcopalians were affected. The society was in disarray. The Bishop was kept extremely busy as he joined efforts with other Christian clergy and later an inter-religious council of Christians and Muslims to mediate in the tense environment. He spoke often in his attempt to calm tempers while seeking to interpret what was transpiring both to his flock and to the society at large. His relationship with the political authorities was both cooperative (member of a National Constitution Commission) and testy as reflected in tense sessions at the Executive Mansion with junta leader Samuel K. Doe and his military colleagues.

As the decade moved to a close in 1989, one began to hear of war and rumors of war. This actually materialized between the end of 1989 and the start of 1990 as it became clear that a National Patriotic Front of Liberia (NPFL) insurgency had taken arms expressly to bring down the government of President Samuel K. Doe (1986–1990). This was to be the beginning of what later became a fourteen-year carnage of death and destruction across Liberia. Browne lived through and sought to minister to his flock in the first couple of years. He spoke about the need for the church to be pastorally visible amid the social cleavages that wracked the society. The church was to be a critical and prophetic voice to guard the interest of God's children through teaching and sensitizing the leadership to the inalienable rights of the individual regardless of status. He acknowledged the high profile of the church in Liberia and recalled the patronage that the church enjoyed at the hands of past governments.

Amid the crisis, the Liberian Council of Churches (LCC) issued press releases and sought audience with President Doe in February 1990. The month of May saw the emergence of an inter-faith mediation committee. Browne experienced a brush with death. NPFL rebels took him at gunpoint from his home because they saw his social gospel work as a threat to Charles Taylor's political ambition. He strove nonetheless to ascertain the whereabouts of his clergy and congregations. By 1991, the Diocese had lost to exile 35% of its clergy and 65% of its congregations. Fr. Christian K. Y. Mulbah Sr. was instrumental in the establishment of a congregation in Danane, Ivory Coast to minister to exile Episcopalians. Bishop Browne kept up his focus on *the shepherd* and *the flock*, reasoning that when the shepherd is away the flock scatters. Meanwhile, his attention was focused on implementing critical decisions of the 1988 and 1990 Diocesan Conventions.

Health issues intervened. He writes in his Diary of September 22, 1991: "Though sick, I worshiped with St Georges' in Caldwell. I did not robe, and could not celebrate. That previous night my pressure had dropped 80/40. I sat most of the service, but stood to preach on "Lord, teach us how to wait.""[1]

Because Suffragan Bishop Neufville was out of country and apparently out of touch with the Diocesan Bishop, Browne appointed The Rev. Fr.

Emmanuel Hodges Vicar General at the head of what became know as the "team ministry." On September 23, 1991 Browne entrusted the affairs of the Diocese to Fr. Hodges.[2]

Back and forth between the United States and Liberia as his health condition allowed, Bishop Browne's last return to the United States is December 29, 1992. On January 8, 1993, he traveled by way of London and once in the States tarried at the "815" headquarters of the Episcopal Church in New York City before returning to Milwaukee where he was in residence with his elder son, Daniel Browne. The last Diary entry I could locate is dated January 11, 1993: "Went to the doctor today at 11:15. Pressure low 90/60, wt 147, potassium low. Met Dr. Earnest. She reinforced the medication."[3] Six weeks later Bishop Browne died.

## A MEASURE OF THE MAN, GEORGE DANIEL BROWNE

Browne was a pastor, a scholar, a theologian, an avid researcher, and a prolific writer. He left behind a rich personal archive perhaps second to no Liberian clergy in recent memory. He also left three completed manuscripts—account of twenty-year episcopacy, his autobiography, and a revision of his master's thesis, "The Christian Approach to the Adherents of the African Traditional Religion."[4] Two have been published posthumously—the autobiography and account of his episcopacy. He was also a complex man as reflected in his dual identity in the Liberian context—paternal line Grebo-Liberian and maternal line immigrant-Liberian. This may have explained his dual ministry in Liberia and beyond, in the Church of the Province of West Africa (CPWA). He felt he needed both for effective ministry, and he was thus at the center of national crises in the 1970s, 1980s, and start of 1990s, even as he collaboratively engaged with social issues in the Province through the periodic issuance of joint pastoral letters with the Bishops of the Province.

He was bold in affirming both indigenous and immigrant heritages. He spoke touchingly of his relationship to his mother, and her circumstances where she had to hand-"wash other people's dirty clothes" to help support him in school. And in affirmation of the Grebo heritage he made clear his thinking in a "Dare to be Different" speech at the inauguration of an ethnic organization, the Popolepo Organization in Monrovia on August 11, 1989 to which he was invited "based on my credentials as a member of the ethnic group described in the constitution [of the organization] as Klao." He was a native of Garraway, now in Grand Kru County. "All my paternal relatives have their roots among the Klao, and I was even born in that township over a half century ago." His theme always was one of national unity, a real symbol of Liberia.[5]

## DOMESTIC AND INTERNATIONAL CONTEXTS OF BROWNE'S MINISTRY

Browne's election as Bishop in 1970 occurred in the context of a slowly changing Liberia. The presidency of William V. S. Tubman (1944–1971) was in its twilight and he was supportive of change that did not challenge his political primacy. George Browne's profile fit well with that view. He would bring a steady Liberian hand to the socially prestigious ECL, certainly not taking it on any radical or unpredictable course as Tubman had sensed Missionary Bishop Dillard Brown was attempting.

One must mention here as well the configuration of the Liberian clergy in 1970. There were the seasoned seniors such as Fr. T. J. O. Gooding, Fr. Samuel Ford Dennis, Fr. Christopher Kandakai, and Fr. William Vanii Gray. Then came the middle level clergy who were shinning products of the new Cuttington but who had yet to attain graduate level education. The one other clergy with impressive credentials was The Rev. Canon Burgess Carr, but Carr had opted to avail himself of opportunities abroad upon graduation from Harvard Divinity School. Carr served as Africa officer at the World Council of Churches in Geneva, Switzerland, and subsequently as secretary general of the All Africa Conference of Churches in Nairobi, Kenya. George Browne, on the other hand, returned home soon after earning the Masters of Sacred Theology (STM) degree from Virginia Theological Seminary (VTS), and continued his foot soldier duties in the sacred ministry of the Liberian church.

At the international level in 1970, the American church, also quite prestigious in the American establishment, was having its own crisis of conscience as it faced the civil rights movement and the social fallout of the Vietnam War. Retrenchment from missionary outreach soon became the order of the day as overseas districts or dioceses were prevailed upon to speed up autonomy schemes. Liberia was no exception. The tragic assassination in 1969 of Dillard Brown, then Missionary Bishop, seemed a perfect opportunity to complete the rationalization of the American withdrawal, or the Episcopal Church (USA) (TEC) withdrawal, from the ECL. Cuttington College's Chaplain George Daniel Browne came to fit the profile of a Liberian successor to the last Missionary Bishop of TEC to the ECL.

## STEWARDSHIP AND SELF-SUPPORT

While always integral to the mission and life of the ECL, the issue of stewardship took on a new meaning following the murder in 1969 of Bishop Dillard Brown and the discussions that ensued about the relationship of the Domestic and Foreign Missionary Society (DFMS) of the TEC to the Missionary District of Liberia. As indicated in the first volume of the church's history, when the American Church suggested that Liberians might elect their own Bishop, the first thought among leading Episcopalians was whether this was the opportunity not only to launch a self-governing Diocese but also the withdrawal of financial support that had marked the relationship since the early nineteenth century. As the process of electing a Liberian Bishop got underway, the issue of self-support was raised anew. Though there were other extenuating circumstances, it took the assurances of a politically paternal President Tubman to calm the waters of doubt as Liberian Episcopalians stood on the verge of taking charge of their affairs of self-governance, self-propagation, and self-support. With the election in 1970 of George Daniel Browne as the 10th Bishop of Liberia, the die was cast. There was no turning back, or so it then seemed.

Before narrating what transpired during the Browne episcopacy, it may be helpful to contextualize the stewardship issue. Every Christian church starts with support from another. Even the first apostles, the first church inspired by Christ himself, started first as receivers of the good news and the benefits from Christ, and then went out as good stewards to spread it as charged. The One Holy and Apostolic Church of which Episcopalians are a part is the fruit of the stewardship of the first body of believers from which stewardship is derived. Almost 200 years ago, the Episcopal Church of the United started the ECL. The Liberian church has thus been a beneficiary of the Christian stewardship of the American church. The challenge of self-support, stewardship, and autonomy is a signal of the Lord's call for ECL to give account of the talent received, those tangibles and intangibles that enabled the planted church to grow over the decades. But this Christian responsibility has often been obscured by a complicated historical relationship between the mother Church and ECL, producing what some have referred to as a missionary mindset or a mindset that tends toward dependency as opposed to self-reliance. Or, might it have been an absence of creativity on part of the Liberian church in adapting the inherited theology from the American church to Liberian conditions—the old potted plant metaphor of adaptation?

The tragedy of the assassination of Missionary Bishop Dillard Brown and the subsequent election of Diocesan Bishop George Browne changed the calculus. Soon there were social rumblings on both sides of the Atlantic. Liberian Episcopalians at both grassroots and leadership levels were developing a consciousness of their identity, at least as that related to the mother Church. The American Church on the other hand found itself faced in the 1960s and 1970s with societal challenges that led it to invite overseas missionary districts to take charge of their affairs as expressed in the three "selves" of governance, propagation, and support.

The 62nd General Convention of TEC in 1967 in Seattle, Washington responded to the Presiding Bishop's call on TEC "to take its place humbly and boldly alongside and in support of, the dispossessed and oppressed peoples of this country [USA] for the healing of our national life."[6] The American Church was responding to challenges of an existential nature emanating from the Civil Rights Movement, the anti-Vietnam war demonstrations and other social challenges in American society. Three million dollars was allocated yearly for three years for Americans who were "largely poor and Black."[7]

There was a simultaneous push at two levels—from below and from above, from below in the form of the challenge that Liberian Episcopalians faced in the wake of the assassination of Missionary Bishop Brown, and from above in terms of the social pressures to which the American church felt obliged to respond. It is this convergence of forces that set the stage for the autonomy debate. A process was now set in train with many twists and turns ahead. From minimal self-help as the American church and bishops continued a pattern of giving to ECL, to a local pattern of minimal support from the pews while few Episcopalian notables shouldered the financial responsibility for the church's work.

## Self-Support Issue, Pre-Browne

Until the episcopacy of Bishop B. W. Harris (1945–1964), self-support schemes seemed largely a symbolic attempt at instructing local Episcopalians in the discipline of stewardship. Browne himself suggests four problems with the old approach or the approach he inherited—absenteeism of Missionary Bishops from the Diocese for protracted periods as was the case of Bishop Overs (1919–1925); TEC's steady increase of grants for budgetary support; the absence of a clearly defined method of collection; and the absence of education and incentives. Earlier efforts included the Ferguson Endowment Fund of 1903, which resulted in the collection by 1911 of $1,000. This initiative was apparently rolled over into a Kroll Endowment Fund (Bishop Leopold Kroll was the 6th Missionary Bishop of ECL), which showed the amount of $3,000 in 1943 for the Missionary District of Liberia with the American Church account number 555. Up to March 1991, the accumulated amount totaled $29,931. The latter came with the stipulation that the interest be added to the principal until further notice, probably meaning the amount be held in some sort of escrow account until church authorities decided a course of action.[8]

Bishop Harris's approach to endowment, a more sustainable one, was to invest in an income-generating building in central Monrovia that came to be known as the Chase or Plaza Building. But endowment funding aside, there were generous increases in subsidies from the American church to the Missionary District. In 1928, the subsidy to the District was $80,907. In 1946, it was $61,572. From 1946 to 1964 it had increased to $463,776 (over 750%). Between 1964 and 1969 it had increased by another 9.3%. In a decade (1960–1969) the District's operational budget increased from $214,000 to $511,454, an increase of 58%. Browne adds: "By comparison, in 1989, the Mother Church's subsidy to the Diocesan budget had decreased by 32% since 1970. Their contribution under the Covenant Agreement of 1982 would be only 31.5% compared to 90% in 1970."[9]

## Toward Autonomy: A Rude Awakening

Never absent from discussions at Convocations or Conventions of the ECL, or from the "Charges" of Bishops, Missionary District and Diocesan alike, the assassination in November 1969 of Bishop Dillard Brown placed the stewardship issue into sharper relief. Bishop Brooke Mosley, Deputy for Overseas Relations/USA and Acting Bishop of Jurisdiction (November 10 to December 16, 1969) was in Liberia when the assassination occurred. He met with Liberian clergy on November 25, 1969. Mosley assurances included informing them that the American church was funding the Liberian church to the tune of $511,000 annually, and that the American church's support did not depend on having an American or Liberian Bishop. Browne observed that Mosley's exposure "was quite a revelation that left many of us flabbergasted." Learning for the very first time the simple fact of the amount of support from the American church given the secrecy and non-collaborative nature of relations between missionary Bishops and the Liberian clergy, he even added that heretofore the District operated on two budgets—the "mission budget" and the "district budget." And two treasurers were in place as well, the "mission treasurer" and the "district treasurer." The mission budget was funds from the mother church and was always kept secret.[10]

Some three months later another American Church official, Sam Van Culin of the Executive Council attended in Gbarnga, Bong County the 47th Convention of ECL in February 1970 and informed the gathering that appropriation to Liberia had been reduced. Then at the 1970 General Convention of TEC in Houston, Texas, the Liberian Diocese was informed that TEC was shifting from overseas support to domestic American issues. Browne writes: "We were informed by the Mother church that the Overseas Jurisdiction should be prepared to work out with the Executive Council by 1973 a mutually satisfactory plan or timetable 'to take full support for their institutional and ecclesiastical program and to achieve at least 50% self-support by 1976,'" Browne continued: "We were bemused and bewildered as we faced the stark reality that we were heading a 134-year old Diocese which was one of the minority Christian Denominations in Liberia and still mainly supported by charity from abroad."[11]

The revelations and ultimatum shockingly received by a youthful Liberian leader were digested not with resignation but with both faithful determination and Christian charity. Browne would soon demonstrate his leadership acumen with a two-pronged approach for stimulating his flock while appealing to the mother church and others with a clear plan to show patience in a transition period from the status quo to steady autonomy.

## Stewardship Measures

While reviewing the Diocese he had inherited by constituting a committee of his clergy to tour the country and report on the state of the church's work, Browne soon set out to formulate ideas about how to address stewardship at home while communicating his vision to the mother church. In a telling statement, which he addressed to the Presiding Bishop and Executive Council of TEC, he told them of three things on his mind. The first was the Liberian church's interpretation of independence. He began with Liberian folk wisdom: "There are three ways to take a burden off one's head. You may throw it off; you may stoop down and take it off your head slowly; or you may invite someone to assist you. By the first method you run the risk of ruining the contents. The second method may strain you. By the third method, you share mutually a common responsibility." Browne then expanded:

> When the Diocese of Liberia speaks of independence, we do not think in terms of confrontation but partnership in a venture which is God's. We do not think of becoming enemies, but we think of mutual respect and acceptance of each other as partners; We do not want you to consider yourselves your Brother's keepers; all we ask is you be your Brother's Brother! It is mentioned among American Church circles that white missionaries are no longer wanted overseas. The Diocese of Liberia wishes to go on record for saying that this is not true of Africa. This idea originated in the U.S. and was not checked out with us in Africa. I advocate that the decisions affecting the life of our Church be made on Liberian soil with majority opinion, but a purely nationalistic church loses its catholicity and richness. The Liberian Diocese seeks partnership both in personnel and resources from people of other nationalities.[12]

The second thing he desired to communicate to the American Church was that the building up of Christ's Kingdom through evangelism was an essential demand on the resources of the American church. Liberia was "totally committed to the program of Evangelism," for it had set for itself a five-year plan "to spread the Gospel to the forgotten, illiterate and tribal people of our country—thus restoring their sense of value in the sight of God and man." Browne interpreted the "current thinking" of the American church to mean that since they were no longer appointing Bishops and missionaries and setting "our priorities," their commitment to "our ministry" would wane. He went on to enumerate the "colossal institutional" and other programs inherited. Cuttington College and Divinity School was given as a critical example "which absorbed over one-third of the budgetary grants," underscoring the fact that the school was vital to Christian education and theological training in the Diocese. He specifically proposed that Executive Council establish a committee to work with the Cuttington authorities on a plan of action by which "this school may become independent from the Diocesan Budget but sponsored by the Episcopal Church."[13]

There was a third thing he wanted communicated. It was that against the backdrop of the Overseas Review Committee's recommendations regarding larger measures of autonomy, that the following proposals were advanced for consideration: "1. That by December 31, 1973 the Liberian Diocese and the American Church would have responsibly arrived at a mutual plan of support for its institutional programs; and 2. That by January 1, 1975 the Liberian Diocese assumes 100% self-support for its ecclesiastical programs. That includes the payment of all its clergy . . . and the operation of its evangelistic programs."[14]

That said, Browne and his co-workers soon set to work to lead a self-support campaign. This campaign came to involve a whole church or "every member canvass" led by leading Episcopalian Nathaniel H. S. Baker (chair Diocesan budget and finance committee). Stewardship was to be understood as "the use of your time, talent and treasure to the Glory of God." It was Baker who became the leader of the very elaborate and ambitious "every member canvass" and who reminded his fellow Episcopalians that dependence on "handout, promises for more handouts and a few generous donations from a very few faithful members" was not a viable way of stewardship. Charles D. Sherman (chair of committee on state of the church) wanted the church to "go into business," taking advantage of Liberian talent, land and other resources. The Bishop was aided as well by a number of Diocesan treasurers and development officers that included G. Alvin Jones (Diocesan treasurer 1971–1981), Josiah Brown (special assistant to the Bishop), The Rev. Canon Jellico Bright (started as acting treasurer and served as treasurer a full decade), Robert Ellis (development officer of ECL), Eugene Cooper (head, Standing Committee), Jeremiah Tulay, and Gyude Bryant (chair, Board of Trustees). Following Nat Baker's death Mai Padmore stepped in as she helped raise consciousness of communicants for support to the Diocese and made generous donations of her own.

Browne would employ this rich human resource over the years of his episcopacy to create an atmosphere conducive to stewardship as he set out to teach and encourage his flock. He wanted open disclosure of incomes and expenditures. Above all he wanted the whole church's participation in financial policy decision-making. With his chief lieutenants, he set out his agenda and modus operandi which began with streamlining the budget to offset reduction in subsidy from TEC, raising the level of annual giving beyond the old quota and assessment from parishes, and building through investment and endowment a reserve for the future of the Diocese.[15]

A ten-year budget project was formulated, and toward the end of the first decade the amount of $41,000 had been raised locally for the operational budget (compared to $18,000 in the previous decade). There was investment in real estate and formulation of a sustainable endowment plan. Building on his predecessor's efforts with the Chase Meridien Building as collateral, though the church owed the bank $2 million, it was able to borrow $450,000 to erect the Jean Travis building, the second major investment in real estate. A donor gave the land to the Women's Auxiliary of Trinity Cathedral, which then transferred it to the Diocese. The building was paid for fully in five years. The Church now owned two prime real estates that generated good revenue for the Diocese. And the house for the expatriate treasurer on 15th Street in Sinkor was leased in 1972, so now there were three pieces of property, which by 1990 together came to account for 50% of the Diocese's budget—almost three years to the Bishop's sudden death.

Other measures of support involved organizations such as the men of the church, and Girls' Friendly Society. Parishioners were encouraged to remember the church in their wills. Through such means some valuable property was acquired. The Board of Trustee was entrusted with the responsibility of the Diocese's investment portfolio. Other sources tapped were Trinity Wall Street with grants to education, and the United Thank Offering (UTO) in equipment aid to parishes.

With help along the way from the Executive Council of TEC, the endowment fund was set to raise $3 million. By 1988, $81,925 was raised. The aggregate of all endowment efforts at March 31, 1991 was $364,266 broken down as follows:

No. 555, From Bishop Kroll, $29,932
No. 853, New fund generated since Browne, $146,000
No. 868, Venture in Mission Fund, $170,223

Stewardship effort for the decade of the 1980s yielded the following:

**Table 1. A Review of the Assessment, Rally, and Endowment Balances for 1981–1990**

| Endowment Fund of the Episcopal Church of Liberia—1981–1990 | | | |
|---|---|---|---|
| Year | Assessment | Rally | Endowment |
| 1981 | $3,000 | $13,201 | |
| 1982 | $34,959 | $9,356 | $10,644 |
| 1983 | $34,294 | $8,271 | $14,000 |
| 1984 | $38,000 | $10,351 | $14,671 |
| 1985 | $35,000 | $6,811 | $16,575 |
| 1986 | $33,700 | $7,090 | $15,000 |
| 1987 | $33,000 | $7,198 | $16,462 |
| 1988 | $33,000 | $11,450 | $20,076 |
| 1989 | $33,000 | $19,025 | $36,141 |
| 1990 | $33,000 | $12,000 | $30,000 |
| Total | $310,953* | $104,753* | $173,569 |

Source: George D. Browne, *The Episcopal Church of Liberia Under Indigenous Leadership: Reflections On a Twenty Year Episcopate* (Lithonia, GA: Third World Literature Publishing, 1994), 90. *—in the original document, the column total for "Assessments" was $305,853 and for "Rally" was $495,753.

## Financial Autonomy and Unforeseen Crises

A military coup in 1980 and civil war's commencement in 1989–1990 changed the calculus. In 1980, many Liberians fled the country, had properties confiscated by the State, or suffered political imprisonment. This affected giving to the church. The American church was subsequently asked to increase appropriation for budget support by 33%, which was granted, to be refunded in five years. Target dates for autonomy were adjusted. According to treasurer, Fr. Jellico Bright, by the mid-1980s the church operated an austerity budget for about three years during which TEC granted budget support of $250,000 annually. The Baker Plan envisaged financial commitment of $300 per annum from each Episcopalian. The goal was to raise $3 million to eventually replace the $250,000 from TEC.

But the civil war which started in 1989 and was still raging in 1992, coupled with the effective ending of the Browne episcopacy as he died February 14, 1993, halted developments in their track. The war drove more than 50% of the national population into exile, not counting the internally displaced. The forecast was now quite gloomy.[16]

Browne's was a difficult inheritance, difficult both in terms of the relative lethargy of Liberian Episcopalians on the issue of stewardship, as well as the shift in TEC from overseas mission to challenges in its own proverbial backyard.

Browne rose to the challenge he faced by rallying his flock to think and to act differently, while appealing to the catholicity of the church for understanding in a necessary transition period. Things seemed on course when one looks at the figures in the late 1970s and early 1980s. By mid-1970s the ECL could count on income from its real estate investments to finance much of its recurrent budget. Prospects were upward-looking as late as 1988 when the Chase building agreement was extended to the year 2000 with 26% increase in rent between 1993 and 1997, and a 31% increase for 1998 to 2002. And then the trajectory changed with dual unforeseen crises—the 1980 coup and civil war that commenced in 1989–1990.

By 1989, out of the operating budget of $825,000, the American Church's contribution was 31.5%. And by 1990, the Diocese was able to reduce TEC's subsidy from about 97% of the budget in 1970 to about 32%. Browne was working toward self-support and may have achieved it fully but for the intervention of the military coup d'état, civil war, and his illness and death.

## EVANGELISM

Always a history-conscious prelate, Browne habitually referenced the past, often acknowledging the efforts of his predecessors. This did not mean he did not assess the past critically. Even so, when it came to evangelism he would start with the "Design of Mission" or the mandate the first American missionaries brought to their pioneering work in the Liberia area early in the nineteenth century before focusing on the issue at hand. And as he observed the state of the church he inherited in 1970, he saw a church more focused on "maintenance" than "mission."

He cited statistics to support his observation. Among Liberian Christians, Episcopalians were two percent. There were twelve Episcopalians for every one hundred students in Episcopal schools in Liberia. From an inherited budget heavily subsidized by the American church, a student at Cuttington College in the 1960s and early 1970s was subsidized by $1,500 annually (for 150 student body). The story was similar for students at such Episcopal boarding schools as those of St. John's Cape Mount and the Julia C. Emery Hall Bromley. Only 10% of the budget was raised locally. Sixty percent of the budget went to maintain educational institutions on the premise that education was the avenue to church membership and evangelism. Twenty four percent of the budget was for "New York appointees" meaning, American lay and clerical missionaries. Sixteen percent of the budget for "evangelism" programs, including salaries of the Bishop, Liberian clergy and lay evangelists.

Evangelism under these circumstances was relegated to a few largely untrained catechists and evangelists, the latter paid $10 monthly. Some 80% of Diocesan programs were concentrated in urban areas where 27% of communicants spoke English. The majority rural Liberians and non-English-speaking Episcopalians remained on the margins. Would you allow a nurse to perform surgery on you? The Bishop once asked rhetorically! The inescapable conclusion was that the ECL "was more institutional and charitable in its structures, direction and operation than openly evangelistic."[17]

## An Active Evangelism

Browne saw here a field "ripe for evangelism." And so as the Diocesan Convention in 1972 set goals to "launch a militant program of rural evangelism," two barriers to evangelism were noted:

(1) Inadequate supply of clergy
(2) Inherited parish and institutional structures competing for meager financial resources.[18]

Overcoming the barriers came to constitute a significant objective for his ministry. Browne often advanced the potted plan metaphor, which likened the church to a potted plant brought to Liberia from the New World to spread the Gospel. The question was whether the envisaged evangelism would entail employing the structures and mindset of the sending church, or whether there would be adaptation to the culture and circumstances of the receiving church. Two stories illustrate a problematic structure and mindset. The first was the case of the historic evangelist William Wade Harris who when refused recognition and ordination in the early Episcopal Church, decided to initiate a one-man effort which soon grew into a movement called initially the Church of the Twelve Apostles that has morphed into today's Harrisist Church with in excess of a million followers in Nigeria, Ghana, and the Ivory Coast. Browne was so impressed with this outcome that he was scheming to incorporate the Harrisist Church into the CPWA before his untimely death in 1993.

The second story entailed a visit he was a part of to "Little Liberia" in the Rivercess area where other Christian groups had simply displaced the Episcopal Church because of its neglect of this and similar rural villages. Browne saw his task as one of changing direction and reversing these situations.

The approach came to be a dynamic evangelism with a dual focus: Christ for Liberia, and Christ for the CPWA. The Bishop could not be more emphatic at the outset: "Our top priority as a church is to bring men and women alienated from God by sin, into reconciliation to Him through the blood of

Christ. Our primary aim, therefore, is to win souls. That is the purpose of this Diocese." He would enlarge on this purpose when, a decade later, he was being enthroned as the Archbishop of CPWA. Against the backdrop of 9 million people in the five countries of the province (Ghana, Gambia, Sierra Leone, Guinea, and Liberia) he threw down the gauntlet: "Who will win nine million souls: Christ or Mohammed?"[19]

In time broad and flexible vision would emerge, drawn from the 1989 Lambeth Conference and as reflected in Plan 77 of the All Africa Conference of Churches, held in Lusaka, Zambia, though it took two riveting events to bring home the point: an historic exchange with Mother Wilhelmina Dukuly of the then newly established Faith Healing Temple of Jesus Christ; and a commencement address delivered by the Bishop at the Baptist Theological Seminary outside Monrovia.

In 1971, Browne received an invitation from Mother Dukuly requesting him to speak at the formal opening of the Temple. Prior commitments precluded his attendance; however, he used the opportunity of a reply to set forth a dimension of his broad perspective on evangelism and to indicate the Episcopal Church's endorsement of Faith healing. He began: "We [in the Episcopal Church] consider healing as a vital part of our ministry. As the author of good, God neither wills nor causes sickness. But because man's life is open to disease brought about by himself, by others and the world, our Lord spent one-third of His earthly ministry in healing and teaching about it. This indicates that God wants us to be well." Browne continued: "Faith healing is not a substitute for medical care or surgical skills. Therefore at all healing services we pray for the doctors, the nurses and all who serve the sick in hospitals. The gifts of faith healing are resident in His Church through the Laying on of Hands, the Anointing of the Sick, the Sacraments of Holy Baptism and Holy Communion, Prayers and Counseling."[20]

The Bishop added: "The fact that Jesus commissioned His Disciples to heal and 'drive out demons' does not give them a monopoly on this ministry. There are diversities of gifts allotted by the same Spirit. The Divine Plan allows for a division of labor and a distribution of gifts to all. We rejoice that God has given one of our members [Fact being underscored that Mother Dukuly was an Episcopalian] this gift and the urge to develop it. We hope it will be exercised within the context of the Christian Church and based on the doctrine of the Atonement." He concluded: "People will be brought here to seek emotional, spiritual and physical healing. It is our ardent hope that in the process they will find Jesus Christ personally and have their faith renewed. May this Temple uplift Jesus, so that through its services, men will be drawn to Him. Be assured of my prayers and moral support."[21]

Mother Dukuly was appreciative of the Bishop's "inspiring letter." She wrote: "The valuable explanations of Faith Healing emphasized in your letter left a lasting impression on the minds of the several hundreds who had come to witness this solemn occasion [of the opening of the Faith Healing Temple]. Particularly, I believe that the Episcopal Church's endorsement of Faith Healing pronounced through its Bishop has opened up a new era in the religious concept of the people of this country in general, and the Episcopalians in particular." [22]

The second riveting event was a commencement address the Bishop delivered at the Baptist Theological Seminary in 1986 titled "New Structures for a New Day." "One of the problems of the Christian Church in West Africa," the Archbishop of the CPWA declared, "is that it forces new insights and new visions into the old institutional structures of ministry without planning for what may happen when the new can no longer operate effectively in old forms." The result has been "the breaking away into splinter groups from the main church." He again cited the case of the Prophet Wade Harris who was once a teacher and catechist in the Episcopal Church. He further told his listeners that the founders and leadership of the Faith Healing Temple of Jesus Christ of Bushrod Island, and the Little White Chapel in Logan Town were each of them active members of the ECL. The founder of the Church of the Lord (Aladura), commonly called the Prophet Church, was a catechist of the Anglican Church of Nigeria. "In each of these cases, we said in effect that the leaders were not qualified for the evangelistic work they felt called to perform, and that we were not prepared to adjust our structures to accommodate their calling." He thought such attitudes explain easily the absence of missionary zeal for the task of evangelization. There seemed a clear challenge of "putting new wine in old wineskins without making provision for what happens when the new wine ferments." The time was at hand for imagination, innovation, and constant contextualization for a dynamic evangelism.[23]

His programmatic effort was an evangelism launched with a three-fold focus—clergy, laity, and neglected congregations. For clergy, the new thrust in training would be away from the exclusive model of Bishop B. W. Harris under which Browne was himself trained-BA/BD/ordination, by which he meant four years of college leading to a bachelor's degree in the arts or sciences (BA), three additional years of theological studies leading to the Bachelor of Divinity (BD) degree, followed by ordination. This was actually an imported American model that persists in the United States, though the BD has now become the Masters of Divinity (MDiv).

Now a six-part theological education plan would be the model going forward:

1. Continuing education for ordained clergy.
2. Further training for those capable of pursuing graduate studies (Fr. A. Bane Collins and Bishop Neufville were among the first to benefit from this opportunity).
3. Theological education for college students for the B. Theo at Cuttington.

4. Join Methodists in operating Gbarnga School of Theology (GST) for training clergy (Diploma in Theology).
5. Already college graduates who wished to enter ordained ministry, be offered special training (Seth Edwards Memorial Institute that trained a number of prominent clergy including Bishop Neufville, Fr. Emmanuel Johnson, Fr. Edward King, etc.). A subset of number five was an apprenticeship arrangement whereby already professional persons who felt the call for ordained ministries were encouraged. Labeled Non-Stipendiary clergy, they included Fr. Alexander Cummings (then a deputy minister of education of Liberia), The Rev. C. Abayomi Cole (a former Methodist pastor), and The Rev. David Howard (formerly of the Presbyterian Church who had actually trained formally as a Presbyterian pastor).
6. Identify and train adult people (40 year olds and above) who are potential leaders, fluent in the local languages and literate in English to facilitate the training. Genesis of this was a "teaching ministry" throughout the Diocese led by former Cuttington College Chaplain Oliver T. Chapin who was Bishop Browne's seminary professor. Among the purposes of the exercise was to bring awareness of contemporary theological thought to rural areas where a majority of Episcopalians resided. The effort led to teacher training workshops and seminars conducted by the Christian Education department of the Diocese led by Abeoseh Bowen Flemister who subsequently was ordained a priest in 1998.

For improvement in the quality of service, there was expected a corresponding improvement in clergy salary and benefits (pension plan and insurance plan, all paid by the Diocese, including medical coverage of 80%). Here was a collaborative Bishop meeting with his clergy colleagues with some regularity through conferences and retreats.

The Laity emphasis would entail new initiatives in Christian education designed for church growth and lay witness; the use of the lectionary of the church to help recover the Christian home, and the fostering of the homes as centers of evangelism, through Bible study and fellowship meetings. The church's Christian education unit provided an enabling framework.

## Services to Neglected Communities

The Diocesan Conventions' approval of robust use of local languages marked a shift from evangelism through education to evangelism the old fashioned way—meeting people in their culture through their language. As pointed out in the first volume of the history of the Episcopal Church, the early missionaries were instructed, "to take every opportunity to inquire into the condition of the native nations." Within the first few decades of missionary work both the old and new Testaments, the Book of Common Prayer and the Hymnal were all translated into the Grebo language. Some backsliding happened with de-emphasis on indigenous languages during the Ferguson episcopacy so that English might be used, the thinking went, to form a united people "out of many tribes." The Cape Mount mission which was established some forty-two years after the pioneering work in Cape Palmas continued the old tradition of the use of native languages in elementary schools and interior chapels until the 1940s and 1950s when President Tubman's National Unification Policy led to a return to the practice of the Ferguson era. Given Missionary Bishop B. W. Harris' personal friendship with Tubman, the Bishop was not sympathetic to Missionary Gail Stewart's important research work among the Vai.[24]

In time a fourth focus became evident in Browne's ministry. It was his gender ministry, leading the Episcopal Church (ECL) to accept women as worthy candidates for the priesthood. Though the genesis of women clergy in ECL may actually date back to 1903 when Bishop Ferguson "set aside" as deacon Rosetta D. Gibson, wife of The Rev. R.H. Gibson, the idea in modern times was first broached by Browne right at the start of his episcopate. In his first address to the Diocesan Convention in 1970 he said:

> The question of admitting women into the Orders of Priests and Bishops is a matter of urgent consideration in light of the growing place of women in other professional skills, development of new forms of ministry, and the importance of this issue in ecumenical circles."

He cited statistics on the issue of women lay readers and ordination of women at the last Triennial of the American church to demonstrate the trending towards eventual acceptance. He interpreted the trend "as a handwriting on the wall," for "sooner or later we will be admitting women to the Orders of Priests and Bishops.[25]

Six years later, and taking his cue from TEC's admittance of women to ordained ministry in 1976, Browne first offered the opportunity to Abeoseh Martha Jean Bowen Flemister, then perhaps the first female Episcopalian with graduate training in Christian education. She received a Master's degree in Christian Education from the Church Divinity School of the Pacific in 1965. The Clergy influenced a rejection of her application by the committee on ministry, though decades later Flemister achieved her desire and was ordained to the diaconate and priesthood in 1997 and 1998, respectively. But the Bishop was not deterred by that early setback. A few years later he invited to the diocese from the United States The Rev. Suzanne A. Fageol, a practicing woman priest to demonstrate to Liberian Episcopalians that woman can be clergy.

Rev. Fageol went to Liberia in 1981 and served there for some four years. The invitation came in this wise: Bishop Browne approach his friend and colleague, the maverick Episcopal Bishop John S. Spong of the Diocese of Newark about his search for an American female priest. As Spong had ordained Fageol he immediately called her and the contact was established with the Liberian Bishop. Fageol accepted the offer in three months after it was made. In an interview with me, she pointed out her prior Africa service in Nigeria, Malawi, Kenya, and Zimbabwe.

According to Fageol, Browne's original plan was to post her at Cuttington University (CU), but then had second thoughts and decided she begin her work at Trinity Cathedral, the center of the national church, for maximum visibility. She remained at Trinity for six months weathering many challenges from her all-male colleagues who simply could not abide a woman priest. The congregation seemingly had no problem with a woman clergy and was consequently more accepting.

The Cuttington assignment materialized after the stint in Monrovia. She was named Chaplain of the University College where she would teach in the theology department. Though initially unsettling, she also trained catechists at the Bolahun center of the church in Lofa County. During her time in the Gbarnga/Suakoko areas she interacted with the Methodist GST and the Roman Catholic St. Paul's Seminary. Such interactions would lead to a most interesting and important project.

Let us first consider the impact of Fageol's work on women ministry in the Episcopal Church. One of her students at Cuttington was Theodora Brooks. In an interview Brooks tells about how she felt the call to ministry at Cuttington and thus transferred from the regular degree program to the theology department. Upon her completion of the Bachelor of Theology degree she was employed in the office of Bishop Browne, who was by then also Primate of the CPWA. During their very first meeting following her graduation, as she narrates, the Bishop intimated that she was headed for graduate studies at VTS, his alma mater. She was ordained to the deaconate in 1987, the year of her graduation from Cuttington, and made a priest by Bishop Browne in 1989. Brooks was soon off to VTS where she would complete the MDiv in 1992, only a few months before the death of Bishop Browne. Today Liberia has about 10 female ordained, active and retired clergy, the most ordained by Bishop Neufville.

Back to Rev. Fageol's remarkable sojourn in Liberia: While serving as Cuttington's Chaplain and also lecturing at the GST, she was apparently drawn into conversations with Bishop Browne and the Roman Catholic

Archbishop Michael Kpakala Francis. The two distinguished Liberian theologians wanted to start an interfaith movement and asked Fageol to undertake for them some basic research in preparation. She raised the need for a sabbatical to do the project, as it was not possible with her Cuttington responsibilities. Eventually funding was secured from missionary bodies in the United States and Britain. The thrust of the research project was to design a curriculum for ecumenical education of an interfaith character—bringing together Christianity, Islam and African Traditional Religions (ATR). The curriculum was to be built around themes directed to various age groups for use in Sunday schools and Christian education. The purpose was to teach tolerance and promote living in harmony where people know each other's creed and faith. Bishop Francis suggested to Fageol to study Vatican II documents and seek to make the project compatible with Catholic doctrine. Browne and Francis saw the rapid growth of independent churches in Liberia in the 1980s and were thinking of how to influence the development of Christianity in the country and the region. The intervention of the civil war and the death of Bishop Browne ended this remarkable initiative, though Bishop Francis would soldier on for many more years. Francis actually led the search for peace ad social justice in Liberia, winning many accolades before he suffered a stroke and remained incapacitated for a few more years before his death in 2013.[26]

**Summary**

In the end, Browne eschewed Dean Arthur Holt's mission failure as "agent of change" in Liberia and embraced more "modest goals" where there remained a "visible Church of Christ" served by a congregation of faithful people preaching the Gospel and administering the Sacraments as contemplated in the "Design of Mission" of almost two centuries earlier.[27] The Gospel was proclaimed and planted among a culture, thus the significance of the local language work. Product of this work included the following: The Liturgy in Vai produced by Fr. Christopher Kandakai; the Gospel in Gbandi produced by Thomson and Yengbe; and the Book of Common Prayer in Gbandi as produced by Fr. Yengbe and Fr. Parsell of the Order of the Holy Cross (OHC). There were the inevitable ups and downs as important segments of the church and the larger society remained unsettled about the developments—unsettled as to Liberia joining the CPWA, schools as instruments of evangelism versus government responsibility primarily with a limited resourced church making only modest contributions.

Bishop Browne wanted the "people to hear the Gospel in their own mother tongue" to satisfy St. Paul's admonition of "How can they believe if they have not heard?" He wanted resources shifted from urban to rural areas where resided a majority of Episcopalians and potential Episcopalians. The status quo of old attitudes and old structures posed challenges. The civil war and its aftermath posed challenges of its own which unfortunately led to the undoing of much that Browne had labored to build, so that "restoring the years the locusts have eaten" would fall to others. Browne did, however, train a clerical force into whose hands the leadership of the church has fallen. He identified and supported his eventual successor going back to 1984 when Fr. Neufville was elected Suffragan Bishop. And Neufville's successor formed part of a cadre of graduate-trained clergy still in leadership positions of the church. There is a sad note, however, of a critical mass of highly trained Liberian clergy serving in dioceses of the Episcopal Church in the United States and perhaps elsewhere in the Diaspora made possible by instability and war in the homeland. There is perhaps a silver lining here of their giving back to their home diocese through the organization known as Liberian Episcopal Community in the United States of America (LECUSA). Beyond organizing for mutual support and fellowship, LECUSA provides pooled resources from among its members, the American church, the worldwide Anglican Communion, and other religious and civic organizations to the people and church of the Episcopal Diocese of Liberia.

## EDUCATION

A hallmark of the Episcopal Church has been its triple ministry of evangelism, education and healing. In the "Design of Mission" or the mandate given by DFMS of the American church to the first official missionaries, the triple ministry was underscored. This charge to the first missionaries emphasized evangelism ("You are sent to establish a mission which seeks nothing less than the Christianizing of Africa . . . although it is but a small portion which may be attained by your mission . . ."); and healing (St. Mark's Hospital "for seamen, colonists, and natives," established c. 1860 stood for long as a testimony to this ministry).[28] About education, the following was said specifically:

> You are expected gradually to enlarge the school for native children, as you find it desirable and consistent with the health of the missionaries. In this work you will find Mr. and Mrs. Thomson [pioneers of the work of the Episcopal Church in Liberia], now superintending the schools, which they established, invaluable aids. You will pay attention to the language of the native nations, and their dialects, with a view to their gradual reduction to a written tongue.[29]

Given the founding circumstances, this was an evangelism inextricably linked to modern education. The issue arises about the dynamics of which came first, how to prioritize? Over the course of historical evolution there has been much shifting of emphases often in the light of a given episcopacy. That Browne would have his own emphasis born of experience and the circumstances of his time should come as no surprise.

**The Schools**

Radical budget reduction at the start of Browne's episcopacy seemingly necessitated decisions to close some of the schools. This evoked controversy and Browne was accused of "presiding over the demise of Episcopal schools." So, what was the state of the church's education ministry in 1970 as Browne came to office? He wanted to know and so he took the sensible approach of assessing what he had inherited before applying his leadership vision to the circumstances. A 1971 evaluation came to guide this effort. Two weeks into his episcopacy Browne establish a fact-finding committee to help him establish the state of the church inclusive of its education ministry. On the situation of Episcopal schools and institutions the committee found no clearly expressed purpose, inadequate material resources, almost no Christian education. The schools in 1971 were as follows: forty elementary and junior high schools, five senior high schools, with Cape Mount and Cape Palmas, each having the largest with sixteen schools.

A set of recommendations was adduced which included the following: that schools with "historic ties" such as Bishop Ferguson High School in Cape Palmas, St. John's in Cape Mount, Bromley in Montserrado County and St. Augustine's in Bolahun be maintained; that all other schools be amalgamated with public schools, and that the Diocesan committee on education be restructured. The 48th Diocesan Convention approved these measures in 1971 by a vote of thirty-seven in favor, and eighteen against, with four abstentions.[30]

Engagement with the Government of Liberia (GOL) ensued early in 1972 against the backdrop of the following stark realities. Of the Diocesan school budget of $294,000, the Liberian government gave $29,000 in subsidy, $20,000 for Cuttington College. Help requested was not forthcoming, and so on the initiative of Bishop Browne, the treasurer of TEC, Matthew Costigan, visited Liberia. Stark realities revealed included the fact that Cuttington was operating on a deficit of $160,000, the Diocesan budget subsidizing each student there to the tune of $1,000 per annum. Cape Mount schools operated on a deficit of $32,000; ECL funded Bromley to the tune of 65%; and B. W. Harris School ran a deficit of $23,000, which the Diocese had to provide. To this situation came a projected Diocesan deficit by 1973 of $250 thousand against the backdrop of an ECL being 2% of Liberian Christians and 12% of students in ECL schools.

The cumulative effect of this development was Browne's leadership intervention. He posed this not so rhetorical question: "Are we willing to build and develop a Christian community or simply train children apart from that community as we are doing now?" His response spelt retrenchment and recalibration. Even some schools with historic ties would be affected, angering important segments of his flock. He considered as well the admonition of TEC treasurer: "You have sacrificed your life to the church and now you must sacrifice your families and your level of living for the schools?"[31] The time to shift emphasis was truly at hand.

In spite of the fact that Bishop Harris' triumvirate of primary, secondary, and collegiate education had receded into history because the level of support that Harris enjoyed from TEC was not Browne's lot, he had to adjust, to shift emphasis. Browne read from the figures that schools were absorbing the lion's share of a diminishing budget, while at the same time stewardship was tending toward self-support as expected by the mother church.

With assessment completed, a process of decision-making ensued. Controversy abounded, for leadership at many levels of ECL seemed taken by the remarkable role the schools had played historically in education in Liberia (Cuttington, Bromley, St. John's, Bishop Ferguson, St. Augustine at Bolahun, and Kakata, respectively). They wanted the status quo maintained, or at least maintenance of the revivals in education that came to characterize Bishop Harris' episcopacy (1945–1964). How to reconcile status quoists and change agents, especially change induced by budgetary considerations? That was the unanswered question.

There were certain major considerations that led to decision: lessons learned from the 1971 Committee report, decision of TEC about drastic budget reduction in all its overseas departments, and Browne's own views that the training of Clergy was a more effective means of evangelism and church membership expansion than the past emphasis on education as instrument of evangelism. Things came to a head at the 49th Diocesan Convention in 1972 when the Report of the Committee on the Future of Episcopal Church Institutions was considered. The Council of Advice drew conclusions and decided two years later as follows:

1. Effective 1974 school year only the following schools would continue with boarding facilities: Cuttington, St. Augustine's in Bolahun and Kakata, and Bromley Mission.
2. The senior high school at Robertsport (The famous St. John's) would cease to be a boarding school, but would offer day tuition.

3. Bishop Ferguson and the Fulton Dunbar schools in Cape Palmas were to temporarily close.
4. Because of the implications of such measures on education in Liberia, Browne was charged to convey decisions to the Liberian government.[32]

Public reaction was swift and at times furious. The *Liberian Age*, the ruling True Whig Party newspaper, titled a December 3, 1973 editorial "Running Financial Woes" of the Episcopal Church. In it the essence of the Church's resolution on the matter was underscored: "The Church is spending over quarter million dollars to operate schools while the government subsidized it with only $29,000," and then the government delayed making this meager payment. The editorial continued: "Should the decision to close down schools persist, Liberia may encounter some setbacks in its education program as the ECL has been one of the country's leading instruments for solid educational foundation, especially in the elementary schools which will be most affected by this decision."[33]

Amid this situation the Bishop convened a meeting of the Diocesan Standing Committee (successor to the Council of Advice) to deliberate on the future of Episcopal schools, all things now considered. The committee decided and action was taken to declare nine schools independent or self-supporting or given time to achieve such status. Five schools were considered a drain on the budget and thus permanently closed. Ten schools were to share government and Diocesan subsidies. Those schools remaining open were asked to absorb students from closed schools. This action saved the Diocese $120,000 per annum.

For the twists and turns of implementation, a Diocesan Board of Education took up the challenge. The Rev. Alexander Cummings was the Board's first chairman, succeeded in 1977 by Dr. Melvin Mason. Dr. Mary Antoinette Brown Sherman, who was herself succeeded in 1986 by Professor Mary Tedi Bryant, succeeded Mason in 1979. They all led Episcopal schools in wholesome directions as they interacted with the government and initiated fund-raising schemes. By 1981, the government was spending $500,000 yearly on Episcopal schools though this figure was hardly sustained in the political turbulence that came to characterize the decade of the 1980s. But in the interim the Bishop could claim that political pressure had achieved what the Diocese could not. The government to the tune of $37,000 funded Bromley annually. And the St. John's/Cape Mount community had schemed with government for $100,000 in annual subsidy if the Diocese could commit to a matching $25,000.

Through it all, Browne held to his view that education is a function of the State. The Church's mission is to train clergy to carrying forward the work of evangelism. The Bishop felt vindicated when the government stepped forward or was pressured to fund schools either closed by the Diocese or from which substantial subsidies had been withdrawn.

## The Flagship Institution of Cuttington

As narrated in the previous volume, during the episcopacy of Bishop Samuel David Ferguson, Cuttington Collegiate and Divinity School was established in 1889 to train young men for service to the church and the state. In time—and following such name changes as Cuttington College and Divinity School, Cuttington University College (CUC), and CU—it grew into a respectable educational institution and took its place for decades alongside Liberia College, later the University of Liberia (UL), as the second higher education institution in Liberia. Never quite becoming the vocational school its early founders and benefactors conceived, Cuttington was able nonetheless to graduate a significant cadre of men (and it was all men in the early history) who became leaders in the church and the larger society. The institution thrived through the end of the 1920s, but then was closed for the following reasons: impact of the great depression on funding to overseas missions; leadership challenges involving Bishop Robert E. Campbell, OHC, his preferred "white" priest as president (The Rev. John Kuhns); and a determined opposition of lay and clerical Liberian church leaders. Because the Bishop had the last word, the school was closed in February 1929, forty years since its founding. It would be another twenty years before the institution would be reopened under quite different circumstances.

### *Cuttington at Suakoko, Early Years*

When Cuttington was relocated from Cape Palmas and officially reopened in March 1949 in central Liberia (Suakoko, Central Province, now Bong County), Bishop Harris envisaged the institution as laying "sound foundations upon which an enduring work can be based." The purpose was nothing short of a "sound education" and the building of a "Christian character" in the process.[34] First recruited to head the new or second Cuttington was the African-American cleric, The Rev. Father Seth Carlye Edwards. Edwards was a missionary from New York who held a Bachelor's degree from Morgan State College, a BD from Union Theological Seminary and a Masters in Education from Harvard University. He arrived in Liberia in 1948 and there labored for three decades, serving as the first president of the new Cuttington (1948–1960), first Dean of Trinity Cathedral (1960–1967), and founder in 1963 of Boy's Town Institute for wayward youths in Schieffelin (now part of Margibi County) where he served as director until 1976, when he returned to

Cuttington as head of the theology department. He died in New York City in 1977 at age seventy-two years.

But Edwards was not alone in this pioneering work, for in the first decade (1948–1958), his principal associates were his wife, Vivian Joseph Edwards (English professor who later earned the EdD from Columbia University), the Rev. Paul M. Washington (theology) and his wife Christine, and Dr. Fenton Sands (agriculture) and his wife, Dorothy, who taught home economics with Pauline Miller, while they both also managed the cafeteria. Arriving in Liberia in 1948, they all settled at Bromley Mission, and from there supervised the clearing and building at Suakoko before taking up residency there. Future Cuttington president, Melvin Mason, was the first student at this new Cuttington, followed by a trickle of others. The early curriculum focused on a liberal arts undergraduate program, with an eye to agriculture and theological education.

The first faculties were the Edwards, the Washingtons, the Sands, and the Okies. All faculty members were American except for two German anthropologists (Ingeborg Jaeniche and Renate Tomalla), a French (M. Boudin), and a Liberian (Rae Tisdale one of few women to enroll early). Tisdale subsequently taught Biology and was an administrator upon returning from graduate school abroad. The college also benefited from African Crossroads students from the United States before the arrival of Peace Corps volunteers in the early 1960s.

President Edwards saw the new Cuttington grow from four students in 1949 to 145 in 1961, with an enviable academic reputation. And this was the case despite the differences in perception between the leadership and some of the leading American faculty and staff as Cuttington entered its second decade. Dr. John Gay who came to shape the College's curriculum in the late 1950s has written thusly of Edwards' leadership: "Edwards operates in very personal, father-like way, running college affairs from the quiet of his office and home. He did not share decision-making and did what he felt was the best thing to do. The leadership style was gentle, but at the same time arbitrary."[35]

The curriculum mimicked American liberal arts colleges as all textbooks were imported from the United States, as were most of the professors. John Gay, a freshly minted Columbia University Philosophy PhD, a Cornell undergraduate degree in Mathematics, as well as a Princeton BD degree in theology, arrived in Liberia in 1958 and joined the Cuttington faculty, becoming dean of instructions. He soon sought to introduce the African reality into teaching, and away from a fixation on the western canons. Gay quickly became critical to the development of a new curriculum. Recruited from the American church, he first arrived Liberia with his wife Judy and a two-year old son. Judy would join Dr. Vivian J. Edward (subsequently, another Columbia University EdD) and spouse of President Edwards in the teaching of English and literature. Gay educated himself and came to appreciate both the integrity of African civilization and the revolution of rising expectations then sweeping the African continent. It was in response to this developing worldview that he began giving shape to a new curriculum, challenging in the process the Liberian rote learning method and moving toward critical thinking.

Gay discovered at Cuttington in the 1950s a "missionary culture of a rather staid and conservative" Anglicanism "tied to the belief that the apostolic succession was the only source of true Christian ministry."[36] Change was soon on the horizon. With the ecumenical collaboration of Methodists, Lutherans and Episcopal missionary teachers, Dr. James F. Hopewell (PhD, Columbia University) and Dr. J. Walter Cason (PhD, Columbia) joined Gay and others in establishing Cuttington as a premier private university in Liberia and West Africa. With the government of Liberia's, African solidarity scholarships augmented by United Nations scholarships, all in furtherance of African decolonization, a number of students came to Cuttington from Ghana, Sierra Leone, Cameroon, Nigeria, Kenya, Tanganyika (to become Tanzania), Rhodesia (to become Zimbabwe), Uganda, Swaziland, Sudan, Lesotho, and even Ethiopia.

Thus it was that decolonization developments on the continent and their impact on Liberia soon necessitated Cuttington to change from "being a small, intimate and very personal family" school to one that began opening to the world beyond. In fact the African "revolution of rising expectations" visited Cuttington in 1960 in the person of the charismatic Kenyan nationalist, Tom Mboya. This visit had a significant impact. Gay writes: "He brought the vigor and intellectual excitement of the independence quest to our students."[37] Perceptions of Africa and Africans were fast changing. Scholarship on Africa was also changing and at least some members of the still largely American faculty sought to adjust the curriculum towards a degree of Africanization. Liberia was then defined by President Tubman's (1944–1971) conservative route to development with his twin signature policies of national unification and of an open door to foreign investment. But in the latter 1960s each of these was subjected to critical review by a combination of students, American faculty, and American Peace Corps Volunteers, some of whom served on Cuttington's faculty or as teachers in Episcopal feeder schools.

## Dr. Christian Baker's Presidency

As the decade of the 1950s ended and the 1960s rolled in, tension was palpable on campus. A combination of Edwards' leadership style, echoes of

Africanization or Liberianization of the institution's leadership, and the willingness of some radical American faculty to take a stand explain the tensions. Some of these faculty members led by Dean of Instructions John Gay wrote to Bishop Harris expressing their lack of confidence in Edwards' leadership. Edwards, always a man to insist to his colleagues and friends that he and his wife (and he hoped other expatriates shared this view) had come to Liberia to work themselves out of a job or to prepare the path to Liberian leadership, immediately tendered his resignation as president. Dean Gay also resigned, and Melvin Mason succeeded him, the first Liberian Dean of the college.

To succeed Edwards, Bishop B. W. Harris tapped perhaps Liberia's sole veterinarian, but also a man with a number of other qualifications that seem to suit him well for the task. He was director of the Government Experimental Agricultural Center at Suakoko, and the son of one of Liberia's prominent Episcopal clerics, The Rev. Fr. James David Kwee Baker. As Christian E. W. Baker was named the first Liberian president of the new Cuttington, Harris echoed the changing sentiments as he wrote: "Dr. Baker's appointment will allay this rising tide of nationalism."[38]

With Mason as dean, Liberians were now in charge of the college. Despite this change, Cuttington was still, according to John Gay, "a small, intimate and very personal family" school though challenged to adjust to its rapidly changing internal and external environments. Baker, a "man with academic vision and concern for the politics of education" was now at the helm. His style was to lead in close collaboration with such high stakeholders as Bishop Harris (who was a personal friend of President Tubman's) and a number of prominent Episcopal churchmen such as Charles D. Sherman, C. Abayomi Cassell, and Emmet Harmon, who were on and off the Board of Trustees. Students were expected to focus on academics and little else. Any suggestion to the contrary was swiftly curtailed, as when student Edward W. Neufville (later the 11th Diocesan Bishop) was the only student suspended from the college for a year because he led a student protest. Nonetheless, the mission of imparting a solid education to its students was not affected by these developments as its graduates fitted almost seamlessly into leading graduate schools in the United States and elsewhere in the world. Few, however, would return to boost the Liberian faculty.

Now a Liberian team led by Baker and Mason was to pick up where Edwards and Gay ended and take the school to the next level. They did so between the years 1960 when Baker was installed and 1972 when Baker resigned. In the interim, with support from the Missionary District of Liberia and the Ford Foundation funds they embarked on a course of faculty development that had at its core the use of international faculty while Liberians went abroad for graduate studies. Among the measures were an international outreach effort that entailed a cooperative arrangement with the Associated Colleges of the Midwest (ten liberal arts colleges in the United States), which included faculty and student exchanges, Fulbright scholars, and Peace Corps volunteers. This combination led Cuttington to achieve a high degree of academic excellence during the Baker years and the few that followed. But Cuttington was never able to attract the critical mass of high quality Liberian faculty that it desired with fervency, possibly because of the school's location in rural Liberia and the location of the UL in the country's capital city of Monrovia.

The brutal assassination of Harris' successor, Bishop Dillard Brown in February 1969 by Professor Justin Obi, a Cuttington chemistry professor of Nigerian nationality, changed the course of the history of the Missionary District of the Episcopal Church in Liberia, and with it, the history of Cuttington College and Divinity School. This tragic event led the Church to elect a Liberian native as Bishop. Then the Chaplain at Cuttington, The Rev. George Daniel Browne was elected April 1, 1970 Bishop of the ECL. As Chairman of Cuttington's Board of Trustees, Browne presided over his first commencement at Cuttington in December 1971. In remarks, he opined that Cuttington's problems were not financial but primarily ones of management. Dr. Baker took offense and resigned the next day (interestingly, as Edwards had done in his time). Some observers have impugned a number of motives for Baker's abrupt resignation. It is suggested that while serving as college president, Baker was also an advisor and consultant to the government, taking care of animals at the zoo at President Tubman's private farm and performing other chores for which he was compensated. While both Bishop Harris and Bishop Dillard Brown were prepared to accommodate the arrangement, Bishop George Browne seemingly found difficulty with it especially as he often experienced difficulty reaching President Baker and otherwise working with him. The commencement remarks, the observation goes, were meant precisely to trigger a resignation given the Liberian circumstances. Henceforth, Browne would seek a president from the clergy over whom he could exercise more influence.[39]

## Father Emmanuel W. Johnson's Presidency

And so the politics of the transition from Baker did not produce another lay president, though at least three prominent names were proposed, including that of Dean of Instructions Melvin Mason. The other names were two former Government of Liberia cabinet secretaries of education—Dr. John Payne Mitchell and Dr. Augustus Feweh Caine. Following an interim administration of almost two years led by the Rev. Fr. E. Bolling Robertson of St. John's Mission School legend, The Rev. Fr. Emmanuel W. Johnson was named the next president of Cuttington. Browne had his man to operate a college owned by the church. And as he would later say in a 1977 commencement address, he felt "a great heritage of a sound educational system" was entrusted to him and he intended to keep it private and independent of all authority except its Board while at the same time laying claim to greater government support.[40]

Though affected by a mode of retrenchment that characterized Episcopal institutions in the 1970s, Cuttington continued to thrive academically. But such good fortune was not to last as, like the UL, the sociopolitical climate of civil society challenging governmental authority, most directly manifested by student unrests at Cuttington posed a threat to the reputation that had been built over the years. President Emmanuel W. Johnson tried to contain rather than work with change. An affable and well-meaning cleric, Johnson was a professional educator with a BA degree from Langston University and a Master's degree from Roosevelt University. He had served principalships at a number of secondary schools, including B. W. Harris Episcopal School, and as superintendent of the government-owned Monrovia Consolidated School System. He seemingly wanted to revert to the tranquil days of the 1950s, including disallowing sociopolitical radicalism on campus. He was shaken by the 1980 bloody military coup d'état that toppled the government of President William R. Tolbert Jr. and with it a perceived political hegemony that had enthralled Liberia since its founding some 133 years earlier. President Johnson was not comfortable with the ways of the new military junta. He soon resigned and even briefly left the country, though he returned and was named Dean of Trinity Cathedral, following President Seth C. Edwards' path some sixteen years earlier.

## Dr. Stephen Yekeson's Presidency

It seemed now the turn of Cuttington's number two administrator, the Vice President for Academic Affairs, Dr. Stephen M. Yekeson. A member of Cuttington's class of 1964, he would become the first alumnus president and the fourth president of the new Cuttington. Yekeson held an master's degree in science education from Tuskegee University, and a PhD also in science education from Western Michigan University. There was a political subtext here. Perceived immigrant hegemony in Liberia had been deposed. The military government offered itself as a government of the indigenous majority of which Yekeson was a member. Changed circumstances would lead to Yekeson's removal after six years in office. Military leader Samuel K. Doe struggled to lead as he faced challenges from his military colleagues. He carried out a number of political purges and then through subterfuge clawed his way to the Liberian civilian presidency in 1986. The stage had been previously set with the recall of Dr. Harry F. Moniba (another Cuttington alumnus of the class of 1964 of which, incidentally, I was also a member) from his Ambassadorial post in London to be named vice chairman of an "Interim National Assembly," a body contrived to replace the military junta in preparation for returning the country to civilian rule. Dr. Moniba and Dr. Yekeson were both from Lofa County and married to two cousins who reportedly considered themselves sisters. Yekeson must have felt that he was in political sync with the national governing authority, and this was cemented by a special Moniba-Yekeson relationship.

The unexpected then happened. In the course of conducting a regular audit of the Rural Development Institute (RDI), a United States Agency for International Development (USAID)-funded unit of Cuttington that had existed since 1979, the auditors discovered that the RDI financial management team failed to account for $278,450. President Yekeson adopted a defensive posture as he claimed that responsibility of audit and administration of USAID grant was neither the College's nor his responsibility. Cuttington's Board of Trustees rejected Yekeson's attempt to distance himself from RDI responsibilities by first resolving to relieve Yekeson of all financial responsibilities of the College at large. Said the Board's chairman, Bishop Browne: "As Chief Executive Officer, the president is ultimately responsible for the total operation of CUC and all its agencies." "It would appear," he continued "that over the years the scope and nature of his assignment have grown to such a magnitude that the incumbent can no longer cope with the onerous responsibilities of the expanded presidency."[41]

The Bishop premised his conclusion on the following. He had been invited by the American Church "all expenses paid" to meet with representatives of the Church and the American Schools and Hospitals Abroad (ASHA), a major donor agency associated with RDI, to be told in person of their concern over the worsening financial crisis at Cuttington. In his statement was this remark: "ASHA's program criterion seven, which is part of the basis for evaluating and awarding grants, states: 'An existing institution must demonstrate competence in professional skills and must exhibit sound management and financial practices.' We have concluded that Cuttington is not meeting this criterion. This impacts adversely on Cuttington's ability to compete for grant assistance in this and future years. It already has had an effect on ongoing grants since ASHA withdrew authorization for limited operational support to cover salaries."

As the Board of Trustees decided to withdraw financial management of the University College from President Yekeson, it appointed a special committee to work out modalities to implement its decision. The committee of three included former Cuttington President Christian Baker, Lay Episcopalian leader Harry Greaves, Sr., and Dr. Walter Gwenigale of the Phebe Hospital then jointly owned by the Lutheran and Episcopal churches. Soon the crisis was in full bloom as Yekeson decided to politicize the developments by publicly suggesting that by including Greaves on the committee the Board was replacing "staunch NDPL members" with Liberia Action Party (LAP) members at Cuttington. The National Democratic Party of Liberia (NDPL) was the ruling party, and LAP was the lead opposition of the day. Grasping the political import of Yekeson's remarks, the Bishop decided to go public at a Board meeting: In prepared remarks, he began: "You may not be aware that the first principal of Cuttington, the Rev. M.P.K. Valentine, was killed. There are reasons to believe that the circumstances surrounding the death were both political and ethnic. In 1929 the Diocese took a decision to close down Cuttington. Circumstances surrounding that decision were a mixture of financial, political and ethnic. In 1969 the Bishop of the Diocese was killed because of his involvement in helping Cuttington find solutions to the problems of Cuttington. Again, political and ethnic reasons cannot be ruled out."[42]

The Bishop continued: "I heard from an official from the USAID office in Monrovia that rumor is circulating that the Board is seeking to replace staunch NDPL members at the college with non-NDPL members. If this rumor is in the USAID office then it is on Capitol Hill and in Washington."[43] He then said:

> Allow me to speak as the Bishop of the Diocese in which Cuttington operates. The Episcopal Church operates schools, including Cuttington, in order to assist the Government of Liberia do its work. We have consistently refused to be partisan in our approach to education. We have even refused to be denominational. No one is employed at Cuttington because of his party affiliation. And this Diocese will not, under any circumstances, endorse that association. We are here seeking administrative and financial solutions to the College. I would like to put on the records of the college that, before this diocese permits Cuttington to be politicized, we will suspend its operation. It has been closed down before, and we are prepared to do it any time if its existence will pose problems for the Church.[44]

Browne then concluded: "I hope that this rumor is not true. However, if it persists, I will call a meeting of my Standing Committee and the Board of Education to advise me further. Let us put these personal feelings behind us as we seek objectively some lasting solutions to the problem before us. Thank you."[45]

The upshot of the foregoing was that the Board, which had elected Yekeson as president November 7, 1981, decided in January 1987 to relieve him of the presidency. The Government of Liberia reacted publicly as the education minister said on national television that the government objected to the decision of the Cuttington Board to remove Yekeson without prior consultation with the government.

The alumni association of Cuttington reacted by meeting in emergency session and backing the Board's action, pointing out that their interest was "to protect the integrity and continuity of their Alma Mater." They in fact voted forty-two to zero, with two abstentions, to support the Board. And so with this backing, the Board, the Church and allied bodies pointed out to the government that Cuttington was a private institution answerable to the Board and the ECL. A showdown was now underway as the Bishop replied the government by stating that the Board's decision to remove Yekeson would stand until the Board reconvenes.

A search committee for a new president was appointed by the Board and mandated to complete its work in six months. Meanwhile the College Chaplain, Fr. Samuel Y. Reed, was appointed interim president. His was not an easy assignment as cleavages on campus assured a crisis situation, a situation, which exploded in a riot on July 13, 1987. One observer wrote: "Transition period was fill with disgruntled, dissatisfied, disloyal and disobedient faculty, staff and students."[46]

As old values faced new realities, Chaplain Reed had to step down and former President Christian Baker came to the rescue in October 1987 to remain through February 1988. They were able to do a little better than muddling through, but not without the old Browne-Baker tension as issues of "lack of confidence" and the Bishop "wanting to run the school" resurfaced and prolonged Cuttington's agonies.[47]

Baker considered his second coming a duty "to return calm and quiet to the University College," and "to restore the years that the locusts hath eaten."[48] Was this Baker's latter day response to the 1972 episode when Browne's expression of no confidence led him abruptly to resign the presidency of the college?

### Dr. Melvin Mason's Presidency

The search for a new president produced Dr. Melvin J. Mason as the Board elected him in 1988. Mason did his graduate studies at Yale University where he was awarded a master's degree in science education, and at Michigan State University where he received the D.Ed. in curriculum development and higher education administration. He took over from Interim President Baker in an abrupt manner as Baker refused to stay another day once Mason showed up on campus to begin his presidency. This was no doubt a reflection of a relationship of distrust between the two men since the early 1970s.

Finally, Dr. Mason was a university President after having been the first student to enroll at the new Cuttington on February 15, 1949, one of first four graduates in 1952, the first Liberian appointed to the faculty and the longest serving (fifteen years). Furthermore, he had served as well as Dean of Men, Registrar, Director of Admission, and Dean of Instructions, being the number two in the college during the Baker presidency. And now he had become the second Cuttington alumnus elevated to the college's presidency.

Mason had not been given a chance to lead Cuttington when Baker resigned in 1972, and so he pursued a career elsewhere in education, first with a World Bank project at the government's Ministry of Education, and subsequently with the United Nations Educational, Scientific and Cultural Organization (UNESCO) in Paris, France. He had left Cuttington 1972 and was returning sixteen years later in 1988 as President. Two years into his presidency, civil war erupted in Liberia. The college was forced to close and eventually to go into exile.

Sixteen years after being passed over for the presidency, Mason was elected by the Board as the 5th President of his alma mater. But he came to the office in troubled times in Liberia. The regime of President Doe seemed on the verge of unraveling as he had eliminated virtually all of his erstwhile colleagues of the military junta that had staged with him a successful coup eight years earlier and armed resistance to his own regime was gathering. Though being appointed president of the state institution, the UL, as we have seen, had politically and perhaps otherwise rehabilitated Dr. Stephen Yekeson, his departure from Cuttington left social tension in its wake.

The abruptness of the Baker to Mason transition notwithstanding, Mason conscientiously set out to lead the college. He recruited a competent staff, which included Dr. Henrique F. Tokpa as vice president for administration and planning, and subsequently for academic affairs. He was able to graduate two classes, Dec. 1988 and Dec. 1989, and then the civil war erupted and forced the closure of the university college.

Mason found himself a refugee first in Nigeria and then in the United States. He soon rallied his troops and began experimenting with the notion of a "Cuttington In Exile" (CIE). The first attempt in Accra, Ghana dubbed then as "Cuttington in Accra" failed for want of funds though some one hundred students were poised to take advantage of the opportunity to complete their studies. CIE, headquartered at St. Paul's College in Virginia, United States, did acquire traction graduating more than 150 students between 1991 and 1996. Its slogan of "keeping hope alive" led it not only to enable a few students complete their education, but also planning opportunities for the day when the exiled institution would return to its Suakoko campus.

Mason was keen on ensuring that Bishop Browne approved the idea of CIE devoting a subsection in his memoirs, *Savoring Education, An Autobiography*, to the subject. Mason narrates not only that Browne verbally approved the idea, but that to the pointed question, "Bishop, do you approve of the CIE program as explained to you?"[49] Browne answered in the affirmative.

Yet there is evidence that Bishop Browne was never enamored of the idea of CIE, pointing out in one correspondence to Mason that "majority of Cuttington students [were] in Liberia," not the United States. In another instance in 1991 the Bishop took exception to Mason's decision to relieve Acting Cuttington President Thomas Kromah Gaie of his position without reference to the canonical Board of Trustees of the University College.[50] The death of Bishop Browne February 14, 1993 and therefore the change in Episcopacy a few years later rendered moot the issue of the Bishop's approval.

Mason was now free to pursue his idea which he came to group under the following objectives: secure resources for the reopening of Cuttington when peace was achieved; assist Cuttington students to continue their education, especially juniors and seniors, whose education had been interrupted by the civil war; provide opportunities for junior staff to obtain their Masters degrees through a vigorous staff development program; and develop a plan that would address Cuttington's social problems when school reopened. While hoping that the four objectives would serve as the basis for the full institutional development plan when peace was restored to Liberia, Mason endeavored to do his best, but minimal if any supervision from the Board of Trustees in the rather chaotic interim between Browne and Neufville may have taken a toll on the institution's progress.

Bishop Browne who died February 14, 1993 never fully embraced the idea of Cuttington in exile.[51] In a letter to Mason, Browne wrote: "Your letter of Feb. 1 just arrived three days ago with the concept paper." "While I appreciate your efforts, I think about the vast majority of students who are not able to go to the United States. I hope that we could "keep hope alive in Liberia. . . . A number of Cuttington students are here in Monrovia, and I hope something could be done for them. In my own area, I am toying with the idea of getting the theology students together to keep their hope alive. Please give some thought to the majority of the students who are in Liberia. Sincerely, GDB, Chair, Board."[52]

## Theological Education and Christian Education

Training church workers became an important priority for Bishop Browne right at the start of his episcopacy. This concern was couched in a pamphlet released by the Bishop in April 1972 titled "Our Priority Number One: Theological Education." Two years later in 1974, Fr. E. Bolling Robertson was appointed "Director of Theological Education for the Diocese." These studies and structures were but preludes to launching vigorous training programs.

Such programs would have as backdrop the state of training as of the early 1970s. In fact for twenty years between 1929 (when Cuttington closed) and 1949 when it reopened there was virtually no clergy training. The training by the OHC of Fr. Vanii Gray and Fr. Christopher Kandakai in the 1940s have often been cited as exceptions.

Only twenty clergy were trained and ordained in twenty-one years between 1949 and 1972. In 1962, the Cuttington seminary closed for want of students. Improvisations emerged. A Department of Theology at Cuttington opened in 1972, and between Cuttington and the GST, eight persons formally trained and were ordained; five also with training in accredited U.S. seminaries. A weak evangelistic thrust was a consequence of training interruptions. A 1987–1991 "Revised Plan" was put in place to avert another training interruption.

The 1972 pamphlet advanced the first training plan. For five years between 1973 and 1977 there was a relentless pursuit of Clergy training such that thirty-six Clergy were trained from 1973–1986. The total number of Clergy in the Diocese was forty in 1986, (thirty-two Liberians including the two Bishops, and eight non-Liberians). Non-academic training continued at the Seth C. Edwards Memorial Institute in Monrovia. Twelve clerical students were enrolled. The Diocese then identified thirty catechists.

The Church advanced in 1986 a "Revised Plan for Theological Education, 1987–1991."[53] It envisaged four categories of training as follows:

1. Men who are experienced in their ethnic surroundings and who may not meet all the academic requirements, but may have moral and social leadership and could be useful to the Church in their communities.
2. Men with high school education who could be sent to the GST (an ecumenical seminary that offered a diploma in theology then planning towards a BA in theology program)
3. Men who could take advantage of the theology program at CUC and later enter accredited seminaries abroad, and
4. The postgraduate program to train Seminary professors. (See also Clergy training under Evangelism above)

Bishop Browne stated that the end result of the training program was to improve his evangelistic program, particularly in rural Liberia. His plans were largely realized as is more fully fleshed out in the section on Evangelism.

Where in 1970 there were twenty-seven Clergy, eighteen Liberians and nine non-Liberians, all men, in twenty years, fifty Liberians were trained and ordained including three women—The Rev. Theodora Brooks, The Rev. Roberta Phillips, and The Rev. Maggie Dennis.

## SOCIAL ISSUES, CIVIL WAR, AND THE CHURCH TO 1993

This section combines issues of church-state relations with the total breakdown of social relations as the country degenerated into civil war in December 1989. It seeks to contextualize the environment within which the church conducted its ministry while highlighting a number of issues brought to the fore. Following the book's method of historical account through episcopacies, we will follow the path of the various political regimes, including those of Presidents Tubman, Tolbert, and Doe and the ensuing circumstances of civil war.

Both in prophetic witness as well as for purposes of containing political violence, the vehicles of the LCC and interfaith forums involving Muslims and Christians were employed. As regards LCC Browne once wrote: "If Christianity is to be effective in Liberia it must present a single face to society and the non-Christian world. Hence the unity for which Christ prayed must be our over-riding aim."[54] Mainline Christian denominations were then largely the face of Christianity in Liberia. And the leaders of these churches were quite engaged with the burning issues that faced Liberia. They sought to speak truth to power often incurring the wrath of those in power, and yet they persisted.

The Chairman of the ECL Council of Advice, Charles Dunbar Sherman (who was a former secretary of the treasury and then a sitting senator from Grand Cape Mount County) uttered the following words as Browne sought to advance his ministry amid a changing Liberia. Not suggesting that this was true or false, Sherman wrote: "There is a myth in our society, that there are four pillars on which the society hangs—the Church, the State, the True Whig Party, and the Masons." There was also a telling counterpoint contained in a draft position paper on "issues of today's Liberia" at the 64th General Convention in 1987. Titled "Reconstruction of the Civic Trust and Respect, Cultural and Social Foundations on which the State Rests," it challenged Sherman's expressed myth both as to its inadequacy and its socially divisive character. Bishop Browne challenged this myth, which many took for reality. He was prepared to tackle "the very foundation of Liberian high society." He did so in prophetic witness. He also did so because he saw himself as bridging the social dichotomy that for long seemed to define Liberian society, though he would tilt toward the indigenous (as opposed to the immigrant) as when he self-identified as the first indigenous Liberian Bishop and otherwise identified himself with Grebo-Liberians.[55]

Browne was elected and consecrated Bishop in 1970 toward the end of Tubman's twenty-seven-year presidency. The atmosphere was defined by the judicial trial of Ambassador Henry Boima Fahnbulleh, Sr., which one news organ characterized as Liberia itself being on trial. Given his lowly beginnings and the Chaplaincy of Cuttington from where he was elected Bishop, Browne was able quickly to establish a modus Vivendi with the autocratic Tubman regime, and Tubman reciprocated by first adding pomp and pageantry to Browne's consecration which he attended and at which he presented the new Bishop with a gold cross pendant. Though Browne raised the controversial Masonic issue while Tubman was still president and Tubman urged compromise as between the Craft and the Church, Browne was during this time less outspoken on social issues.

On Tubman's death a year later, however, the Bishop was effusive in tribute to the fallen president. He called Tubman "the greatest patron of religion Liberia has ever known." Tubman "recognized the validity of all religious convictions. . . . He respected all religious authorities whether they were Archbishops or Alhajis,.. Zoes or local preachers." "On this score," he continued, "his motto was 'touch not my anointed and do my prophet no harm.' (Psalm 105:15) "He was not only the father of our nation, but also the chief patron of religion in Liberia," as Browne concluded: "he was the unifying factor of religion in Liberia." "He leaves an indelible mark and enviable example in the history of religion in Liberia."[56]

The 1970s under President Tolbert were years of political liberalization and social tension, which culminated in a major civil disobedience event on April 14, 1979, and then a bloody military coup d'état a year later, which resulted in the assassination of the president and the overthrow of his government. A now increasingly socially engaged George Browne assailed some government policies, mediated in the civil conflict that effectively started with the April 14 riots, even serving on the Nettie Sie Brownell National Commission charged with uncovering the root causes of social discontent in the country. Browne also butted heads with the powerful Masonic Craft of Liberia.

On the April 14 situation Browne joined forces with Pastor E. Toimu Reeves of the Providence Baptist Church to foster reconciliation amidst "the broken relationships within our society." He pledged they would look at the case "through the eyes of the Church," as he admonished his readers not to "give away what has been given to us. Don't let us fail to act like men of reason or to reason like men of action," a smart paraphrasing of Tubman's "think like men of action, and act like men of thought." Browne went on to serve on the Brownell Commission or the presidential Commission on National Reconstruction following the civil disobedience or "rice riots" of April 14, 1979.[57]

The Masonic issue was first broached at a Clergy conference in 1970. The Bishop was concerned about what he considered Masonic disturbance of Church services when attending funerals of their brethren. Some viewed this as a frontal attack on one of the so-called pillars of Liberian society of which the Church was an integral part. In February 1973, the Bishop addressed a letter to all fraternities, including the Masons, urging them to cease the practice during funeral services of "rapping their gavels and keeping guard over the corpse" as they were "disturbing" and an "intrusion" in the Church's worship services. Soon the issue was joined as joint delegations of the Craft and the Church began to meet. A confrontation ensued between the two seemingly irreconcilable positions, the Church citing its Canon Law (III, 20, 1 [a]) "which we swore to defend," while the Masons responded by stating, "Masonry [was] founded on the basic principles of unalloyed belief in God" and faithfulness to Masonic obligations such as use of gavel.[58]

In the end there was an ambiguous resolution as many Clergy and prominent Episcopalians were also Masons, and many apparently accepted the "pillars of society" myth, reiterated in 1973 by Past Master and Vice President of Liberia James E. Greene. He characterized resolution of the matter as leading to "a good relation with the Craft, State and Church." The resolution was curiously accepted by Browne himself in reply to a stinging letter of rebuke to him from Churchman George Padmore as he disclaimed a charge of prejudice towards the Craft, averring that he could not be prejudiced "for I am also a member of one of the orders" (possibly the United Brothers of Friendship; UBF).[59]

There was ambiguity on many fronts as the military staged a successful coup on April 12, 1980, ending more than one hundred years of hegemonic political rule but also plunging the country into unprecedented political violence and uncertainty.

Men of the cloth sought to mediate as Browne ministered to his flock. So did the wider Christian community with the formation of the LCC. But first, the immediate situation was faced—the military coup d'état in which President Tolbert was assassinated and the April 22 executions when thirteen senior officials of his government, some of them prominent Episcopalians, were publicly executed. This writer, then a deposed minister of state for presidential affairs in the now defunct Tolbert administration, was on the same flight as Bishop Browne from neighboring Sierra Leone precisely on the date of the executions of former government officials. In their efforts to minister to a traumatized society, church leaders were already mediating with the government and preaching reconciliation. Bishop Browne considered Junta leader Samuel K. Doe cooperative and responsive to the churches only through 1983.

Thereafter, the goals of the two parties, the church and the government, began to diverge for a number of reasons. Chief among these reasons was the junta's determination to consolidate power and to ensure that the processes set in motion to return the country to civilian rule would not be inimical to its political interest. Such a goal soon clashed with a social gospel oriented church determined on its part to uphold the rule of law, human rights, and the ideals of democracy.

The mainline Christian churches had since 1982 worked together with the creation of the LCC, with Bishop Browne serving as the group's first president. LCC came in time to be deeply involved in many areas of the life of the Liberian people. Issues that came to exercise the LCC and that became conflict point between the organization and the military leader included the 1984 UL crisis when students protests were severely crushed by the military leaving death and destruction in its wake. It was the aftermath of the 1985 attempted Thomas Quiwonkpa coup d'état when an angry Doe went after his opponents, real and perceived, with massive blood-letting, and the CUC crisis of 1986–1987 when the government attempted to block a decision of the Cuttington Board of Trustees to remove President Stephen Yekeson for cause.

In the post-1985 elections period, there were other issues bearing on human rights violations and a studied disregard for the rule of law on the part of the military government. Doe accused church leaders of immorality and corruption. When Baptist minister Walter Richards challenged the government a response of silence ensued. In a letter to Doe the LCC viewed "with consternation Decree No. 88—A as a backward step which negates the constructive efforts which you made so far for the return of our country to civilian rule." Doe retaliated with the withdrawal of customs and duty free privileges from the churches.[60]

Based on a sermon preached on November 3, 1985, it seems that either Browne was unwittingly providing Doe a way out of the crisis or Browne was positioning himself to sustain a mediatory role for himself and the LCC. In the sermon on national reconciliation which was broadcast live on state radio, the Bishop seemed to be taking the official American line about the outcome of the controversial 1985 elections regarding Doe winning "only 51%" of the vote when elsewhere in Africa presidents were winning with 99.9% of the vote. Browne appealed to opposition parties to reverse their positions of protest by refusing to take their seats, and instead take the seats they had won in the legislature. It was the typical optimist/pessimist glass half full versus half empty urgings. If this was intended to provide Doe a face-saving opportunity, it hardly achieved its reconciliation intentions.

Then came Doe's surprising offer to Bishop Browne to deliver the "Inaugural Sermon" on the January 5, 1986 eve of his inauguration as the elected president of Liberia. Given a second chance Browne preached above the fray, invoking "beating swords into plowshares" and offering a parable about the fate of a bird hidden from a wise old man who was being asked to say whether the bird was dead or alive. The wise old man's response: "My sons, I do not know whether the bird is dead or alive, but one thing I know: its life is in your hands," for depending on the response of the old man the boy had it within his power to either squeeze to death the bird or produce it alive. And so came the words of the Bishop to the president-elect that he alone could decide the fate of the Liberian people for their lives were now in his hands as the life of the bird depended on those holding the bird.[61]

But President Doe did not heed. He persecuted the church as he closed the Roman Catholic radio station, deported a prominent American Catholic priest, ridiculed and scandalized at will such church leaders as Bishop Arthur Kulah of the United Methodist Church, Rev. Walter Richards of the Baptist Church, and ceased the passport of Bishop Browne. Browne has written that these were only some of the reasons "why church leaders were unsympathetic to the 1989 crisis which toppled the president."[62]

The 1989 crisis developed into a full-fledged civil war, which came to ravage the country for some fifteen years. In its initial stages, a church in peril attempted nevertheless to mediate between the contending forces. The ECL channeled whatever assistance it could muster to war victims through the LCC, and the LCC urged dialogue in meetings with Doe. In May 1990, Christians and Muslims came together in the Interfaith Mediation Committee (IMC). Doe asked the IMC to partner with a Joint Committee of the government of Liberia, political parties and others to attempt mediation, but this was to little avail.

Three years into the war's genesis, Bishop Browne died in February 1993. He was able in late 1992 to speak to the state of the church before flying to the United States to seek medical attention. He reported that only seven active clergy were left in the country during what became the first stage of the war, as he expressed optimism that those who were forced to leave the country would return. ECL lost to exile or death fourteen out of forty clergymen, or about 35% of its pastors within a year of the war. "When the shepherd is away from the flock, it is natural for the flock to scatter in search of green pastures." In this early stage of the crisis the church had lost to exile or internal displacement 65% of its congregations and 35% of its clergy.[63]

Bishop Browne considered President Tubman "a benevolent patron" of the church, President Tolbert as "a herald of a new Liberia" that was then derailed, and President Doe as "a military dictator who in his last days tried to destroy the church."[64] Concluding his twenty-year Episcopacy book, Browne recalled decisions taken at the 65th Convention in 1988 projecting "1992 and Beyond" which focused on a proposed program regarding church property, clergy salary, clergy deployment, and theological education. These would remain some of the major issues to challenge Bishop Browne's successors.

## IDENTITY WITH CHURCH OF THE PROVINCE OF WEST AFRICA AS COVENANT REDEFINES RELATIONS WITH AMERICAN CHURCH

"The identity crisis was a major problem for the Diocese of Liberia. It was ecclesiastically based in the United States yet domiciled in Africa."[65]

To address this perceived identity situation Bishop Browne employed his passion for history by referencing a 1912 incident during the episcopacy of his sole Liberian predecessor, Bishop Samuel David Ferguson (1884–1916). As we related in the first volume of the church's history, a suggestion was floated by the American church in 1912 that the Missionary District of Liberia consider jurisdictional transfer to the Church of England in exchange for American ecclesiastical jurisdiction over Central America. The Liberian District rejected the proposal largely on political and nationalistic grounds. Political, because the British colonial government in neighboring Sierra Leone had in 1885 forcibly annexed the Gallinas Liberian territory to Sierra Leone, and nationalistic, because Liberian Episcopalians then thought that "when the mother Church ceased her immediate work in this field, she would have reared up an independent Native Church to be left to pursue a career under its own leaders."[66]

There were other attempts by the Liberian church to grapple with the identity issue: "In 1948 the Bishop of Lagos invited Bishop B.W. Harris as West African Bishops contemplated establishing a Province. His low-keyed response was to send The Rev. Father J.D.K. Baker as an observer. The assembled Bishops called Baker's presence marking "a new page in the history of the Province." In 1963, the Bishop of Sierra Leone represented the Archbishop of the Province at the Liberian convention and remarked: "We are in an age when we ought to consolidate our forces in the Lord's vineyard in the countries of West Africa." It is important to recall the context of political decolonization and intense African engagements with the organizing of African unity on the horizon."[67]

Four years before his brutal assassination Bishop Dillard Brown predicted in 1965 what he considered inevitable closer contacts of the District with the Province of West Africa. But obvious constitutional barriers had to be removed. All dioceses of the American church and most missionary districts were identified with one of its nine provinces. "Liberia was one of the few that did not belong, but remained an extra-provincial Diocese." The prompting of sorts came from the United States in the form of a non-binding resolution "to limit the General Convention to the 50 States of the American union and to release all other Dioceses to their own geographic provinces as we did long ago in Japan and Brazil."[68]

Bishop Browne and the Standing Committee of the ECL saw an eventual move into the Province "as a natural process of growth, maturity and search for identity within their geographic region." This was the context that led Bishop Browne in 1971, barely a year into his episcopacy to make a ten-day study visit to the Church of Uganda to learn about its operations and structures. This was the church that came to be led by Archbishop Janani Jakalioya Luwun of the Anglican Province of Uganda, Rwanda, Burundi, and Boga-Zaire. The Archbishop was executed by the Dictator Idi Amin in February 1977 and years later was proclaimed the first martyr of the Church of Uganda's second century. Browne was impressed with the fact that that Church had developed so well that it had already produced martyrs. He looked at stewardship patterns. For him this was all proof positive of the benefits derived from belonging to a province in the same geographic region.

As he moved from idea to action for its realization he felt buoyed by developments in the West African region at the political level. Economic Community of West African States (ECOWAS) was on the horizon, as was the Mano River Union. "While the church was nursing its ecclesiastical and cultural differences, the political leaders were striving for unity and solidarity among themselves. Second only to being Christians, Liberians were all Africans and had historical, ethnic and cultural ties with the rest of Africa." Thus Browne embarked in 1972 with a high-powered delegation at a meeting of the Provincial Standing Committee of the CPWA. Issues of constitutional alignment were raised and suggestions proffered. The Province seemingly was eager for Liberian membership. The Liberian delegation wanted all proposals presented to their Convention for deliberation and action. The proposals from the Synod of the Province were in 1974 presented to ECL convention where an "acrimonious debate" ensued, though the issue was resolved by a vote of seventy-two for, twelve against, and eleven abstentions. Browne was then authorized to seek approval for Liberia to obtain associate membership in the Province. The older generations of Liberia embraced change with reluctance. They were among those resisting Liberia's embrace of Africa and distancing from the American church.[69]

Browne's implementation entailed seeking approval from the American church for the Liberian church to obtain associate membership in the Province of West Africa. The proposed action included that the Diocese would take all necessary steps to also decide no later than five years from associate membership to become a full member. The American church was consulted and at General Convention in 1976 a resolution was approved supportive of the action of ECL in seeking associate membership in the province. On the strength of this approval Liberia was in August 1977 admitted an associate member of the Province. Among measures taken both to account for the association status and also in anticipation of full membership were the American church's development of a Covenant Plan, the need for constitutional amendments both for the Province and the ECL.

A joint Committee on Covenant Relationship involving the Liberian and American churches was soon established. On the Liberian side were Charles Dunbar Sherman who served as chair, and Joseph Rudolph Grimes who was cochair. Bishop William Folwell and the Rev. Samuel Van Culin led the American delegation. Representing the Province as observer was the Bishop of Accra. The committee produced a Covenant document establishing the basis for a new relationship with the proviso that the Covenant Plan would be subject to revision as warranted by changing circumstances.

Things soon moved in rapid succession. Along with constitutional adjustments, the 59th Diocesan Convention authorized the Bishop of Liberia to finalize the steps necessary for Liberia to become a full member of the Province. Finally, a petition from ECL to TEC through the World Missions Department sought permission to seek full membership in CPWA. In reporting to the General Convention the Department said: "The Diocese of Liberia requested permission to transfer its Metropolitical authority to the Province of West Africa during 1982, and this request was approved by the Executive Council last November (1981)."[70]

Some six months following ECL's admission to full membership of the Province, Browne was elected Archbishop of the CPWA. He would lead the Province until his death in February 1993. As with the Episcopal Church challenges he inherited at his consecration in 1970, he wanted to know the full scope of the challenges he was inheriting from the CPWA. Among the many initiatives he took in this regards was the commissioning of a study to meet the "dire needs for a path with goals and objectives which we all can accept. In spite of our various national, cultural and linguistic differences, we need an organizational structure that will be the focus of our life together." The study was carried out by J. Robert Ellis, a development officer of ECL and grew out of Archbishop Browne's "Provincial Presentation" to the Third Partners-In-Mission Consultation held at Ducor Hotel in Liberia, November 20–24, 1983, a year into his Archbishopric. External partners funded the study and Ellis was attached to the office of the Archbishop for a year.

Essential recommendations from the Ellis study included: strengthening existing links regarding talent, time and resources; improving administrative and provincial structure (secretariat to be in Archbishop's country); establishing firm financial plan for the future regarding "enabling and empowering"; establishing work in Francophone countries; and making better use of existing programs. Outgrowths of this fact-finding effort led to the following: the Liberian senior clergyman, The Rev. A. Bane Collins served the church in Gambia, as did The Rev. James B. Sellee subsequently; The Rev. Momo Kpartor served for many years the church in Cameroons; and The Rev. Father Kwame Amamoo of Ghana served at Trinity Cathedral in Monrovia and at CU.

Archbishop Browne also issued pastoral letters jointly with the Diocesan Bishops of the CPWA. A first letter issued December 1, 1983 spoke of people prone to "quack spirituality." "We must not only preach the Gospel but speak also of its social implications, such as healing the sick, alleviating suffering, feeding the hungry, caring for the poor, teaching the children and guiding the youth, all of which are part of Christ's concern."

Some of the advantages of Liberian membership in CPWA include fulfillment of the 1836 "Design of Missions" that envisaged a missionary enterprise to encompass the whole of western Africa; acknowledging and advancing the work of Evangelist William Wade Harris in Ivory Coast and elsewhere along the coast; many other points of contact with students coming to Cuttington and priests from other West African countries serving in Liberia. Then there are the issues that Liberia shares in common with West Africa: Polygamy and church membership, the advance of Islam, human rights, and political and economic challenges. Browne wrote: "It was therefore important that the Diocese of Liberia join efforts and resources with fellow Africans to provide answers rather than to sit comfortably in the household of the American Church and ignore these formidable issues that affect its very existence."

Liberia's move into the Province did not end its relationship with its historic partner, the American church. It merely redefined a new relationship that would entail serving as a conduit between TEC and the Province. Chancellor J. Rudolph Grimes writes: "There is no doubt in my mind that the Episcopal Church of the United States sees our full membership in the Province of West Africa as a new link for them with the Province. New opportunities now opened on both sides and I hope that they will be pursued." And Presiding Bishop John Allin concurred: "This transfer does not terminate the relationship of this church and the Diocese of Liberia; but it opens up new dimensions of relationship for which I rejoice. It provides the Episcopal Church of the United States with a new opportunity to welcome new forms of partnership in mission with the province." Among the many benefits were those of identity and self-determination. Also, had Liberia not acted it would have been coerced to join one of nine American provinces that its overseas dioceses were placed in willy-nilly.[71]

There were disadvantages or challenges in the Liberian move to the Province. They include non-contiguity of the Dioceses; infrastructure challenges including communications and transportation, and the dual language situation. But these were more opportunities than hindrances. The secular West African organizations faced the identical challenges, which they were working steadily to overcome. Perhaps the real challenge for Liberian Episcopalians was finding new ways and means to grow ministry within the framework of the Province and thus begin to overcome their own problem of identity.

The path taken by the Covenant arrangement at this time was largely dictated by civil crisis in Liberia, for no sooner had the ink dried on the first document than the ECL was adversely impacted by chronic political instability which eventuated in the launching of a full-fledged civil war in late 1989. About a decade later, a needs assessment was carried out "with the view of determining the status of the ECL and the rehabilitation required early on in the civil crisis." But these updates occurred during the episcopacies of Bishop Browne's successors.

The genesis of the struggle for identity is the American origin of Liberian Episcopalianism and the ever-present challenge of adapting to an African environment. The struggle for identity has both internal and external dimensions. Internally, it entailed a complicated but necessary blending of cultures at all societal levels. Externally, the issue was perhaps first put in sharp relief in 1913 when the suggestion was proffered that Liberia consider leaving the American Church and becoming a part of the Anglican Church in Africa. The Liberian Church stated its un-readiness and there the matter rested until the post-war era of African decolonization, which eventuated in closer associations of all sorts among the newly independent states of Africa.

This new dispensation provided an opportunity for the first Bishop of the Liberian church elected by Liberian Episcopalians themselves. Browne clearly led the charge for change, meticulously studying the situation and making strategic moves as, for example, when he allowed himself a visit of observation to a dynamic Province of Uganda and parts adjacent under the iconic leadership of Archbishop Janani Luwum a year following his consecration. Browne's strategic moves included sending Liberian Clergy on tours of African Dioceses and commissioning studies to guide his thinking and decision paths. The political processes that led to the 1963 creation of the Organization of African Unity (OAU), the 1973 establishment of the Mano River Union (MRU), and the 1975 birth of the ECOWAS were not negligible influences on African Anglicans/Episcopalians. But Bishop Browne did not only commission studies. He acted on the recommendations and thus interactions notably involving clergy exchanges were beginning to see the light of day. Though some of them produced challenges of their own, they were teething challenges that awaited creative action.

In the end, the church seemed to be faced simultaneously with the dictates of catholicity and the requirements of culture and history. This entailed a difficult balancing act in the hands of skillful leadership. It would prove bewildering to congregations where leadership is in unsteady hands.

## BROWNE'S MINISTRY ASSESSED

A review of Bishop Browne's ministry places him in league with predecessor Bishops John Payne, Samuel David Ferguson, and Bravid Washington Harris. Payne pioneered the church's work in Cape Palmas and Parts Adjacent. Ferguson deepened the work such that the mission was nearer "being a significant and responsible agent of planned change in Liberia." And Harris so renewed and revived the work that at his retirement, effusive praises came from both his Liberian flock and his American colleagues in TEC's National Council. Harris' ministry also produced a George Daniel Browne.

Ten years into his episcopacy Browne considered that he had made significant strides in his quest to achieve for the church self-governance, self-propagation, and self-support. Leading the ECL away from TEC and into CPWA clearly signaled self-governance. Self-propagation was reflected in pertinent numbers. During the first decade, the numerical strength of the church grew by 76% and congregations by 82%. Rural membership grew by 146%, a signal of a more socially inclusive church. Congregations grew from sixty-six in 1970 to 120 in 1980. Those baptized grew from 10,151 in 1970 to 18,552 in 1980. And, seventeen of thirty-two clergy were ordained since 1970.

Though 56% of the budget was raised locally by 1980 as opposed to 4% in 1969, the self-support effort was stalled both because of the 1980 military coup d'état and the economic downturn that came about a couple of years prior to the coup. Prominent Episcopalians who were generous in their support of the church either fled the country or had their properties confiscated by the military junta.

Twenty years into his episcopacy Browne was still hard at work strengthening self-governance, expanding and further deepening self-propagation, and pressing ever forward on the self-support front. In 1986, there were 116 congregations, with membership in 1985 of 20,105. By February 1990, there were 140 congregations and a membership of 25,000.

Significantly, the following persons were ordained between 1970 and 1993: Paul Korvah, 1970; Samuel Reed, 1972; Thomas Savage, Daniel Harris, and A. B. Cummings, 1973; William Newton, Charles Cole, and Edward Hoff, 1975; Benedict Vani and J. Jellico Bright, 1976; Emmanuel Hodges, Lawrence Bainda, and Thomas Smith, 1978; Jonathan Hart and John Jallah, 1979; Momo Kpartor, 1980; Sayonkon Jarteh, Samuel Harmon, and John Griffiths, 1981; Tamba Songar, 1982; Budu Shannon, 1984; Harmond, Tumu, William Travers, Peter Washington, Horatio Morais, 1985; Dee Wellington Bright, Wheigar Bright, Desmond Williams, Kweetor Velemee, and Wilmot Merchant, 1986; Hne Thompson, James Sellee, Theodora Brooks, Herman Browne, Prince Wreh, Christian Mulbah, and James Wilson, 1987;

Roberta Gray and James Tamba, 1988; and Thompson Yengbe, Alphonso Dormu, Letomba Passewe, Joseph Greene, Wilfred Gbusseh, Maggie Dennis, Hne Merriam, and Elijah Harris, 1989. John Harmon was ordained at ECL's request by the Bishop of Southern Virginia.

Of the fifty ordained, twelve held either the MDiv or BD degrees (post Cuttington training); ten held diplomas from the GST. Eight already had their BA or master's of arts (MA) in other disciplines, and they were given some training in theology. Ten were ordained as seniors equipped ethno-linguistically to serve rural communities.[72]

Even on the verge of ill health, the Bishop made valiant efforts to report to his flock the state of the church, making projections for 1992 and beyond. He wanted to be carried forward programs proposed in 1988 at the 65th Convention regarding assembling and organizing church property, improving clergy salaries with congregations expected to pay half of all clergy salaries, a more streamlined, collaborative way of clergy deployment, and theological education that benefitted from a cadre of trained Liberian theologians and others equipped with graduate education.

As regards "cadre of trained Liberian theologians," Bishop Browne ordained to the diaconate (and some to the priesthood) a small number of promising young graduates of Cuttington's 1980s theology classes. While most of them went on to acquire graduate degrees, two went further to earn the PhD degree in theology: The Rev. Dr. James Bombo Sellee, Dean of Trinity Cathedral since 2017, earned his PhD in theology (biblical studies, Old Testament) in 2004 from the University of Gloucestershire, United Kingdom; and The Rev. Dr. Herman B. Browne, President of CU since 2016, earned his PhD in theology (systematic theology) in 1994 from the University of London. Browne and Sellee were thus the first two Liberian clergy ever to earn terminal academic degrees in theology.

Bishop Browne even laid out his own retirement plan: "The Canons of the Diocese and the Province require the Bishop and clergy to retire at 65 years of age. For the incumbent, that date is December 17, 1998, if God wills it. It is our plan for the Diocesan Convention of 1997 to elect a Bishop Coadjutor and have him consecrated shortly thereafter. Then we will ask for an extended vacation to give him the opportunity to run the Diocese. Some time in December 1998 we will have him enthroned as the 11th Diocesan Bishop of Liberia."[73]

The quality and character of Browne's leadership has been extolled by many, among them a former Chancellor of ECL and CPWA, J. Rudolph Grimes, TEC Presiding Bishop Edmund Browning, and the Archbishop of Canterbury George Carey. Grimes said in tribute to the fallen Bishop: "He was a very brilliant, quiet, reserved, courageous, optimistic, decisive and effective religious leader." Bishop Browning wrote: "George Browne was a true shepherd in the deepest sense of what that means . . . the good shepherd who lays down his life for his sheep." And Archbishop Carey: "George Browne was a great African bishop. He brought to his Episcopal ministry gifts of discernment that proved invaluable."

Truly these gifts place Bishop Browne in the pantheon of great Liberian and African bishops who impacted in significant ways the church and the society in which it is embedded. He has consequently left a lasting legacy despite the intrusion and disruption of a military coup and a prolonged and brutal civil war. Among his legacies are the irreversible Africanization of the Liberian church, a trained clerical force to be reckoned with long into the future even if many now function in the Diaspora, and a decided expansion of the church beyond historic interiors such as rural Cape Palmas, rural Cape Mount, and rural Lofa Counties, into now most of the rest of rural or interior Liberia.

Africanization means joining West African Anglicanism, and increasing liturgical uses of Liberian languages and modes of worship. There were men ordained to work in eight of Liberia's indigenous languages including Gbandi, Bassa, Grebo, Kissi, Kpelle, Kru, Lorma, and Vai. The trained clergy carried the implication that such a minister can do more effective evangelism. As we earlier pointed out, the Bishop once quipped, "Would you allow a nurse to perform surgery on you?"[74] A renewed rural shift means going into the old hinterland regions and elsewhere where reside a majority of Liberians.

Browne seemed set apart from his predecessors and contemporaries by his ecumenicalism and catholicity; his social gospel disposition; his irreverence for the social status quo; his wide embrace of evangelism; and his appreciation of history.

Though he advocated for addressing Liberia's perennial identity problem and advanced the Africanization of ECL, this was no stance of pure nationalism. He wanted an ecumenism rooted in Scripture (the incorporation of "other sheep not of this flock" [John 10:16]), and a church in partnership with people of other nationalities in order to secure its catholicity and its richness.

As to his social Gospel disposition, Browne would remind us that as fully God and fully man, Jesus enjoins us to engage with the human condition. Our relationship with God must be both horizontal and vertical. Thus Bishop Browne was at the center of the unfolding drama in Liberia in the 1970s into the 1980s—member of the Brownell Commission, a national commission charged with investigating the root causes of the social malaise that erupted in the civil disobedience of April 14, 1979. Browne also served as the first president of the Liberian Council of Churches, and was a member of the National Constitution Commission charged with drafting what was edited into the present or 1986 Constitution of Liberia.

His irreverence for the social status quo: Where his missionary predecessors had to be circumspect because they were foreigners, secured in his nationality, Browne (like Bishop Samuel David Ferguson before him) often spoke truth to power. He took the church to rural Liberia, or to the rest of it, where the majority of Episcopalians lived, he challenged the political myth that tended to sustain minority immigrant rule including clashing with the Ancient Free and Accepted Masons of Liberia; and he joined forces to defeat a gambling bill before the national legislature in the 1970s.

Browne widely embraced evangelism through means that were both orthodox and unorthodox. He did so through the constitution, canons, and institutions of ECL, but also outside those frameworks. He sought belatedly to bring the work of William Wade Harris into the fold of CPWA; he endorsed faith healing as carried out by the then Mother Wilhelmina Dukuly's Faith Healing Temple of Jesus Christ, and the Little White Chapel of Logan Town, among others. In the end what mattered was that more souls were won for Christ.

Finally, Bishop Browne's appreciation of history also set him apart. He made himself a researcher and prolific writer because he wanted to appreciate the past of the church and other social institutions, the better to chart a course for the challenges before him. He churned out articles, pamphlets, and learned sermons over the span of his ministry. He left three completed book manuscripts, two of which were published posthumously. His rich personal documents are deposited with the Archives of the Episcopal Church in Austin, Texas, United States.

Cumulatively then, these qualities of ecumenicalism and Catholicity, social gospel disposition, irreverence for the social status quo, wide embrace of evangelism, and appreciation of history set Browne apart and mark him as a great religious leader for all times.

## NOTES

1. George D. Browne, "Diaries and Log Books," September 22, 1991.
2. Festive Thanksgiving service at Trinity Cathedral, noon of November 27, 1992. Well attended by state and church officials. See also Bishop Browne's open letter to Episcopalians, September 20, 1992 (Dunn Archives).
3. Browne, "Diaries and Log Books," January 11, 1993.
4. See Browne, *Autobiography of George D. Browne (1933–1993): Tenth Bishop of Liberia, Sixth Archbishop of the Province of West Africa* (Praha, Czech Republic: SÍŤ—Ecumenical Publishing, 1998); and Browne, "Christian Approach to the Adherents of The African Traditional Religions," unpublished manuscript, complete with acknowledgment by author and dated Spring 1993, Milwaukee, WI, in 97 pgs.

5. See open letter to Episcopalians in Browne (Dunn Archives); and Browne, "Dare To Be Different," address to the Popolebo (Kru/Klao Organization), Monrovia, Liberia, August 11, 1989, 6 pages (DFMS Papers). The DFMS Papers are located in Archives of the Episcopal Church, Austin, Texas, Domestic and Foreign Missionary Society, boxes 2–18 (hereafter cited DFMS Papers).

6. Episcopal Church USA (ECUSA), *Journal of the General Convention* (1967): 482. Available online at the Archives of the Episcopal Church, https://www.episcopalarchives.org/governance-documents/journals-of-gc (accessed October 9, 2019).

7. ECUSA, *Journal of the Special General Convention* (1967): 455, https://www.episcopalarchives.org/governance-documents/journals-of-gc (accessed October 9, 2019).

8. George D. Browne, *The Episcopal Church of Liberia Under Indigenous Leadership: Reflections On a Twenty Year Episcopate* (Lithonia, GA: Third World Literature Publishing, 1994), 75; Trust Funds, "Report of the Committee on Trust Funds of the DFMS of the Protestant Episcopal Church," March 31, 1991 (Dunn Archives).

9. Browne, *Indigenous Leadership*, 80; see also Covenant Agreement between TEC and ECL (Dunn Archives).

10. Browne, *Indigenous Leadership*, 82.

11. Browne, *Indigenous Leadership*, 82; *Journal of 47th Convention* (1970): 77; Bishop Browne's Log Book, 1970 (Dunn Archives).

12. Browne, "A Statement from the Liberian Diocese to the Executive Council," May 1972, 3 pages (DFMS Papers).

13. Browne, "A Statement from the Liberian Diocese to the Executive Council," May 1972, 3 pages (DFMS Papers).

14. Browne, "A Statement from the Liberian Diocese to the Executive Council," May 1972; See also The 1977 "Plan For Autonomy," and influence of the Lusaka Conference of the All Africa Conference of Churches (AACC), which called upon the church in Africa to embrace liberation from dependency in order to experiment and develop a style that is distinctly Africa—a theme of self-reliance, inspired these measures (Dunn Archives).

15. *Journal 63rd Diocesan Convention of ECL* (1986); Statement, *Journal 56th Diocesan Convention of ECL* (February 8, 1979), (Dunn Archives).

16. Browne, *Indigenous Leadership*, 92.

17. Browne, *Indigenous Leadership*, 90.

18. Browne, "A Statement from the Liberian Diocese to the Executive Council," May 1972, 3 pages (DFMS Papers).

19. "Who will win 9,000,000 Souls, CHRIST OR MOHAMMED? Bishop Browne Throws out Challenge at colorful Enthronement Ceremony," *Daily Observer* (Monrovia, Liberia) 2, no. 187, November 22, 1982, front page.

20. Browne to Dukuly, November 9, 1971 and November 11, 1971; Dukuly to Browne, November 24, 1971 (DFMS Papers, AR 2005.007, box 5, 1972–1979, 2).

21. Browne to Dukuly, November 9, 1971 and November 11, 1971; Dukuly to Browne, November 24, 1971 (DFMS Papers, AR. 2005.007, box 5, 1972–1979, 2).

22. Dukuly to Browne, November 24, 1971 (DFMS Papers, AR 2005.007, box 5, 1972–1979, 1).

23. George D. Browne, "New Structures for a New Day," commencement Address, Baptist Theological Seminary, Schieffelin, Liberia, December 8, 1986 (DFMS Papers, AR 2005, box 6 untitled folder, 16th in box, 6 pages [last page missing]).

24. E. Bolling Robertson Papers (Dunn Archives).

25. *Journal of the 48th General Convocation*, February 3–7, 1971; also 47th General Convocation, February 4–8, 1970; and The Special Convocation (Continuation of the 47th), April 1, 1970 (Dunn Archives).

26. The Rev. Suzanne Antoinette Fageol, telephone Interview with the author, June 27, 2018 (b. December 2, 1949, D. 1979, P. 1980, Diocese of Newark).

27. For "Design of Mission," see Parson, "Beginning of the Church in Liberia," *Historical Magazine of the Episcopal Church* 7, June 1938, 162–63; and his "Spirit of Missions, 1836," *Historical Magazine of the Episcopal Church* 7, June 1938, 339–42. See also Dean Arthur Holt, "Change Strategies Initiated by the Protestant Episcopal Church in Liberia from 1836 to 1950 and Their Differential Effects," Ed.D. diss., Boston University, 1970, 393 pages.

28. "Design of Mission," see Parson, "Beginning of the Church in Liberia."

29. "Design of Mission," see Parson, "Beginning of the Church in Liberia."

30. *Journal of 48th Diocesan Convention* (1971) (Dunn Archive).

31. Browne, *Indigenous Leadership*, 63.

32. *Journal of 49th Diocesan Convention* (1972) (Dunn Archives).

33. Quoted in Browne, *Indigenous Leadership*, 65.

34. D. Elwood Dunn, *History of the Episcopal Church in Liberia, 1821–1980* (Metuchen, NJ: American Theological Library Association and the Scarecrow Press, 1992).

35. See unpublished manuscript of Dr. John Gay (Dunn Archives); also John Gay, *A Letter To My Children, With Much Love* (Self-published, 1999), chaps. 6–16.

36. Gay, unpublished manuscript (Dunn Archives).

37. Gay, unpublished manuscript (Dunn Archives).

38. Dunn, *History of the Episcopal Church in Liberia*, 230.

39. G. Alvin Jones, Treasurer of ECL, for a decade, and close aide of Bishop Browne, telephone interview with author, December 26, 2018.

40. Browne, "Commencement Address of 1977" (Dunn Archives).

41. Board of Trustees, "Statement from the Chairman," December 16, 1986, 3 pages, Bishop Browne's Diary (Dunn Archives), in Browne, "Diaries and Log Books." See also Edward A. Holmes, "The Rural Development Institute at Cuttington University College: Its Founding," *Liberian Studies Journal* 13, no. 1 (1989): 67–75.

42. Bishop Browne's Diary (Dunn Archives), in Browne, "Diaries and Log Books."

43. Bishop Browne's Diary (Dunn Archives), in Browne, "Diaries and Log Books."

44. Bishop Browne's Diary (Dunn Archives), in Browne, "Diaries and Log Books."

45. Bishop Browne's Diary (Dunn Archives), in Browne, "Diaries and Log Books."

46. Acting CUC Chaplain Emmanuel Hodges to Bishop, August 30, 1987 (DFMS Papers).

47. Exchange of letters, Baker to Browne, December 14, 1987; and Browne to Baker, December 16, 1987 (DFMS Papers).

48. Exchange of letters, Baker to Browne, December 14, 1987; and Browne to Baker, December 16, 1987 (DFMS Papers).

49. Melvin J. Mason, *Savoring Education: An Autobiography* (Columbus, GA: Brentwood Christian Press, 2007).

50. Cuttington's Board meeting of February 19–20, 1992; and Mason to Gaie, April 1991, appointing him acting president of Cuttington; and Browne to Mason, February 28, 1992 and May 16, 1991 (Dunn Archives).

51. Bishop Browne's Diary, "Majority of Cuttington Students in Liberia," 1991, in Browne, "Diaries and Log Books."

52. Letter Mason to Browne, written after February 1, and before Browne's death on February 14, 1993. (Dunn Archives).

53. Browne, *Indigenous Leadership*, 45.

54. Brown, "1982 Address of the Bishop," *Journal of the 59th Diocesan Convention* (1982), 44 (Dunn Archives).

55. See *Journal of the 64th Diocesan Convention* (1987) (Dunn Archives), with regard to the myth mentioned by Sherman. See also Browne, "Dare to be Different," remarks at POPOLEBO (a Kru/Krao ethnic organization), Letter of invitation to Browne from C. Forth, August 11, 1989 (DFMS Papers).

56. "A Tribute to the Late President Tubman," July 26, 1971, 3 pages (DFMS Papers); See also Browne, *Indigenous Leadership*. With all the tolerance ascribed to Tubman, note his confrontation with Jehovah's Witness folks in 1960s. See Ijoma Flemister recalls "Violent Religious Persecution in Liberia," At JW Convention, Jehovah's Witness arrested in Gbarnga for refusal to sing National Anthem and pledge allegiance to the Flag, beaten and detained by Liberian government soldiers;" "Jehovah Witnessed expelled from civil service jobs" Gbatala, Bong County, March 1963.

57. "A Statement Addressed to our Friends in Liberia." (From Bishop Browne and the Baptist Prelate, The Rev. E, Tormu Reeves) April 27, 1979, 5 pages (Dunn Archives). See also D. Elwood Dunn, Amos J. Beyan, and Carl Patrick Burrowes, *Historical Dictionary of Liberia*, 2nd ed. (Lanham, MD: Scarecrow Press, 2001), 23–24, for summary of April 14, 1979 developments.

58. See Browne's letter in *Indigenous Leadership*, and E. Reginald Goodridge to Browne in which he copied Tolbert as Grand Master Emeritus in apparent sustenance of the myth? And Browne, *Indigenous Leadership*, chap. 5, on social issues and Free Masonry.

59. Greene to Bishop, May 31, 1973; Padmore to Browne & Browne to Padmore, June 13, 1973; Browne to Padmore, June 14, 1973, Browne to Harris, September 14, 1979 (DFMS Papers, AR 2005.007, box 6, 1972–1979).

60. See Bill Berkeley, *Liberia: A Promise Betrayed: A Report on Human Rights* (New York: Lawyers' Committee For Human Rights, 1986), for a full account of the developments touched on; also see Liberian Council of Churches to Doe, August 21, 1984 (Dunn Archives).

61. Browne's "Our Responsibility For the Future Life and Character of Liberia," Inaugural Sermon, January 5, 1986, 7 pages, at Intercessory Service on the eve of the Inauguration (DFMS Papers).

62. Browne, *Indigenous Leadership*, 14–15.
63. Browne, *Indigenous Leadership*, 163.
64. Browne, *Indigenous Leadership*, 15.
65. Church of the Province of West Africa (CPWA), *The Church of the Province of West Africa: Constitution And Canons*, revised (Accra: Anglican Press, 1990), arcticle 10, section 3bb.
66. Dunn, *History of the Episcopal Church in Liberia*, 146–50, quote from "Memorial to the Board of Missions and General Convention of the Protestant Episcopal Church, USA"; See also *Journal of the 12th General Convention*, 53–54, and the "Memorial, 1913," 11.
67. *Journal of the 25th General Convention* (year) 35; *Journal of the 39th General Convention* (1962), 75–76; *Journal of the 41st General Convention* (1964), 22–23.
68. G. Browne, *Indigenous Leadership*, 45.
69. George D. Browne, *Ten Years Episcopacy: A Reflection* (Sandpoint, ID: St. Agnes' Vicarage, 1980), 54–55.
70. Browne, *Indigenous Leadership*, 52; Dunn, *History of the Episcopal Church*. Background notes on CPWA: Five countries constitute the Province—Gambia, Ghana, Guinea, Liberia and Sierra Leone. Plus missionary activities in Cameroon, Cape Verde, Guinea-Bissau and Senegal. Demography in 1980s: young population of 44–48% under fifteen years old and 55–65% under twenty-five years old. Religious pluralism: Christianity, Islam and African Traditional Religions; 28% Christian, 27% Muslim, and 45% ATR. Sierra Leone is the oldest Diocese of the Church of England in West Africa since 1852. Though Diocese of Liberia is a year older, it began to associate constitutionally with the Province only in 1977. See J. Robert Ellis, Jr., "Assessment and Recommendations on the Church of the Province of West Africa," Monrovia, Liberia, December 2, 1985, 105 pages (Dunn Archives).
71. Browne, *Indigenous Leadership*, 53–54.
72. Browne, *Indigenous Leadership*, 39–40.
73. Browne, *Indigenous Leadership*, 167.
74. Browne, *Indigenous Leadership*, 90.

*Chapter Two*

# Interim Between Bishop Browne and Bishop Neufville (1993–1996)

## BROWNE'S HEALTH CONDITION AND AD HOC ADMINISTRATIVE ARRANGEMENTS

Bishop George D. Browne fell ill in 1991 and sought medical attention in the United States. His illness necessitated the establishment of an ad hoc arrangement given the absence of Suffragan Bishop Edward Wea Neufville II from the Diocese. Both men had experienced extreme, even life-threatening difficulties as the country was plunged into civil war in 1990. Where Browne's circumstances had allowed him to remain in the country until his health began to falter, Neufville seemingly found it necessary to secure his young family in the United States while remaining in touch with the Diocese, even making occasional visits. But before chronicling the events as they transpired, the health issues that contextualized Browne's ministry between 1990 and his death in February 1993 must first be made clear.

From the United States on September 20, 1992, Browne addressed an open letter to his fellow Episcopalians: "Many of you are concerned about the state of my health," he began. "After the heart surgery and we were planning to return in mid-August, it was discovered that I was allergic to some of the medications the doctors had given me and the blood plasma I took in March (1991) at the time of the surgery. They had induced hepatitis." "In late June," he continued, "I was readmitted for six days. At the time a liver biopsy was done. It revealed an infected liver. The doctors informed me of the natural sequence: retention of body fluid resulting in a swollen abdomen, swollen feet and easy exhaustion. They advised that I remain in this country (U.S.) so that when these symptoms appear they can treat it."

The Bishop continued: "By August 2 all these symptoms had appeared. On the 6th I had to be readmitted. I was nearly unconscious that day and the doctors had given my family a 50–50% chance of survival. They immediately performed a paracentesis, which revealed again an infected liver. My weight prior to this day was about 150 lbs. The doctors said that I must reduce considerably before adding weight. I was put on restricted fluid intake; one and half glasses of water a day and a pinch of salt a day! As I write this letter I weigh 140 lbs. having reduced by 25 lbs. in a month. The abdomen has reduced considerably to about 25% of the original size, and the feet are normal size. I am to see the doctors early next month, and I hope he will place me in a protein diet to build up before returning." And then he added in conclusion: "Those of you who know me will recall that I have never been out of the diocese for more than 8 weeks at a time, regardless. We are anxious to return to the work God has entrusted to us. God's blessings! Yours, George D. Browne, Bishop."[1] So, we have here a very sick Bishop and Shepherd of his flock anxious to return to them.

To appreciate what lay ahead in terms of the relationship between the two Liberian bishops, one Diocesan and the other Suffragan, it may be useful to recall the words of Bishop Browne on the occasion of the consecration of The Ven. Edward W. Neufville as Suffragan Bishop on May 6, 1984. Speaking to the topic "Are Bishops Essential to the Church? What can we Expect from our Suffragan?" Browne pointed out that he had called for a Suffragan because the church was growing and there was need for Episcopal assistance. He then added significantly: "As a Suffragan Bishop he has all the authority of a Bishop in the Church of God, and can perform Episcopal functions of all kinds." He informed the congregation that he and Fr. Neufville had had a retreat at which they talked briefly about the relationship between the Suffragan and the Diocesan. Archbishop Browne was expansive:

> We decided it would be a team ministry between us. We expect to work like brothers. Where disagreement comes in, we pledged to be opened with one another and talk and pray about it. We have agreed that our first loyalty should be to God and the Diocese. With that in mind, we realize that we have a challenge. This is the only diocese with a Suffragan Bishop that I know of in Western Africa, and maybe on the whole continent. We must prove that we can work together as co-equals, and we look to the Diocese to support us in this joint ministry.[2]

Those words were spoken almost a decade earlier. Evidently the two bishops had had their trials and tribulations but they seemed at that point not to have impaired the work of the Diocese.

They were together as the church anticipated the disruption of war in early 1990 (the civil war beginning on Christmas eve, 1989). The 67th Convention of the church had endorsed a proposal for the administrative rearrangement of the Diocese into three major units as follows:

1. Office of Evangelism and Ecclesiastical Matters, to include commission of ministry, examining chaplain, Christian education, evangelism & outreach, theological education, ecumenical & interfaith matters and Liturgy. This unit was to be headed by the Rev. Emmanuel Hodges.
2. Office of Education and Social Matters, to include board of education, development office, health and social welfare. This unit was to be headed by Mr. J. Robert Ellis.
3. Office of Finance and Budget Matters, to include board of trustees, pension plan, trust funds, endowment, and committee on finance and stewardship. This unit was to be headed by the Rev. John Jellico Bright.

The confluence of a number of circumstances led the Bishop incrementally to install teams of clergy and lay leaders to administer the affairs of the diocese during his protracted but intermittent absence from the diocese in the interest of his health. Those circumstances include a now increasingly evident difficult working relationship with Suffragan Bishop Neufville, the uncertainties of the civil war including the adverse effect on the church in common with all societal institutions, and the displacement of much of the clerical force. One wonders whether the Convention's action was already a reflection of distrust between the two bishops. Where did the Suffragan Bishop fit in the new administrative arrangement? Though still charged with the Northern Archdeaconry, such major administrative overhaul might have at least hinted a role for the assistant bishop.

Many parishioners seemed surprised when differences between the Diocesan Bishop and his assistant, the Suffragan Bishop, showed its ugly face at the funeral of Bishop Browne at Trinity Cathedral on March 9, 1993. A tense situation developed, as the late Bishop's family did not want the Suffragan Bishop to participate in the funeral ceremonies, even marching in the procession. This attitude on the part of the family necessitated Neufville's issuance of a communication to the Clergy of the Diocese urging them to inform their parishes about why he was being low-profiled during the period of the funeral.

Individuals in the position to know informed me that the rift began almost immediately following the consecration in 1984 of Bishop Neufville as Suffragan Bishop. Bishop Neufville has himself written the following in his incomplete draft autobiography. "My Episcopacy," about the origins of the differences: "At the inception of my Episcopal ministry," he writes, "and throughout following my election on the first ballot in 1984 at Epiphany Chapel Cuttington University, the obvious unreadiness, in my view, of the Diocesan to accept and live with another head wearing a MITRE created an atmosphere unconducive to camaraderie and Christian brotherly team ministry."[3] While personality differences often figure in such situations some have pointed to specifics. "From the beginning, the working relationship between George Browne and Edward Neufville was not good," one Clergy, recalls. He continued: "It appeared that as far as he (Neufville) was concerned, he and Bishop Browne were bishops and in a sense equal. . . . It appears that Neufville felt that he could make his own decisions and do things his own way within the diocese. That approach or behavior didn't sit well with George Browne. Also, George Browne had already been a diocesan bishop for over 10 years when Neufville became suffragan in 1984. Thus, relinquishing power or control to another person would never come easily."[4]

But there were many other perspectives. One suggests that long before the start of the civil war, Bishop Neufville had felt slighted when Browne went to Nimba County, without his knowledge, to investigate him and the congregations under his charge due to inconsistencies in the Suffragan's reports to the Diocese. Browne then subsequently removed the Cuttington community from the jurisdiction of the Northern Archdeaconry, which Neufville administered. There seemed to have been an issue of ambiguity regarding the role of the Suffragan, with Browne holding one view and Neufville another. Neufville, on the one hand, seemingly took an exclusivist view of his assigned area of the Northern Archdeaconry, believing that Browne's supervisory role was to be minimal. Browne, on the other hand, held the Suffragan as his assistant, by no means at liberty to do as he wished.[5]

The mutual suspicion deepened as Browne grew increasingly non-collaborative, providing his Suffragan with minimal information about the operations of the Diocese. A rift began to emerge in the church between sympathizers of the Diocesan and Suffragan Bishops.

"When the Charles Taylor war occurred in 1990," Fr. Jellico Bright has written in response to my research questions to him:

> Neufville and I were displaced on the campus of CUC. At the request of Eugene Cooper to Bishop Browne to secure round trip tickets for both of us (Bishop Neufville and me) to visit our families in the United States, Bishop Browne agreed and provided the tickets. This was around 1991. I believe that Bishop Neufville came earlier in the year and I came to the US later in 1991. It is important to note that Bishop Browne remained in Liberia throughout the Liberian civil war until the time that he needed to seek medical attention.[6]

Other observers have said that Browne was disappointed with Neufville on grounds that he deserted his flock in crisis. But Neufville informed Browne about his movements during the initial stages of the war. For example, he wrote a note to Browne on reaching Monrovia from displacement on the Cuttington campus. "Due to recent developments in Gbarnga," the note of March 18, 1990 began, " I was constrained to bring my family to Monrovia for security reasons." Neufville has also detailed his harrowing war experience in a document titled "Some of our Experiences in Liberia during the civil war" by The Rt Rev. Edward W. Neufville, II, Bishop (Suffragan) Liberia. In it he details the travails of himself and family and how American friends assisted them, including a plane ticket for Mrs. Neufville from the Presiding Bishop of the American church that explains their presence in the United States. Nothing was said about the role of the Diocesan Bishop in the effort, or the account of Fr. Jellico Bright about tickets provided by Browne. What seems clear in the varying or conflicting accounts is that civil war conditions had created difficult circumstances for both Bishops and prior relations of distrust did not make for good working relations going forward.[7]

Other circumstances that led Bishop Browne to install ad hoc administrators include the uncertainties of the civil war. Through the Liberian Council of Churches (LCC), Browne had been in contact with the Interim Government of National Unity (IGNU) in Monrovia while other LCC colleagues tried to communicate with National Patriotic Front leader Charles Taylor and other warring factions, all in an effort to end the carnage. But it was becoming increasingly clear that the conflict was perhaps not yet "ripe for resolution." Then more than half of the Diocese's clerical force was displaced and an even larger percentage of the congregations were in peril. Browne tried to consolidate what he could from his Monrovia base until his health became an issue.

In late November 1990, when he was rescued from his Virginia home outside Monrovia, his first act was to establish a council of advisors. The council consisted of members of the Diocesan Council and Standing Committee still in country. He consulted this body with regularity, periodically reporting to them his every action. Prior to his first departure abroad for health reasons he appointed a Vicar General to work with the Council reportedly in keeping with canonical provisions of both the Diocese and the Province for, according to Article 10, Section 3b:

> If the Diocesan shall be absent from the Diocese for more than six weeks and there be no Bishop Coadjutor, Suffragan Bishop or assistant Bishop to whom he could delegate authority to administer the spiritualities of the Diocese, and to maintain discipline according to this Constitution, he shall make appropriate

arrangements through the appointment of a Vicar General with requisite authority or through such means that are provided in his Docesan Constitution and Canons for an Ecclesiastical Authority.[8]

To clarify the purely legal issues of what should obtain in the absence of the Diocesan from jurisdiction, as well as succession in case of incapacity or death of the Diocesan, I sought the views of current Diocesan Chancellor Seward M. Cooper. He referenced the *Constitutions and Canons* of the Diocese and the Province deemed to have been in effect during the 1992–1993 period and offered the following as what legally might have obtained:

1. Absence the Diocesan from jurisdiction for more than six months, coupled with absence of the Suffragan, "the Diocesan may appoint a Vicar General with requisite authority." This translates: "If . . . both Bishop Browne and Suffragan Bishop Neufville were absent from the Diocese, then Bishop Browne could have legally appointed a Vicar General."
2. In case of death of the Diocesan [See Art. VII (Vacancy) of Provincial Constitution] "and there is no Bishop Coadjutor, election is to be held for a new Bishop." This would obtain even if there were an incumbent Suffragan Bishop since the office of Suffragan Bishop "[C]arries with it no presumption that the holder will be elected to the office of Diocesan Bishop on the occurrence of a vacancy, not that he would be precluded from such election . . ." [see article 7 (Suffragan Bishop) of Provincial Constitution].[9]

What actually obtained, though not outside the pale of the law, was dictated by circumstances including an unhealthy working relationship between Bishop Browne and Bishop Neufville. As Browne was back and forth between the United States and Liberia, Browne found it necessary to renew the ad hoc arrangement. To guide Vicar General Hodges in his work, Browne convened the chairs of the different committees of the Diocese and formed the Team Ministry. Upon what eventuated in his last return to Liberia on November 19, 1992, to assess the work of the Diocese and make provisions for its ongoing programs, and his departure December 16, 1992, the same circumstances obtaining, Bishop Browne arranged again for a Vicar General to work along with the Team Ministry.

Then without warning on January 20, 1993, Suffragan Bishop Neufville arrived in the Diocese with no evidence of his having communicated with the now gravely ill Diocesan Bishop.[10] Perhaps a combination of the tense relationship between the two Bishops and the gravity of Browne's illness precluded communication in the normal course of things. At any rate, while the Vicar General and the Team Ministry were trying to address the quandary they faced they received news that Bishop Browne had died February 14, 1993. The Bishop died at the Milwaukee Regional Medical Center at 8 a.m. on the 14th, moments after my spouse and I had just driven into the city and visited the unconscious and now dying Bishop. I was privileged to have worked with Bishop Browne on the manuscript of his book, *The Episcopal Church of Liberia Under Indigenous Leadership: Reflections On a Twenty Year Episcopate*, from 1991 through late 1992.[11]

## STATE OF THE CHURCH ON BROWNE'S SUDDEN DEATH: LEADERSHIP CONTROVERSY

Given the ad hoc administration Browne was constrained to put in place as he shuttled between the United States and Liberia seeking medical attention, and Neufville's own perception of his role as Suffragan Bishop in the Diocese, controversy seemed inevitable. The Suffragan Bishop had arrived from the United States in the Diocese three weeks to the death in the United States of the Diocesan. The Suffragan had seemingly not communicated with the Diocesan or his family. The Suffragan asserted that the affairs of the Church had devolved upon him pending election of a successor Diocesan. The Team Ministry refused to cede, referencing instead the Provincial canons, which they claimed stipulated that the Dean of the Province would serve as Metropolitan pending election of a new Diocesan Bishop of Liberia.

The background that culminated in the foregoing is traceable to the old Browne-Neufville differences. Not only had Neufville abandoned his flock in the view of Browne, he had taken canonical residency in the U.S. Diocese of South Carolina. Neufville saw things quite differently. He felt that he had struggled on his own under dire civil war circumstances to first secure his family in the United States and then to provide for them. To do this without abandoning his flock, he had to seek assistance in any way he could to pay the bills of his family. He returned to Liberia when he could, assisted with relief activities, and carried out the functions of a Bishop in the Diocese such as confirming and ordaining as the opportunity allowed.

Neufville's family preceded him to the United States as he joined them in August 1991 and settled with them in the Diocese of South Carolina. In a letter of November 4, 1992, Browne wrote:

> I can understand the circumstance [that brought you to South Carolina] but it is irregular. If you would like a canonical change of residence for a while then please let me know, and I will send a formal letter to that effect. In the meanwhile, until I hear from you I will put hold on your canonical residence in Liberia, for you cannot be resident in two dioceses at the same time.

Neufville retorted in a reply a week later:

> You suggest in your letter that if I desire a change of canonical residence for a while I should let you know so that you can send a formal letter to that effect. I was taken by surprise that such a suggestion should come from you in this critical period of our history when our people need us most. Please note that it was never my intention neither is it now to withdraw from my ministry to our people, especially at this critical time, to which the Lord Almighty has called me, regardless. If in the future I ever decide a change in canonical residence I am well aware of the canonical and constitutional procedures regarding it. [Neufville added that he would return to Liberia] right after the American Thanksgiving.[12]

Bishop Browne replied to Neufville, for the last time as it turned out. "If you had explained these facts [About temporary arrangements in his family's interest] to me in July or August, " he wrote, "I would not have had to ask the Church Life Insurance for explanation." One of Browne's concerns was that the life insurance plan for the Neufville family would not lapse as a consequence of attempted adjustments as between coverage in the dioceses of Liberia and South Carolina. But the misunderstanding had already led Browne to withhold regular salary payments to Neufville as at July 1, 1992, though the hold was lifted and Neufville received a lump sum of $21,193.50 on August 25, 1992 for June 1990 to July 1992 salary.

Though Bishop Browne's death ended this phase of the saga, it was not before Bishop Edward Salmon of the Diocese of South Carolina had chimed in with a sarcastic letter to Bishop Browne only a few weeks before Browne's death. "I know that you must be rejoicing knowing that Bishop Neufville is back in Liberia taking care of the Diocese." And the American cleric did not relent as following Browne's death he wrote to the Rev. Jellico Bright, acting treasurer of the Diocese of Liberia: "I believe that response [Browne's to Salmon] is irregular and I am forwarding a copy of this letter to the Archbishop of Canterbury," perhaps in like manner as Browne had copied his letter to Salmon to the Presiding Bishop of the Episcopal Church.

Bishop Browne died February 14, 1993 at age 59 years. Funeral Services were held in Milwaukee, Wisconsin and New York City before the body was flown home for last funeral rites at Trinity Cathedral in Monrovia, and burial at Bamboo Town, Virginia, Liberia, on March 9, 1993. The unresolved bad relationship between the Diocesan and the Suffragan reared its ugly head at the funeral service. It was agreed that the Browne family did not want Neufville to participate in the service for all the reasons earlier mentioned. Bishop Browne had held the view that Neufville's physical and canonical residence in another diocese had undercut his place as Suffragan in the Diocese of Liberia, and some claim that Browne had consequently suspended Neufville until otherwise ordered.[13] And then Neufville's encounters with the Vicar General and Team Ministry induced suspicion because when Browne was present in Liberia, Neufville was absent, and when Browne was absent Neufville somehow showed up, becoming particularly assertive, according to Vicar General Emmanuel Hodges, following Browne's death.

And so, on the day of the funeral as the procession had assembled with The Rev. Herman Browne (son of the Bishop and Homilist for the funeral) near the rear of the line, Herman Browne was summoned by the Provincial Church's hierarchy, particularly the Dean of the Province to help settle "whether or not Neufville should process." Bishop Browne's widow, Mrs. Clavender Railey Browne insisted at this point that Neufville should not process. There was much back and forth about the matter. I recall encountering the Rev. Christopher Kandakai, a senior priest of the Diocese who was late in arrival, and pleading with him to intervene and try to save the day. Another senior priest of the Diocese, The Rev. Canon A. Bane Collins reportedly expressed things in theological terms, suggesting that processing was part of the liturgical prerogative of any Bishop of the church, and to deny that to Neufville or any other Bishop would be tantamount to dethroning him. Herman Browne was persuaded and succeeded in bringing his mother to agree. Thus the impasse was broken and the procession proceeded into the Cathedral for the funeral services. A most impressive service was executed at which presided Dean Joseph Dadson of the Church of the Province of West Africa (CPWA) who had now by canonical requirement become the Metropolitan of the Diocese of Liberia pending the election of a new Diocesan bishop. The Diocese of Liberia, the Province of West Africa, the Episcopal Church of the United States (ECUSA) and the Church of England made moving tributes. Bishop Browne was also accorded a State Funeral by the wartime government of Liberia dubbed IGNU.

## CHURCH OF THE PROVINCE OF WEST AFRICA OVERSIGHT AMID UNEASY RELATIONS BETWEEN NEUFVILLE AND TEAM MINISTRY

Upon the Bishop's death authority for the ECL devolved on an interim basis upon The Rt. Rev. Joseph K. Dadson, Dean of the Province and now Metropolitan of the Diocese. Following the funeral, Bishop Dadson convened a meeting at the Spriggs Payne Airport in Monrovia involving all the relevant parties upon whose shoulders the responsibility of the ECL had devolved—the

Standing Committee, the Team Ministry, Vicar General Emmanuel Hodges and the Suffragan Bishop. Discussing the key question about how to assure a workable interim arrangement between the death of Bishop Browne and the election of the next Diocesan bishop, comparisons were made between the provisions of the *Provincial Constitution* (1990), and the *Constitution of the Diocese of Liberia* (1984). It was decided that the *Provincial Constitution* being the supreme law, its provisions should guide the deliberations. Accordingly, it was decided as follows:

1. The Vicar General, together with the Team Ministry appointed by the deceased Bishop of Liberia for the administration of the Diocese during his absence from the Diocese, should continue to be responsible for the administration of the Diocese.
2. The Suffragan Bishop who is now at post should be responsible for Episcopal Acts.
3. All should be seen to be cooperating in the smooth administration of the Diocese (All, that is the Suffragan Bishop and the Team Ministry). Any matter that the corporate body could not resolve should be referred to the Dean of the Province (who would find a solution through consultation).

Dean Dadson then put a question regarding the fairness and workability of the guidelines as above stated, to which both Bishop Neufville and the Team Ministry answered in the affirmative. That Neufville had mental reservations would surface later, as when he separately engaged both Bishop Dadson and the Chancellor of both the Diocese of Liberia and of the Province, Counselor J. Rudolph Grimes.

To Dean Dadson Bishop Neufville wrote: "I have found myself obliged to address this letter to you for, in my own judgment, I thought it best not to raise questions or issues in the presence of others, as the interim head of the Diocese was discussed at the James Spriggs Airport just prior to your March 10 departure for Ghana." Neufville continued: "With your kind permission, your Lordship, I beg to draw your kind attention to a matter of concern regarding the smooth operation of the Diocese. There appears to be a certain degree of incongruity occasioned by the dichotomy of leadership presented by continued use of a Team Ministry whilst I am present in the Diocese. If the Team Ministry remains the Administrative Head of the Church, perforce of circumstances, I thereby become obliged to answer to the Vicar General, a Priest in charge of the Cathedral where I spiritually preside." After expressing his views on the Canons of both the Diocese and the Province, Neufville wrote in conclusion that "we need a confluence of spiritual and administrative leadership under one umbrella, so as to put to rest, once and for all, the germinating seeds of divisiveness."[14]

Then in a letter to Chancellor Grimes to which was attached copy of the letter to Dadson, Neufville said the Spriggs Payne Airport "arrangement confuses me." "The glaring dichotomy of leadership occasioned by this arrangement makes it difficult for me to properly function. I therefore humbly request that you kindly do all you can to rectify, at your earliest, what I consider a deviation from the canons." It took several months before an opinion was forthcoming from Grimes and it was triggered by other circumstances. On the specific issue of the Team Ministry and also expressing his reservations on the decision of keeping in place the Team Ministry, Grimes wrote: "Since the "TEAM MINISTRY" is not included in our Diocesan Constitution and Canons, I consider that Archbishop Browne's appointment of the 'TEAM MINISTRY' to administer the Diocese at best can only be interpreted as a temporary one especially since he seemed to have administered the Diocese even though ill and physically away from its seat, because otherwise it would be beyond the pale of legality."[15]

In all these developments, the Church remained painfully divided and Liberian Episcopalians confused. None of this might have happened had mutual trust characterized the relationship between Bishop Browne and Bishop Neufville. Under normal circumstances most people would support the team ministry, as there was no Bishop on the ground. The return of the Suffragan might have resolved the matter and the team ministry dissolved. But one observer suspects that "the manner in which the existence and role of the team ministry was spoken of by Bishop Neufville—demonized and denigrated—made many feel that Bishop Browne had set up an illegal body to deprive Neufville of his Episcopal charge over the diocese." There was the added suspicion "that Dadson's action was to counter just such an impression, and establish the team's legitimacy." Henceforth "the team was now on a war path post-Dadson and was determined to hold off Neufville for as long as possible whom they perceived as a destroyer of Browne's legacy."[16]

Dadson visited Liberia July 1993, and in a series of meetings with the awkward leadership team in place, succeeded in amending the arrangement so that instead of vicar general there was a nomenclature change to chairman of the team ministry. Dadson conveyed the following information, which did little to clarify the situation:

1. The Suffragan Bishop of Liberia, the Rt. Rev'd Edward W. Neufville, has asked for leave of absence to travel to the United States of America for medical and other matters from July 21st, 1993 'til September 5, 1993.
2. The Rev'd Emmanuel D. Hodges of Trinity Cathedral Monrovia is therefore asked by copy of this letter, to administer the Diocese of Liberia as

vicar general from the dates the Suffragan Bishop leaves the Diocese until his return, that is July 21st to 5th September 1993.

To this letter Bishop Dadson attached a memo dated July 7, 1993 directed to the Diocese of Liberia, Suffragan Bishop, Team Ministry, Chairman and Members Congregations, Parishes and Clergy, Acting Chancellor/Registrar titled "How The Diocese is to be seen operating." It was a diplomatic affirmation of the March 10, 1993 Spriggs Payne Airport understanding or agreement. The Church actually muddled through to elections, which were then still two years away.[17]

## ELECTION OF SUCCESSOR DIOCESAN BISHOP

The countdown to elections began to materialize in April 1993 as the Diocesan Registrar and Acting Chancellor, Joseph P. H. Findley established the Church's Standing Committee as "the Ecclesiastical Authority of the Church" and thus the proper instance for calling "a Special Convention for the election of a Diocesan in succession to Bishop Browne." A Bishop nominating committee was elected at a special convention held July 16, 1994. The year following through consultations involving the Suffragan Bishop, the Archbishop of the CPWA, the Standing Committee and the Team Ministry, May 17–21 was established as the dates for a Diocesan Convention to elect a new Bishop.[18]

Thus it was that the 146th Special Diocesan Convention was held at Trinity Cathedral in Monrovia on May 19, 1995. The three candidates that were advanced by the nominating committee were The Rev. Jonathan B. B. Hart, The Rev. Momo B. Kpartor (then distant and serving in Cameroons), and Suffragan Bishop Edward W. Neufville. But settling on the three names did not go unchallenged as some raised questions about a process that excluded some obvious "hopefuls," not to speak of the use or misuse of the name of Fr. Kpartor who was resident abroad—a situation reminiscent of the use of the name of the Rev. Canon Burgess Carr in the 1970 election that brought Bishop Browne to office. There was here the proverbial elephant in the room in the person of Vicar General, The Rev. Father Emmanuel Hodges. But this was a muted matter that soon became moot. On the basis of the three names, therefore, the election got underway. During what became a first round, no candidate received the two-thirds requirement for outright election. Neufville received ninety-three votes, Hart forty-eight, and Kpartor four votes. A required second round had Kpartor eliminated with the two top vote getters remaining. Neufville polled ninety-seven votes to Hart's forty-four, and thus on second ballot Neufville was elected the 11th Diocesan Bishop of the Episcopal Church of Liberia (ECL).

In keeping with Church protocol this information was conveyed to the Archbishop and Primate of the CPWA, The most Rev. Robert G. A. Okine, who then sent a memo to the following: The Diocesan Bishop-Elect, The Rt Rev. Edward W. Neufville II, The Vicar-General, ECL, The Rev. Fr. Emmanuel D. Hodges, The Diocesan Registrar/Acting Chancellor and Chairman, Special Diocesan Convention, Mr. Joseph P. H. Findley, The Secretary to the Convention, Mr. William T. Diggs. In the memo Archbishop Okine intimated that the letter of notice of the election's outcome was followed by a series of correspondences from aggrieved Episcopalian individuals and groups alleging that the election was marked by irregularities and controversy. Okine dutifully circulated all correspondence from Liberia to all the Bishops of the Province, the Provincial Chancellor and Registrar for study and comments.

Okine then wrote: "Due to the absence of some of the Bishops from their dioceses, and with the seemingly explosive situation in the Church of Liberia which merited a consensus response, my reply has taken some time for which I render humble apology." He was now happy to report that all of the responses were now in from the Provincial Chancellor and all the Diocesan Bishops at post (seven altogether, including the Archbishop), which were now being shared with the Clergy and people of ECL.

Bishop Neufville's election as Diocesan had been accepted by Okine and unanimously confirmed by the Episcopal Synod of the Province. Neufville had accordingly been notified. In accordance with Provincial Constitution an Instrument of Confirmation had been sent to the Vicar General, Rev. Fr. Emmanuel D. Hodges "to be proclaimed in the Cathedral and in all Parish Churches during Divine Service on two Sundays following the receipt of this notification." The Vicar General in his capacity as Priest-in-Charge of Trinity Cathedral was issued a mandate for the Enthronement of Bishop Neufville as Diocesan Bishop. The Liberian authorities were now free to issue a release to the press on the matter.[19]

Okine moved next to the main complaints raised by aggrieved persons and organizations, commenting on each. The Ghanaian prelate considered why certain names did not emerge as candidates "frivolous" and not worthy of entertainment. With the stroke of his pen the elephant in the room issue was quickly laid to rest. On the allegation during the election of politicking, bribery, tribalism, etc., they were considered unsubstantiated "mere generalizations" and thus warranted being ignored "with the exception of one name (withheld) [no doubt that of Fr. Hodges] which was mentioned." And finally, regarding complaint on the run-off election, the mechanics were explained of going into a second round as no one obtained the required two thirds vote in the first round, and that Kpartor was properly eliminated because he was not among the two top vote winners.

Then came some penetrating observations from Okine. It was "with deep pain" that he had read the complaints of the aggrieved persons, though protest against any election result is not unusual, and so the complaint against the election of Neufville was received in this light. "What I was not so sure of," he continued, "was whether any of you four officials were served with copies of the complaints. I was particularly disappointed that these complaints came after the election had been 'successfully' completed. I sincerely believe that if these seeming irregularities had been deeply impressed upon members of the Special Convention, as they sat, the likelihood of their being ignored would have been slim since they were delicate enough to demand some attention, provided they had been substantiated."[20]

There was more: "I have had the opportunity to visit your Diocese. I, therefore, know at first hand some of the grievances of the members. What saddens me greatly is the fact that there seems to exist factions within the Church who 'may' be classified as 'pro-Browne' and 'pro-Neufville.' There is nothing wrong with having deep admiration for a person and being strongly attached to him/her. What is wrong is doing this for the wrong reasons and/or motives. Worst of all is it for one to be so set in his/her ways and/or thinking that nothing else matters, however reasonable."[21] "In the interest of brotherly/sisterly love, peace unity and progress," Okine counseled that the ECL should "let bygones be bygones. You should bury all your differences in the name of Christ and give Bishop Edward Neufville a chance to prove himself as a Godly and capable Shepherd. This will help him to bring about the much needed healing and reconciliation that the Church of Liberia so badly needs."

And then the chief pastor of the CPWA launched into a sermonette: "The divisive issue has dragged on for far too long. To encourage its perpetuation will serve no useful purpose to any individual or group of persons and the Church; for that matter, it is unholy for the Church to wash her dirty linen in public. It is unholier still for the Church to continue to be at war in the midst of a once-devastated nation which is gradually beginning to see some signs of peace. As the 'salt of the earth' and 'light of the world' it behooves us to lead exemplary lives to give positive meaning to our preachments and pronouncements."[22]

"St Paul's exhortation in 1 Corinthians 13 is still relevant to your present situation, particularly: 'Love is patient and kind; love is not jealous or boastful; it is not arrogant or rude. Love does not insist on its own way; it is not irritable or resentful; it does not rejoice at wrong, but rejoices in the right. Love bears all things, believes all things, hopes all things, endures all things." (1 Cor. 13:4–7). Remember also our Lord's legacy to us his followers: "This is my commandment, that you love one another as I have loved you." (John 15:12) Let us learn to forgive and forget! I know it is not easy to overcome and forget months of deep hurt and suffering overnight. But with earnest prayer and fasting, this can be done with God's help. 'Not by might, nor by power, but by my Spirit, says the Lord of hosts.' (Zech. 4:6)"

On the same date as the memo to Bishop Neufville was written, a letter confirming his election as Diocesan Bishop of Liberia was dispatched with much of the information in the memo summarized. Okine extended congratulations to the new Bishop-Elect and counseled him as "the new Shepherd of the Episcopal flock of Liberia," to take with utmost seriousness his "solemn task" of reassembling and healing his scattered and wounded flock.[23]

Yet another letter came from Archbishop Okine to the Episcopal Church, this one a mandate to the Rev. Fr. Emmanuel Douglas Hodges, Vicar-General and Priest-in-Charge, Trinity Cathedral enjoining and commanding him, against the backdrop of the election and confirmation thereof "to INSTALL and ENTHRONE the said Right Reverend Edward W. Neufville, II as Diocesan Bishop of the Diocese of Liberia." "In the name of the Father, and of the Son, and of the Holy Spirit, Amen." And this was "Given under our Hand and Seal this 31st day of October in the Year of our Lord One thousand nine hundred and ninety-five in the Fifteenth Year of our Consecration and Third Year of our Archiepiscopacy. Signed by The Most Revd Robert G. A. Okine, Archbishop, Church of the Province of West Africa."

That this may have been a most difficult assignment for Hodges is an understatement. When I asked Mrs. Korto Hodges, widow of Fr. Hodges for a brief interview she painfully declined. When I pressed gently for her reconsideration, she politely said that she knows how to reach me if she changes her mind. I did not hear from her before going to press. No Provincial Bishop attended the enthronement and installation of Bishop Neufville as Diocesan Bishop of Liberia. Bishop Donald Hart, a retired Bishop of the Diocese of Hawaii, represented the Presiding Bishop of the American church.[24]

## ASSESSING THE INTERIM PERIOD

The experience of the ECL and the CPWA negotiating a transition from the episcopacy of George Daniel Browne to that of Edward Wea Neufville II may be comparable in scale and scope to the post-Samuel David Ferguson transition of more than a century ago. Differences in time and circumstances notwithstanding, the task was no less daunting. Bishop Ferguson, the first and only Liberian among the missionary bishops died 1916 at the end of a remarkable thirty-one-year episcopacy. His legacy was encapsulated in this statement: "This much can be said about [Ferguson's] ministry, he did in fact build a base . . . and the Mission was nearer in 1916 than any previous time to being a significant and responsible agent of planned change in Liberia."[25]

Bishop Browne, the first Liberian-born bishop, elected by Liberian Episcopalians, died at age fifty-nine years, following a twenty-two-year episcopacy. Chancellor J. Rudolph Grimes said the following about Browne's legacy: "He was dedicated to his ministry and everyone can see the demonstration of his courage and determination. His success will be emblazoned in the history of the Diocese of Liberia and in the Anglican Church of the Province of West Africa." Father Jellico Bright had this to say about Browne's legacy: "Though affected in the 1980s and beyond by political instability and civil war that followed, Browne was able to lay a solid structural foundation and make great strides in the development of the Clergy."

Yet, a combination of civil war and the Bishop's health circumstances left the church reeling in division and distrust, ripe for a reconciling chief pastor. Could Bishop Neufville have led reconciliation efforts given that his person was enmeshed in the controversy? It took all of twenty-nine years between Bishop Ferguson's death in 1916 and the start of the episcopacy of Missionary Bishop B. W. Harris in 1945 to see vibrancy restored to the Church in ways that were both tangible and intangible. Might post-civil war conditions and a traumatized Church today (comparable to the inertia of missionary bishops between 1916 and 1945) define the challenge today of the ECL?

## NOTES

1. Browne to Dear Fellow Episcopalians, September 20, 1992, 1 page (Dunn Archives).

2. Sermon by Archbishop George D. Browne, "Are Bishops Essential to the Church? What can we expect from our Suffragan?" Sermon by Archbishop George D. Browne on the occasion of the Ordination and Consecration of The Ven. Edward W. Neufville as Suffragan Bishop, Trinity Cathedral, May 6, 1984, 6 pages (Dunn Archives).

3. Bishop Edward W. Neufville II's draft manuscript, "My Episcopacy," (Dunn Archives; courtesy of Mrs. Louise M. Neufville).

4. Neufville's letter to the Clergy, "Memo from Suffragan Bishop Neufville to "All Clergy of the Diocese. Subject: As you know, the late Bishop Browne requested that I should nothing to do with or at his burial ceremonies, as relayed by his widow and children." March 5, 1993, same message faxed to Bishop Edward L. Salmon and Bishop Allen L. Bartlett Jr., 1 page (Dunn Archives); Fr. Jellico Bright, interview by telephone and email with author, 2016; Mrs. Clavender Railey Browne, interview with author, January 11, 2017, Milwaukee, WI; Mrs. Louise Neufville, interview

by telephone and Sumter, SC, with author, March 1, 2016; Dr. Herman B. Browne, interview with author Cuttington, Suakoko, October 18, 2016. They reflect the full force of the conflict as in the sharp differences of perspectives.

5. Herman B. Browne, interview with author Cuttington, Suakoko, October 18, 2016.

6. Bright, interview by telephone and email with author, 2016.

7. Reference Nuefville's letter of 3/18/90, and Neufville's article, "Some of our Experience in the Liberian Civil War," 8pp (Courtesy of Mrs. Nuefville)

8. See ECL, *The Episcopal Church of Liberia: Constitution and Canons*, Amended (Accra: Anglican Press, 1987), article 10, section 3b (revised as at 1990).

9. Counselor Seward M. Cooper, Chancellor, ECL, email communication between author, June 20, 2019.

10. American church officials, aware of the communication issues between Bishops Browne and Neufville, attempted to be helpful. A letter of January 8, 1992 from Secretary General of The Anglican Communion, Canon Sam van Culin says: "I am sure that George [Browne] looks forward to your return and to your continuing ministry together as soon as you feel able to do this." A more poignant letter to Neufville, dated November 23, 1992 came from the Africa Partnership Officer of The Episcopal Church (USA) (TEC), The Rev. Dr. E. Nathaniel Porter. "By now, I am sure you have learned that Archbishop Browne has left the States for London on his way to Liberia. We do hold him in our most sincere prayers as he embarks on a bold and potentially dangerous mission,. However our prayer and faith is that God will guide and protect him and his beloved family. Please keep us informed about your ministry progresses" (both letters in Dunn Archives).

11. Letter to publisher Taryor of January 11, 1993 regarding the second galley. See also J. Rudolph Grimes, "A Tribute to the Memory of THE MOST REVEREND GEORGE DANIEL BROWNE, BSc, BD, DD, KGB, BISHOP OF LIBERIA AND ARCHBISHOP AND PRIMATE of the ANGLICAN CHURCH OFK THE PROVINCE OF WEST AFRICA." Grimes as Chancellor of ECL and CPWA, New York, February 27, 1993. 5 pages (Dunn Archives)

12. Browne to Neufville, November 4, 1992; Neufville to Browne, November 10, 1992 (Dunn Archives).

13. See Jellico Bright, interview by telephone and email with author, 2016. For reasons associated with Neufville's functions in the Diocese of South Carolina without Browne's approval, "he suspended Bishop Neufville from his duties as Suffragan Bishop. As part of the suspension, Bishop Browne instructed me as treasurer to immediately withhold all and any payments to Bishop Neufville until his authorization." According to Fr. Bright, the CPWA was duly informed.

14. Neufville to Dadson, n.d., 2 pages (Dunn Archives).

15. Memo to The "Memorandum To: The Team Ministry," Episcopal Diocese of Liberia, From Chancellor J. Rudolph Grimes, June 28, 1993, 3 pages. Grimes was actually reacting to an "undated letter sent to Episcopalians." Neufville to Grimes, March 16, 1993.

16. Herman B. Browne's comments on the Grimes memo (interview with author, October 18, 2016, Cuttington, Suakoko, including email exchanges).

17. Note Dadson to The Rev. Prince E. S. Thompson, Episcopal Secretary CPWA in Freetown. See CPWA, D, 10A, July 6, 1993 (Dunn Archives).

18. Findley to Mitchell, April 2, 1993 (Dunn Archives).

19. CPWA, "Memo from Archbishop Robert Okine to ECL Officials. Subject: Election of a Diocesan Bishop of Liberia." October 31, 1995, 5 pages.

20. CPWA, "Memo from Okine to ECL," October 31, 1995, 5 pages, items from Okine.

21._CPWA, "Memo from Okine to ECL,", October 31, 1995, 5 pages, items from Okine.

22._CPWA, "Memo from Okine to ECL,", October 31, 1995, 5 pages, items from Okine.

23. CPWA, "Memo from Okine to ECL," October 31, 1995, 5 pages, items from Okine; Okine to Neufville, October 31, 1995.

24. ECL, "Souvenir Programme, Installation and Enthronement of The Rt. Rev. Edward Wea Neufville II, BA, MTS, DD, the 11th Bishop of Liberia," Trinity Cathedral, Broad Street, Monrovia, January 6, 1996. Feast of The Epiphany,

25. D. Elwood Dunn, *A History of the Episcopal Church of Liberia, 1821–1980* (Metuchen, NJ: American Theological Library Association and the Scarecrow Press, 1992), 155–56.

*Chapter Three*

# Episcopate of Bishop Edward Wea Neufville II (1996–2007)

## ANOTHER CHALLENGING BEGINNING

The episcopacy of the second Liberian Diocesan Bishop elected by Liberian Episcopalians had a beginning as inauspicious as was his predecessor's, though the circumstances of the two men were fundamentally different. While Bishop Browne inherited a Missionary District with umbilical cord tied to the American Church, Bishop Neufville inherited a tragically divided Church embedded in a country at war with itself. Such circumstances significantly shaped the episcopates of the two Church leaders. Browne was challenged to set a new course after 134 years of missionary leadership. For his part, Neufville was challenged to reconcile his flock and reconstruct the physical plant laid waste by civil war.

Edward Wea Neufville II had a distinguished background in the history of the Episcopal Church of Liberia (ECL). The 11th Diocesan Bishop and the 2nd Suffragan Bishop, he was also a scion of at least two Grebo-Liberian Episcopalians of the early Church—The Rev. Edward Wea Neufville (–June 6, 1871) and P. Keda Neufville, an alumnus of the old Cuttington and a faculty member of the school in Cape Palmas, Maryland County. Born to the union of Edward Dosa-Wea Neufville I and Sarah Hneanyene Elliott on December 16, 1937 in Gedetarbo, Maryland County, Liberia, Neufville II's ministry spans forty-one years, twelve years as Suffragan and eleven years as Diocesan Bishop. He was ordained a priest in 1970, consecrated a Bishop (Suffragan) in 1984, and enthroned Diocesan Bishop in 1996. He retired in 2007 after serving as Diocesan for eleven years, and died four years later at the Medical University in Charleston, South Carolina, on January 10, 2011.

Upon retirement Bishop Mark Lawrence licensed Bishop Neufville to function in the American Diocese of South Carolina. Neufville seemed to cherish his Bishop-in-Residence opportunity at the Good Shepherd Episcopal Church in Sumter, SC, for he would say at the end of one service, "I am grateful that I was able to serve my Lord at an altar today."[1]

## JOURNEY TO THE EPISCOPACY

Neufville graduated from Cuttington College and Divinity School with a bachelor's degree in political science in 1963. He began implementing his call to ministry following a few years working as a banker. Between 1964 and 1968, he served as a Lay Reader at Trinity Cathedral while reading theology through a correspondence course. But his formal theological training effectively began with his enrollment at the Seth C. Edwards Institute, then a tutorial option for theological training given that Cuttington's Divinity School had been closed since 1962 due to a lack of students. Duly certified by the Institute in 1969, Canon-Missioner Seth C. Edwards wrote in his 1969 report to ECL that those who had entered the program

> should be commended for their perseverance. They have weathered adverse criticism from within and without and, thanks be to God, He has brought these men to a high place. . . . These men are well seasoned and mature. Do not despise them! Your leadership in the next few years may very well be in their hands. We look forward to the training of other men for the priesthood, until such time under the Providence of God, we are able to open our own seminary or to work out a plan with other denominations for a union seminary geared to the high level we demand.[2]

Among those who benefited from the program were: Emmanuel W. Johnson (former president of Cuttington and former dean of Trinity Cathedral), Edward King (former dean of Trinity Cathedral, and former principal of B. W. Harris Episcopal School), Jonah N. Togba (Vicar at St. Augustine's, Kakata), and Fr. Philip Sherman (Rector at both St. John's Lower Buchanan, and St. Paul's Greenville). There were subsequent efforts to institutionalize the program as the Seth C. Edwards Memorial Theological Institute.

Missionary Bishop Dillard Houston Brown ordained Neufville a deacon February 11, 1968, and Bishop Alfred Voegeli, Interim Bishop of Liberia, ordained him priest February 15, 1970. Neufville was assigned to St. Martin-on-the Mount in Nimba County as Vicar and Priest-in-Charge at St. Valentine's, Sanniquellie, Nimba County. Thus beginning his ministry as a rural priest, Neufville would serve for some fifteen years, building church, rectory, and school in Yekepa, and initiating the building of a church edifice in Sanniquelle. Also appointed Archdeacon of the Northern Archdeaconry,

Neufville brought vibrancy to the work of the church in three important counties, Nimba, Lofa, and Bong.

He was married to Louise Himmiede Morais, herself a descendant of the prominent Morais family of Cape Palmas, May 14, 1967. The union was blessed with four children. A break occurred in his work in 1972 as he pursued theological studies in the United States. August 1972 to May 1974, when he was awarded the master's degree in theological studies at Virginia Theological Seminary (VTS). He returned to his posts in Yekepa and Sanniquellie upon his return home. In 1981, he was appointed Archdeacon of the Northern Archdeaconry (Nimba, Bong, and Lofa Counties).

Growth of the church in Neufville's jurisdiction was underscored with the hosting in 1978 of the 55th Diocesan Convention in Yekepa at St. Martin-on-the-Mount. Growth of the church at the diocesan level soon necessitated a Suffragan Bishop.

Liberia had, in 1982, acceded to full membership in the Church of the Province of West Africa (CPWA) and had thus begun ministry in a new and challenging context, the African context that actually defined and was defined by its parishioners. Additionally, Bishop Browne had been elected Archbishop of the Province with significantly increased responsibilities. He asked his Church for assistance and the Convention obliged. Four priests/candidates emerged. They were The Rev. Amos Bani Collins (then Archdeacon of the Southwestern Archdeaconry and a priest since 1958), The Rev. J. Jellico Bright (rector, St. Stephen's Episcopal Church, Monrovia and a priest since 1977), and The Rev. Edward W. Neufville (then Archdeacon of the Northern Archdeaconry and a priest since 1970).

Neufville was elected on the very first ballot, beating back the challenges from his older and more experienced competitors. On May 4, 1984, Father Neufville was consecrated Bishop Suffragan by Archbishop Browne, assisted by a phalanx of Bishops of CPWA including retired Archbishops Ismael Le Maire of Ghana and Moses N. C. O. Scott of Freetown, Bishop John B. Arthur of Kumasi, Bishop Prince Thompson of Freetown, Bishop Michael Keili of Bo, Bishop Joseph Dadson of Sunyani Tamale, Bishop John Ackon of Cape Coast, Bishop Robert Okine of Koforidua, Bishop J. Rigal Elisee of Gambia, and Bishop Francis Thompson of Accra. With the late Suffragan Bishop T. M. F. Gardiner as the 318th in Apostolic Succession, and Bishop Browne as the 652nd, Suffragan Bishop Neufville became the 653rd in apostolic succession.

While the Church is God's kingdom here on earth, it is also a human agency. As such, it is subject to human foibles. The American Church made Bishop Gardiner a Suffragan Bishop in 1921 because there was sentiment for a Liberian bishop, but not one with the authority to lead an American missionary church. And though he carried out his ministry as best he could, it was not without "the unwitting and undeserving focus for many of the American and [his fellow] Liberian prejudices and assumptions." Gardiner was never consulted in the decision-making process of the Diocese by the three Missionary Bishops under whom he served, neither was he consulted by the mother church. His role was therefore not a large one.[3] History is always instructive. The first Suffragan Bishop was a humble and unassuming man. He served faithfully and with devotion until his death in 1941. Neufville's election marked a second such experiment.

At the colorful ordination and consecration of Bishop Neufville at Trinity Cathedral on May 6, 1984, Bishop Browne preached a sermon expressly intended to educate. Titled: "Are Bishops essential to the Church? What can we expect from our Suffragan?" Browne offered a two-pronged answer: His first point was that for the Anglican Church the historic episcopate, traceable to Christ's Apostles, is essential to maintaining the integrity of the faith, including "our portion of the One, Holy Catholic and Apostolic Church." The second point was a new theory gaining ground in Christendom as espoused by contemporary New Testament and church history scholars, namely, that Bishops are essential to the church, "but churches without bishops also have manifestations of the true church and have real ministers and valid Sacraments."[4]

In a prescient message, Browne detailed opportunities for collaborative ministry even as he pointed to pitfalls. A Suffragan Bishop was sign of church growth and the consequent need for Episcopal assistance. "As a Suffragan Bishop he has all the authority of a Bishop in the Church of God, and can perform Episcopal functions of all kinds." The Diocesan Bishop revealed that he and his Suffragan-elect went on a retreat prior to the consecration. "We decided that it would be a team ministry between us. We expect to work like brothers. Where disagreement comes in, we pledged to be open with one another and talk and pray about it. We have agreed that our first loyalty should be to God and the Diocese." That there would be challenges was fully recognized as Browne threw down the gauntlet: "We must prove that we can work together as co-equals, and we look to the Diocese to support us in this joint ministry." Bishop Browne continued: "The temptation to be overly sensitive, and to listen to fellow clergy and lay people who may try to plant seeds of discord between us, will be great. With a deepening prayer life, and loyalty to one another, we can meet the challenge with God's grace."

Even more expansive and prescient, Browne spoke to the ministry he and his fellow Bishop Neufville would expect of the Diocese of Liberia. "We ask the people of this diocese to remember that we, like them, are but dust and ashes—human beings with all the limitations and frailty that go with it. We all live in the same political and economic climate. We have our egos, feelings, hopes and dreams. We too, like them, are subject to illness and fatigue, and are often sinners. Bishops are many times lonely. They are only Bishops by the grace of God and through the power of the Holy Spirit."

Bearing in mind their Bishops' humanity, the diocese has a responsibility to minister to them, for Christ himself was recipient of such ministry. "The bishops and their families have personal and social needs to be met. They need continuing education, and a period of rest and recreation. We have a right to expect from our people, their prayers, their sincere compliments, their frank and yet respectful feedback from time to time, as well as their loyalty."[5]

The human failings that ensued have been highlighted in the chapter above on the interim period between Browne and Neufville. Such failings were soon exacerbated by war conditions and Browne's ill health and subsequent death.

But first, an account must be given of Bishop Neufville's work as Suffragan or assistant to the Diocesan Bishop. It was actually a continuation or an up scaling of his ministry as Archdeacon of the Northern Archdeaconry, supervising the work in the Counties of Lofa, Bong, and Nimba or the LOBONI region (envisaged for the first autonomous diocese of ECL), and reporting on his stewardship to the Diocesan Bishop and the Conventions of ECL over the years. As priest in charge of several congregations in Nimba, Lofa, and Bong Counties for a decade before being elected Bishop, Neufville had registered an enviable record—a church and school had been built from scratch in Yekepa; a congregation kept alive in Sanniquellie; and congregations sprouting in Gbarnga and its environs.

With the authority of a bishop added to his profile he soon found cause to accelerate what he was already doing in the region, as well as begin the implementation of a mandate given him by Bishop Browne regarding the Northern region. The mandate was to grow the region in accordance with specified criteria such as enlarging its economic base through agriculture and other self-supporting initiatives, and otherwise prepare the region for diocesan status within the wider ECL. Envisaged as well were three other regions to be developed into autonomous dioceses, with all four eventually becoming constituent dioceses of the ECL.

Neufville seemed well on his way toward preparing the Northern region for diocesan status. Spiritually vibrant congregations were growing especially in the Gbarnga area, with each church planted followed by a school. Such was the case of St, Peter's Gbarnga and the Sugar Hill church and school also in Gbarnga. For the latter, a rural congregation was developing, 98% of its membership outside the money-earning economy but highly committed to the mission of the church. A Kpelle literacy program was begun there in 1988, which enabled Services to be conducted in both Kpelle and English. Not only did Bishop Neufville speak of a master plan for evangelism, education and health in the region, he also began envisaging St. Peter's Gbarnga as the future Cathedral for the new autonomous diocese. An early 1989 convention of the Archdeaconry featured a revival-like atmosphere. There was Bible study in Kissi, Gbandi, and English, and a sharing of testimonies, even "hair-raising melodies and prayers" as Neufville himself reported in early 1989 to the 66th Diocesan Convention, about a year before the onset of civil war in December 1989.

Unfortunately, war conditions were not conducive to collaborative work. With things falling apart all around and the struggle for survival a paramount concern, there was much temptation to move away from the structures and strictures of the institution of the church.

We now meet two Bishops and their respective war experiences. In recounting his personal experiences, Browne details his travails, never leaving his flock, always endeavoring to remain the good Shepherd. What turned out to be Browne's last return home from medical treatment in the United States occurred in December 1992 following an eight-month stay abroad. Evidently still sick, he attended a special thanksgiving service at Trinity Cathedral. As a result of poor communication with his Suffragan, Neufville was not in country. Browne would die some two months upon his return to his doctors in the United States.

Bishop Neufville who had first endeavored to report to Browne at the initiation of the civil war, had come down from his Gbarnga Archdeaconry to see Browne in Monrovia in March 1990. Not finding him at his office at Trinity Cathedral, Neufville left a note dated March 18, 1990 in which he described war developments in Gbarnga that constrained him to bring his family to Monrovia for reasons of security. Neufville would later elaborate his own war experience in his "In the Valley of the Shadow in Liberia," address to VTS, October 24, 1991 during his temporary residence in Sumter, South Carolina. Captured here, as elsewhere is the story of a man desperately struggling to secure his young family as civil war erupts in Liberia. With all systems down critical communication breaks down between Browne and Neufville. Browne falls ill as he too struggles to keep the Diocese afloat not knowing the whereabouts of his Suffragan. Old suspicions and distrusts took over. The Church suffered.

Following an interim period fraught with controversy (See chapter 2 on interim period between Browne and Neufville), a Special Convention was agreed for election of a Diocesan Bishop in succession to the late Bishop Browne. Bishop Neufville was elected on the second ballot and installed and enthroned at Trinity Cathedral in Monrovia on January 6, 1996 as the 11th Bishop of Liberia. The officiating clergy included Bishop Donald Hart, retired Bishop of Hawaii, United States, and "Mandated Presiding Presbyter and Neufville's nemesis," The Rev. Fr. Emmanuel D. Hodges, Priest-in-Charge, Trinity Cathedral. Bishop Donald Hart, representing the Presiding Bishop of the American Church, was the guest preacher.

Presiding Bishop Edmond L. Browning had earlier sent to Neufville greetings and a warm "Dear Brother Edward" letter of re-assurance in which he wrote, inter alia:

> My day has been brightened by good news, for I have learned of your election as Bishop of Liberia and I hasten to send my personal congratulations and the assurance of my prayers for your new ministry. Liberia has been a part of our prayer life for many years, and rightly so, and I am pleased now to be able to add a note of joy to the ongoing intercession of concern. I know your election will be received joyfully in the Episcopal Church of Liberia, throughout the Church of the Province of West Africa, and wherever Liberians have been scattered by this terrible war; you bring a promise of new hope to these people of God, dispersed and aching to come home. As Suffragan you have been faithful, and you have taken upon yourself the responsibility that circumstances required. That same faithfulness has been noted throughout the Anglican Communion, and your people have responded appropriately to it. You are now called to take on even more responsibility and the church is obviously confident of your capability, your spiritual strength to strive for nothing less than peace in a nation too long bereft of it. My brother, I thank God for your election and I give you my blessing and my promise of continued support.[6]

No Bishop from the CPWA attended this important event. Bishop Donald Hart emphasized in his sermon the historical relations between the two churches, their covenant relationship's importance, and called for church unity and a new focus and direction of the Liberian Church, which faced a great challenge of rebuilding.

Preaching the following day, Bishop Neufville dwelt briefly on the Church's external relations as he stressed the urgency in becoming an independent and self-sustaining church, realizing that support from the American church should not be expected indefinitely, adding that ECL had the will, and, with the cooperation and support of The Episcopal Church (USA) (TEC), he foresaw a new and vibrant church developing in post-war Liberia. And in a more pointed message to his Liberian flock the new Diocesan wrote:

> The challenges facing us as a Diocese are myriad and defying. We must therefore unite and direct our energies in developing schemes that will help us respond to these challenges. The breakdown of law and order in our society, violence, moral decadence, hunger, high illiteracy rate, poverty, drug abuse, juvenile delinquency and the deterioration of family life are only a few of the

many social evils which beset our Liberian society. Thus, as a nation and a Church, we must break loose from us the handcuffs of bitterness, greed, hatred and selfishness so that we can direct our efforts in addressing these ills. Brothers and Sisters, we have a unique and colossal task to evangelize, educate, and to do social work. This is the mandate and mission given all Christians by Jesus our Lord. As your chief servant and pastor, I pledge and re-dedicate myself to this great calling. Toward this end, I need your talents, cooperation and prayers so that we can work together as partners in this great venture.[7]

## VISION AND THRUST OF LEADERSHIP

Neufville situated his vision by recalling the environment of his episcopacy. "I assumed the Episcopacy of the ECL in one of the most difficult and scary periods in the history of our country." "I must have been perceived as a fool treading where angels fear to tread when I consented to my election to take over the helm of Episcopal leadership of ECL." But a sense of calling places all this in perspective. "God normally calls us to perform stressful and hardship assignments. But his grace is always sufficient and available to help us through." The biblical Moses and Jeremiah complained but God had answers. Jonah tried to run away from preaching to the evil people of Ninevah, but who can run away from God, Bishop Neufville asked. "In my particular case," he continued: "my call was a gradual persistent process. It was not instant. I did not have the 'burning bush' experience. Neither did I receive the call through a prophet or by dint of persuasion by my parents, spiritual mentors or comrades. My discernment process was personal and inward, and a prolonged journey. It was a real struggle to allow my personal and selfish agenda to be subsumed by God's agenda for me."

Bishop Neufville had more to say in this extraordinary draft autobiography entitled "My Episcopacy." His cousin Gridor Togba who was not literate in English but in the Grebo language taught him to read and write in that Liberian language. "This allowed me to come to grips with the culture of the people, as indeed language is the vehicle of culture. This experience has greatly enhanced my ministry among my own people." Paying tribute to his mother, he called her his "first school teacher and seminary professor." He went on to self-describe as "studious" with "a great gift of committing things to memory." From his youth, he wrote, he was a shy person, a personality trait he carried to adulthood. "Because of this shyness some people take me as being selfish and proud especially when I came to hold leadership positions. I virtually practiced how not to be shy. This is common to a type A personality person. This I struggled to overcome over the years and I believe I made some break-throughs. "And then came a window into a personal outlook on life and his calling: "Some one described life as the waiting period between birth and death. I define life as the period to use our gifts and talents—the opportunity to serve God and man before death, if time allows." "Our ministry is to glorify God through our labor and faithfulness to our calling."[8]

At the resumed 68th Diocesan Convention after an interregnum of five civil war years, in February 1996 barely a month into his installation, the Bishop was forthright: "I am taking over a diocese fraught with bitterness and unhappy division." "As a concrete testimony of my desire to foster reconciliation and unity within the Episcopal Diocese, I am declaring the month of February 1996 'Reconciliation Month!'" "All Parishes within the Diocese shall be expected to organize relevant services, programs and retreats to pray for the unity, moral and spiritual strength of the Episcopal Church of Liberia." The "task before us is onerous and frightening. . . . I plead with all detractors in the name of Jesus Christ, our Lord, to 'beat their swords into ploughshares and their spears into pruning hooks' (Isaiah 2:4) so that we can rise and build our Church and our country.[9] Would there be a strategy to unpack these words of inspiration and wisdom?"

Those who came to know well the Bishop attest to the fact that despite the challenging circumstances under which he came to office, or perhaps precisely because of those circumstances, he was a reconciler who was also able to advance evangelism and education. A prominent lay minister and cradle Episcopalian, Elizabeth Selee Mulbah, saw Neufville as "a pastor, a reconciler and a God-fearing leader" who was also "mission-minded in his search to resurrect dead or dormant churches and schools." Fr. A-Too Williams also remembers a reconciler as he offered an olive branch to those perceived as detractors. Fr. Edward Thompson who also served as Bishop Neufville's first administrative assistant says that the thrust of his ministry was "to revive diocesan failed or closed schools and revitalize fledgling ones." And following the April 6, 1996 bloody episode of Liberia's ongoing civil war, Neufville undertook the rebuilding of morale among Episcopalians and the rebuilding of damaged infrastructure (schools and churches). As opposed to the Diocese, the churches themselves carried out some of these projects out. Thompson then offered this measure of the man: "Neufville," he wrote,

> projected the persona of a deeply spiritual, prayerful person. I once asked who was responsible for the spiritually grounded leader he had become. He was unequivocal in pointing to his mother. The Neufvilles hail from Gedetarbo in Cape Palmas, and everyone in the Cape Palmas area of the Diocese knew Ma Neufville as a deeply spiritual, "praying" Christian. At a service of ordination to the diaconate over which he was presiding at Trinity Cathedral, he was so overcome during the Prayer of Consecration as to almost launch into a mumbling that sounded like "speaking in tongues."[10]

Though some experienced Bishop Neufville as "morally rigid," even a "rigid pastor," many more remember him as a "deeply spiritual, praying person" whose life, echoing 1 Timothy 3:2, was above reproach, as he exercised self-control, lived wisely, and had a good reputation. Though not always successful, he strove to reconcile a divided church, and concerted with other religious leaders through the Liberian Council of Churches and the Inter-Religious Council to carry forward the Liberian peace process.

## STEWARDSHIP MINISTRY

Stewardship is leadership inspiring resource mobilization and management in service to the total ministry of the church—evangelism, education, healing. Yet perhaps a more pertinent or fundamental question regarding stewardship is: How does a church in disarray in a country emerging from civil war approach stewardship? Unlike his predecessor whose stewardship thrust was linked to preparing the church for financial autonomy, the point of departure for Neufville was "planning for sustainability." This approach was against the backdrop of post war Liberian circumstances and donor (TEC) inclination toward community-based development projects.

An ECL "philosophy of development" was put forward. It was reportedly rooted in "biblical and theological mandate and the operational experiences of the church since its inception." Derived from 2 Corinthians 5:18 that "In Christ, the world is being reconciled to God, and we have been entrusted with the ministry of manifesting that reconciliation and redemption," two target goals were articulated: (1) "Church planting to all communities through results-focused development projects that will meet the overall needs of people returning from war exile or displacement to their communities by empowering the church, parishioners and community members," and (2) "That the most vulnerable persons and communities affected by social, economic, and political oppression, especially due to the Liberian conflict, will be supported in their efforts to rebuild their lives, develop socially, economically, politically and environmentally sustainable communities to achieve a better quality of life." The plan came replete with an organizational structure where the Convention and the Bishop were at the apex, followed by a Development Planning Board staffed to cater to three Archdeaconries—Southwestern, Northern, and Southeastern.[11]

To give effect to the plan, the 68th Diocesan Convention in January 1996 established a Planning and Development Committee of the ECL by dissolving a prior development committee that had been established by the 62nd Convention in February 1982. This all-embracing planning and development approach was designed to address "the problems of the total being, thereby reviving the churches and institutions and restoring hope and confidence not only to parishioners, but the people of Liberia in general." Such a development plan was derived from a 1999 needs assessment report. That report suggested that due to war conditions the church had to heavily rely on support from donor agencies and American church partners to support programs and projects, with the understanding that in time the Liberian church would be able to sustain and independently undertake its own programs. But despite the new nomenclature of development planning accompanied by new administrative arrangements endorsed by Conventions, there is little evidence that the plans were pursued. Instead, Neufville's assessment of the state of the church in the aftermath of civil war led him to adopt the notion of transitioning from the reality of relief to the aspiration of development.[12]

These initial efforts and challenges soon gave rise to a variety of other approaches, chief among them was a resort or return to a "special relationship" arrangement with the American church, and an otherwise stewardship ad hocism that saw the ECL "scouting for resources" largely from abroad, including Canada, Europe, and elsewhere. The special relationship was problematic as the partners' perceptions differed widely. It came to be driven by pragmatic revisions of the Covenant agreement that defined the relationship since 1979.

First came the inheritance. No doubt the various assessment reports had noted the challenges of domestic resource mobilization in a collapsed national economy and massive flight of capital and know-how in the wake of political violence and civil war. Attempts were made to assemble such church assets as land, buildings, farms, etc. Bishop Neufville did not take too kindly to the part of his inheritance that had to do with his predecessor as he reportedly lamented the implications of Browne's three-pronged policy of self-governance, self-propagation, and self-sustenance, opining that it had the effect of "distancing the diocese financially from 815 [Headquarters of TEC], which then contributed to "the demise of the [Episcopal] schools."[13]

There were many exhortations or expressions of aspirations in the Bishop's various annual addresses to ECL conventions. Already Neufville had engaged in relief work while still Suffragan Bishop in the early 1990s. There is a video of his distribution of relief supplies to churches in Lower Buchanan and Upper Buchanan in Grand Bassa County early in 1994. There are reports as well of visits behind rebel line in Bomi County, even the Bishop's performance of a confirmation service on the campus of the Booker Washington Institute in Margibi County in November 1993. Upon his election as Diocesan Bishop he employed the services of a number of economic development expert Episcopalians in fleshing out a development plan replete with a concept paper driven by donors' priorities, as was the norm with the Liberian government.

At his first Convention as Diocesan in 1996 Neufville lamented that the church was not impacting the lives of Liberians in the midst of war, as he announced that he was embarking upon a "Relief Assistance and Rehabilitation program—Operation Episcopal Relief Assistance" to be coordinated by the Bishop's office. Reiterated convention after convention, the plan was plagued with a challenge of implementation, which was a combination of meager resources and lack of focused attention to what was possible under the circumstances. Or, as one Clergy observer who worked closely with the Bishop noted, the Bishop left the impression that the force of his office would ensure implementation of decisions taken. Neufville himself said that the administrative mechanism he had in place allowed things to be done even while he was away, and that the Bishop's office had an "efficient coordinator" with whom he is always in contact, even when out of the country. Yet such expectations were not always compatible with the facts.

There appeared a return to the notion of a special relationship between the Liberian and American churches, for as Neufville welcomed a joint Covenant Committee consulting in Liberia in April 1999, he thanked TEC for wartime assistance through the Presiding Bishop's Fund for World Relief and the continued support to the Liberian church from TEC's Executive Council. Painting a grim picture of war-devastated Liberia, he averred that the task ahead was enormous. Presenting a laundry list of needs, Neufville reported on the state of the church—clergy shortage, education, and evangelism challenges. He highlighted as well his administration's maintenance of Boys Town for wayward urban youths. This was a project that was initiated in the early 1960s by Fr. Seth C. Edwards when he served as Dean of Trinity Cathedral. Eighty-six former combatants were enrolled at one point. He referenced as well his innovative lecture series for spiritual and intellectual stimulation, the revival of a news organ, the Episcopal Church Drums, as well as his development plan documents. He added that an assessment tour of 95% of the church's property nationwide suggested that the Diocese needed $2.5 million for the rehabilitation of its educational institutions, a critical arm in his view of evangelism.

Neufville reported to the 76th Convention in 2005 on ECL's financial position. Locally derived rental income was unreliable as a 1999 projection of $235,000 yielded only $92,000. The Diocesan treasurer reported that foreign travels by the Bishop and team created perennial budget deficits. In 1998, $38,936 was spent on foreign travel, exceeding the budget by $6,936. The year following $32,800 was spent, exceeding the budgeted amount by $2,880. And in 2000, $63,287 was spent on foreign travel, exceeding the budget by $23,870. This deficit spending was rationalized with "you must spend money to get money." A gift of $250,000 from an anonymous American donor for education in Liberia was used to reconstruct schools, but those schools were soon completely destroyed in renewed warfare in 2003, though the Bishop kept rebuilding as resources and circumstances allowed.

The Covenant agreement with TEC provided diminishing budget subsidies to ECL, though Neufville pointed out that the subsidies would be supplemented with a series of companion Diocese relationships and "aggressive fund-raising campaign in the [American] House of Bishops and in some caring parishes" of the American church, noting the role of Bishop Robert Scruton of Western Massachusetts. But soon the Bishop was drawn into an American hot button social issue, that of human sexuality or same-sex relations. He took issue with certain guidelines that seemed prerequisites to the establishment of companion diocese relationships. Bishop Neufville noted, "The guidelines to the formation of a companion diocese relationship require that we accept the lifestyle of each other." "My friends, brothers and sisters," he declared, "we do not hate homosexuals but we loathe their deviant sexual orientation because we believe it to be unscriptural." We prefer dioceses "who are orthodox in their theology and approach to this troubling and crippling issue of homosexual and lesbian practices in their church." Might this position have alienated him from predominant liberal American church folks, keeping him close to his American base in the Diocese of South Carolina and other more conservative parts of the American church?[14]

Here is a picture of financial transfers from TEC to ECL 1995 through 2006. In addition to these block grants, there are about one hundred trust funds established for Liberia's benefits. Sampling the funds which are apart from ECL Endowment Fund of 1982 vintage, there is a Jane Bohlen Fund marked 1857, No. 1 as "Gift of her children. Income to be used to promote the cause of the Bible and the Gospel in foreign lands, preferably Liberia." Miss Josephine Collins of Hillsboro, OH Fund marked 1918, No. 1 as Bequest of, "In memory of Colonel Wever and family; Income for the support of the Julia C. Emery Girls School, Liberia; Income to the Diocese of Liberia, restricted to girls education." There is as well the William B. Stephens and Orlando Crease Scholarships (1889) "A gift to endow two scholarships at St. John's School, Cape Mount, Liberia." Such funds aggregating to more than one hundred dating back to the early twentieth century, even the late nineteenth century. Their accumulated appreciation was frequently accessed by ECL to pay for certain items such as the construction of the 15th Street apartment building in Monrovia. Such borrowings against the trust funds were reportedly never refunded, and TEC apparently took the view that the money was ECL's and so they were released upon request.

Table 2. A Review of Transfers from the TEC to the ELC, 1995–2006

The Episcopal Church (USA) Transfers to Episcopal Church of Liberia 1995–2006

| 1995 | 1996 | 1997 | |
|---|---|---|---|
| $234,112 | $234,112 | $234,112 | $702,336 |
| 1998 | 1999 | 2000 | Triennium |
| $234,112 | $234,112 | $234,112 | $702,336 |
| 2001 | 2002 | 2003 | Triennium |
| $235,000 | $235,000 | $235,000 | $705,000 |
| 2004 | 2005 | 2006 | Triennium |
| $228,000 | $221,000 | $214,000 | $663,000 |
| Grand Total | | | $2,772,672 |

*Sources*: Covenant Agreements; Budget General Convention, adopted 1994; Budget of the Episcopal Church, 1998-2000, 26; *Supplement to the Journal*, 144; Journal Reports, Overseas Covenants/Liberia, 888, 826. Kind assistance of Archives of the Episcopal Church, Austin, Texas (DFMS Papers).

One year to retirement Bishop Neufville began speaking of "autonomy and financial independence." In his 2007 address to the Diocesan Convention, he lamented a declining subsidy to the operating budget since the 1990s, pointing out that that decline was accelerating. He talked about local resource mobilization such as vast agricultural land that lay fallow in the fifteen counties of the country (though the church then had no presence in Gbapolou County), adding vaguely other potential economic ventures. In exhortation, he called upon all Episcopalians "to be more conscious and sensitive to their stewardship responsibility to the local congregations by the regular payment of pledges, and by practicing the biblical requirement of tithing or 10% of your income, however small, be it salary, gifts, vegetables, cattle, goats. Offering is not limited to cash. It could be in kind. This is also a Sacramental act." The Bishop added at this eleventh hour "that we begin to do for ourselves and stop depending on hand-outs." He was mute on the ambitious development plan that was rolled out at the start of his episcopacy. He spoke as well of investment ventures to add to the Plaza and Jean Travis commercial buildings of the church.[15]

As Neufville departed the office of Bishop of ECL, here is what the church's assets looked like: In addition to what was internally generated from such sources as the church's investments in real estate such as the Plaza, Jean Travis and 15th Street buildings, as well as the meager quota and assessments from the congregations of ECL, external resource came from block grants from TEC, trust funds, endowment funds, and a functional pension plan for the clergy. There were as well ad hoc donations from various dioceses of the American church and Trinity Church Wall Street.

The Pension Plan for Clergy cost the Diocese $85,000 yearly as deducted from the $225,000 block grant from TEC. This was an arrangement meant to ensure regularity and stability of the pension plan. The Rev. Bruce Woodcock, an American cleric friend of ECL, facilitated things as partnership manager of Church Pension Fund. Ten American dioceses and congregations committed to paying $5,000 per annum toward pension premium for five years " to give us some breathing space," though it is unclear that such commitments were met with regularity.

## EVANGELISM MINISTRY

Long before his election as Diocesan Bishop, Neufville's fervor for spreading the Gospel had become widely known. Perhaps beginning with his first assignment as a priest at St. Martin-on-the-Mount in Yekepa, and throughout his years as Suffragan Bishop, evangelism has remained central to his ministry. He "projected the persona of a deeply spiritual, prayerful person," a close priest associate has written. As his predecessor had said before him, Bishop Neufville often made it clear that the church exists primarily to evangelize, and as such this was the mission "to which we are called, 'And ye shall be my witness. . . .' Act 1:8v." But there must be enablers of evangelism as St. Paul wrote to the Romans: "And how are they to believe of whom they have never heard, and how are they to hear without a preacher, and how can men preach unless they are sent" (Rom. 10:14–15). Neufville joined to these considerations his disposition of personal piety often citing the words of the dying American missionary-evangelist Lancelot Minor: "What! The Mission?" he asked. "Let it go forward more than it has ever done!"

The following events or circumstances highlight Neufville's ministry:

1. At the 69th Diocesan Convention Bishop Neufville sought at Bible studies and in his sermons to encourage a war-weary congregation. For example, he posed during one Bible study session a question meant to guide: "How are we afflicted?—Leading to his now famous signature phrase: "afflicted but not crushed."
2. The historic 77th Convention at Cavalla in 2007 commemorating the 170th anniversary of the establishment of the Episcopal church in what became Liberia;

3. Spiritual and intellectual development and renewal through lecture series and marriage retreats;
4. Significant numerical increase in the Clergy force in ten-year episcopacy;
5. ECL focuses anew Lofa County as 2008 Convention convenes at St. Mary's, and Order of the Holy Cross (OHC) transitions to all African Celtic style Monastic Missionary Order called The Community of the Love of Jesus Christ (CLJC); and
6. New outreach ministry of a Seaman Church Institute.

The 69th Diocesan Convention convened at St. Thomas New Kru Town on February 5–9, 1997 under the theme "The Lord is speaking. Are you listening?" The Bishop made it clear at the outset that the Convention would be not all business, politics, and resolutions, but worship and Bible study. He told the Convention that if anyone had a burden and desired prayers, there would be prayer teams in designated areas to offer prayers. On the second day sitting Neufville announced Bible study, which he reiterated, was one of the main features of the Convention. He offered a series of questions to guide the study: "How are we afflicted?" "Are we experiencing agony?" Given the atmosphere of war-weary and a traumatized Liberia, such questions seemed to resonate in the hearts of many, and thus they all came to realize, in the words of the Bishop that indeed "we are afflicted but not crushed." The Bishop's sermon theme was "The Lord is speaking. Are you listening?" This inspired the then head of the Interim Government of Liberia, Madame Ruth Perry in her own remarks to the Convention to speak of a "people afflicted but not crushed."

Bishop Neufville led hundreds of Episcopalians on a pilgrimage in 2007 to the birthplace of the Church in the southeastern region of Cape Palmas to convene the 77th Diocesan Convention and celebrate the Church's 170th anniversary (anniversary was 2006, but meeting in 2007 due to logistical and other challenges). The year 2006 marked the 170th anniversary of the formal launching of the work of the Episcopal Church in Cape Palmas and Parts Adjacent. The Bishop, a Cape Palmas native himself, wanted to use the occasion to inspire a new zeal for evangelism in the Diocese. The Convention met March 15–26, 2006 in Grand Cavalla at the Epiphany Church, perhaps the first church edifice erected by the official missionaries sent by the American church.

Evangelistic fervor was evident at this 77th Diocesan Convention under theme "What would you do if you had the upper hand? (1 Samuel 24:11). Theme song: "Dear Lord and Father of Mankind, forgive our foolish ways." Neufville called the site of the gathering "Holy grounds of Cavalla where the seed of Christianity was planted by our forefathers and the Holy Spirit moved men and women to propagate the Gospel with the gratifying results of enlightening the minds of the native inhabitants of this village and beyond." He wanted the anniversary celebrations "at this very cradle" of the Episcopal Church to be done 'with reverence, humility and thankfulness for the productive work of the early missionaries." The celebrations were climaxed with the symbolism of baptism in the Cavalla River separating Liberia from the Ivory Coast. This experience moved the leaders of Kablakeh town to request a school. Through the generous gift of the Paul Frank Foundation in the United States, a church was planted and an elementary school established. Forty-four people including young children were baptized in the Cavalla River by immersion, perhaps a first in the history of the church. It was a glorious occasion and a sight to behold with a stirring sermon by the Rev. Fr. Thompson Yengbe.

In his own message marking the occasion, Bishop Neufville said: "One cannot but imagine the tremendous sacrifices made by the early missionaries who obeyed the call of God to sail to this part of His vineyard which was some time referred to as the 'Dark Continent.' Leaving behind them their loving families, friends and safe homes just to share the good news of salvation which God offers to all through the birth, life, death and resurrection of Jesus Christ our Lord and Savior." "These stalwart men and women," he continued, "deserve to be honored and eulogized for their shining example of faith in God and dedication to duty coupled with a powerful sense of mission and deep love for Jesus Christ. . . . These heroes and heroines of faith blazed the trail 170 years ago with confidence in the power of God and arrived safely in Cavalla and Mount Vaughn where they sowed the seed of the Gospel which has blossomed over the years."

Bishop Neufville added: "We have come to celebrate and appreciate their struggles and to thank God for them and for the succeeding generations of Christians whose faith has kept the flame of the Gospel ablaze despite many odds. It is my prayer and ardent hope that these celebrations will renew our hearts and strengthen our faith in our Lord and Savior Jesus Christ to love and serve Him."

What followed were services for the unveiling of a mural, the dedication and blessings of Epiphany Cemetery, Epiphany school, St. James school, St. Stephens's school, Epiphany Rectory and Vicarage, and service for the rededication and blessings of the Monument and Cemetery at Mount Vaughn (St. Mathias Church, the site at which the Thomson couple initiated the work before arrival of official missionaries in 1836). The celebrations also featured pertinent lectures such as an "Historical overview of the Episcopal Church of Liberia" by Bro. Henry D. Woart; "The Role of the Episcopal Church in

Health Care Delivery" by Sis Elizabeth S. Mulbah; "The Role of the Church in Education" by Bro. Clement V. Kimber, and "The Episcopal Church's Contributions to the State and Government" by Bro. Sandei A. Cooper, Sr.

Then there was a focus on the church in Lofa County with the 78th Diocesan Convention convening at St. Mary's Episcopal Church, Bolahun, March 7–11, 2007. The convention was meeting at this church in rural Liberia perhaps for the first time. The planning process involved many including the Bolahun Alumni Family and Friends Association (BAFFA), the group principally responsible for restoring the famous St. Augustine High School Bolahun.

The transition from OHC to CLJ was also a highlight of the church's work in Lofa County. As with the anniversary celebration at Cavalla, Bolahun was a celebration of another significant church-planting site, the work of the OHC. In 1972, the Order ceased somewhat its independent operations in Lofa County as it turned things over to the Diocese of Liberia. It would nonetheless remain in Liberia for another thirteen years operating schools and a Leper Colony. In the mid-1980s, OHC focused its attention on training Liberians to take full charge of its important activities. As related to me in an interview at the West Park, New York headquarters of the Order by Brother Lawrence, OHC, who had served many years in Liberia, since the 1972 turnover to the ECL, a number of circumstances conspired that eventually resulted in a transition of OHC to a new African Order.[16] They included a reluctance of the graduates of the schools to return to sustain a teaching staff, leaving authorities to import teachers from Ghana as the best Liberian graduates gravitated toward politics and other non-teaching vocations. Furthermore, where the ECL apparently could not, it took the Liberian government quite some time to undertake responsibilities for the Order's educational, medical, and related institutions.

OHC had ceased or scaled down its Liberia operations prior to the civil war. War conditions led to a full suspension of activities. With peace restored, OHC symbolically returned in the person of Fr. Anthony-Gerald Stevens. In 2005, at age 93 years, he returned to Liberia but lived for a while with the Neufvilles in Monrovia because conditions were not yet safe in Lofa County, as peace remained elusive. After eight months in Monrovia, he was constrained to return to the United States and to the Mother House of the Order at West Park, New York. There he encountered young Emmanuel Dunor whom he had helped educate many years earlier. Dunor was at West Park to fulfill his desire to become a monk himself. With friendship renewed, Dunor in time decided to return to Liberia, the desire to become a monk still burning in his heart. In God's mysterious way, Fr. Stevens returned to Liberia in 2006 and established an all African Celtic-style Anglican Monastic Missionary Order called The Community of the Love of Jesus Christ (CLJC).

CLJ's purpose is to bring people back to Jesus following fifteen years of war. The new Order was overseen by a Liberian Mission Committee whose members were Bishop Alex Dickson (retired Bishop of West Tennessee), Bishop Neufville and his wife Louise Neufville, Fr. Anthony Kowbeidu, a Liberian Diaspora priest, and Joe Namie, Chair of the Mbalotahun Leprosy Rehabilitation Program (MLRP) Foundation for the education of children of Leprosy patients, and others.[17]

After mentoring Dunor for several months, Dunor was made Prefect of the Order. He soon recruited five young men who joined him, among them Br. Francis Saah, and Bro. Frank F. Foday. Bishop Neufville who then entrusted the remnants of the work of OHC to the new CLJ, ordained Dunor. In January 2007, Father Stevens moved back to Bolahun with Dunor and the five men to begin their work in Lofa County. Some nine months later, on September 22, 2007, Fr. Stevens died peacefully in his little cell at the St. Francis Monastery at age 95 years. "He was wrapped in a banana leaf at his request and buried in the cemetery of the leper colony at Mbalotahun." It was a hallelujah occasion indeed![18]

Spiritual and Intellectual development and renewal via lecture series and marriage retreats: An important feature of Neufville's ministry was the holding of a lecture series in the Diocese. For example, in 1998, there was a Lent lecture series attended cumulatively by 400 people for an average of 80 people per session. These events at Trinity Cathedral, St. Thomas Camp Johnson Road, St. Thomas New Kru Town, and St. Stephen's, Good Shepherd featured speakers, which included Rev. Abeoseh Flemister, Fr. James Sellee, Trinity Dean Jonathan B. B. Hart, Rev. Roberta Phillips, Fr. Emmanuel Hodges, and Fr. Victor King, among others. In 2002, 645 people in aggregate attended the lecture series.

There were also marriage retreats intended to meet the spiritual and educational needs of parishioners and the larger Christian community. In October 1999, Good Shepherd again hosted a retreat that featured Bro. and Sis. William Diggs, with presentations by Fr. Jonathan B. B. Hart of Trinity Cathedral, and Rev. Andrew Afolabi. A message from Bishop Neufville noted: "It is important that we run such retreats in order to foster and encourage healthy and functional Christian marriages in our communities."

Beyond Monrovia in the Bassa region there was a Pentecost lecture series September 23–26, 1999 with presentations by The Rev. Victor King, The Holy Spirit and the Church; The Rev. Emmanuel Hodges, The Episcopal Church and the Anglican Church; The Rev. Thomas S. Smith, The Worship of the Church; The Rev. Christian Harding, The Sacraments of the Church; The Rev. Abeoseh Flemister, Church Mannerisms; and The Rev. Elijah Harris, The Holy Bible. Eighty-two in all attended.

For the Advent lecture series in November 1999 a total of 230 people attended over a four-week period. Some of the topics addressed included "The Seasons of the Church" (Fr. James Yarsiah), "Preparing in Advent for Christmas" (Rev. A. Flemister), "The Old Testament Prophesies and the Messiah, Jesus Christ" (Fr. James Tamba), "Jesus and the Millennium" (Fr. Emmanuel Hodges), and "The Second Coming of Jesus" (Fr. Lee O. D. Mitchell).

Significant numerical increase in the clerical force as the Bishop marked a decade in office may not immediately be translated into significant clerical action, though the historic first of the largest number of females ordained to the priesthood warrants acknowledgment. The Bishop said in his 77th Convention Charge that between 1996 and 2006, twenty-seven new Clergy were added to the twenty-one active clergy he inherited, eighteen priests, and nine deacons. There is little evidence that significant church growth occurred or that the Clergy was able to make a difference, for the Bishop himself spoke often of the need to resurrect "our dying and stagnant churches and to plant new ones." The Bishop also acknowledged a problem of clergy shortage. The entire Grand Kru County had a single Deacon serving nine congregations. Clergy demands were unreasonable: "Anything short of a rectory and a car is considered demeaning by some priests."

Relations with his clergy and postulants were not always cordial. In fact, there were instances of uncharitable hostility unworthy of people of God. The Bishop refused to ordain one postulant, and publicly berated one of his priests who then responded in a stinging letter of rebuke. Consider Neufville's apprehension: "Though we need more ordained men and women, we will be extremely careful and prayerful in order to be able to discern those applicants who just want jobs from those who show sincerity and are really called."[19] Consider also Resolution 14 of the Bolahun Convention: "That the issue of shortage of clergy be urgently addressed by improving the conditions of service of the clergy and postulants, as well as providing appropriate level of opportunities for training and capacity building of clergy and postulants." This was yet another resolution that would remain unimplemented.[20]

The final of the highlights of Bishop Neufville's evangelism efforts was the initiation of a Seaman Church Institute Outreach Ministry. This innovative ministry of ECL was established in 1998. Rev. Edward Gbe became its founding Chaplain, and the Institute was registered with the Liberian government, with access granted by the National Port Authority. In 1998, Fr. Gbe visited forty-seven vessels and interacted with seventy-three seafarers at the Freeport of Monrovia, headquarters of the National Port Authority. There were successors to this initial new ministry of ECL.

Overall then, we have highlighted, but not exhausted the many manifestations of Bishop Neufville's evangelism thrust. The Church celebrated the faith of Christ crucified at its historic cradle in 2007, though the 170th anniversary year was 2006. The Church returned to Lofa County for Convention in 2008, but also to mark an important transition from OHC to a new African Order, the CLJC. Valliant attempts were being made to bring back spiritual vibrancy to a church that, because of war and unhappy divisions, had fallen on hard times, a church "afflicted but not crushed." Bishop Neufville was the prime mover in these events. Many hailed his spiritual leadership, among them his successor, Bishop Jonathan Hart who has noted: "In his sermons, teachings and in practice he promoted spirituality in the ECL. He insisted on his clergy living moral lives and taking good care of their families. He fought to ban the open taking in of alcoholic beverages at Church gatherings to the annoyance of some Episcopalians."[21]

Neufville was a highly spiritual individual who used every opportunity for prayers, Bible study and reflection. The thrust of his evangelism ministry was reflected in his sermons at the start and end of his episcopacy. At the New Kru Town Convention in 1997, the theme was: "The Lord is speaking. Are you listening?" It was also at this convention that he coined the phrase "we are afflicted but not crushed." And then came Bishop Neufville's closing address to the Convention at St. Mary's in Bolahun in 2007: "Carry your cross, I will carry mine, you pray for me, I pray for you. God bless us all."

## EDUCATION MINISTRY

As he viewed the landscape of post-war Liberia, Neufville estimated that education was the greatest challenge to ECL and its institutions. For this reason he sought not only to prioritize education at the start of his episcopacy but also to relink education to the church's mission of evangelism. While this linkage may not have been new, the long history of the church bearing witness to this fact, Bishop Neufville seemed keen to underscore what he termed the need for the ECL's Convention "to lift the ban on education which it imposed in 1972 in order to give us a free hand to do education." By this he was signaling that the controversies associated with the closure of some Episcopal schools for financial and related reasons had now become moot and that the Diocese should now move forward full throttle with its education ministry broadly conceived. This ministry would have a two-prong thrust—to the end of evangelism, but also as a "mission to liberate the whole person," tending toward "the formation of a wholesome well-rounded citizen."

### The Schools

Historically, ECL has been in the vanguard of education in Liberia even prior to the country's political independence. Well documented is the pioneering work of missionaries in Cape Palmas, Cape Mount, Bolahun, Bromley, and a number of parish day schools such as the Trinity Parish Day School, forerunner to the B. W. Harris Episcopal High School. In the 1970s, ECL determined that pressures on its resources did not allow it to continue with the operation of all the schools and consequently there were closures and mergers. This development did not augur well for the reputation of Episcopal schools, which during their heyday took pupils from primary and secondary levels all the way to the church's flagship institution of higher learning, Cuttington College and Divinity School (later name changed to Cuttington University College, and finally, Cuttington University) (CUC/CU).

Neufville wanted to do two things: to join the government in addressing the crippling education deficit in post-war Liberia, and somehow to restore the years the locusts had eaten regarding quality education that emanated from Episcopal schools. Thus at the 69th Diocesan Convention in 1997an education secretariat was proposed with a Board whose mission was "to encourage the re-opening of schools, reawaken the spirit of quality education and rekindle in the institutions other values which made the Episcopal schools enjoy the high moral and academic fame for more than a century."[22] The Board of Education soon partnered with the Board of Trustees and the Planning and Development Board to carry forward this purpose.

One of the first issues tackled was that of a sustainability package of funding. Identified initially as funding sources were education funds from the churches of the Diocese, special fundraising locally, and contribution from the Diocesan budget. While these sources for a variety of reasons did not yield the desired expectations, there was some funding from foreign sources that gave an initial fillip to the educational effort. The Presiding Bishop Fund for World Relief and Development provided $50,000 for education, which was used to renovate schools and pay teachers. A gift of $250,000 from an anonymous American donor toward education in Liberia was used to reconstruct Episcopal schools, though the restored schools would again be destroyed during a second phase of Liberian civil warfare.

This did not dampen enthusiasm. The school Board and teachers rebuilt where they could and otherwise kept the school doors opened. One report noted the following as among the best functioning schools in the Diocese: St. Peter's Comprehensive Episcopal School in Gbarnga was considered in 2006 the most progressive institution in the Episcopal school system. It had an enrollment of 1,625 students and ran morning, afternoon, and evening sessions, catering to people of all walks of life in Bong County. Bromley Mission, a girl's boarding school that went up to eleventh grade, had more than one hundred students enrolled. B. W. Harris Episcopal High School in Monrovia started the year 2004 with an enrollment of 412 students. St. John's Episcopal

High School and the elementary school of Cape Mount County were seemingly back in operation though not at their high reputation-era levels.

In the year that followed, there were twenty-seven Episcopal schools in operation throughout the country—seventeen elementary schools, three kindergartens to ninth grade, four from kindergarten to twelfth grade, and one junior and senior high school. In 2007, there was a total of 4,890 students in Episcopal schools throughout the country, 40% of them being female.

Though functioning under different management boards, Boys Town Institute was back in operation, catering to almost a hundred ex-combatants. And on the initiative of Episcopal churchman Winston Tubman and his wife Nehsee Tubman, RAFIKI (Swahili for "friend") Foundation was introduced to ECL. This international philanthropic organization worked to rehabilitate young boys and girls. "The mission of Rafiki Foundation is to help Africans know God and raise their standard of living." Its agreement with ECL led to formal establishment in 2007 on fifty acres of land located near Boys Town in Margibi County and owned by ECL but donated for the construction of a village of "hope and help." A $2.5 million children village was formally opened in 2007.[23] The training village has since been implementing stated goals in the agreement between ECL and RAFIKI which include service to orphan and vulnerable children by addressing their physical, spiritual social, outreach and educational needs. The latter entailed providing "a classical Christian education from pre school through primary school (grade 6)," and opportunities to orphans for a quality secondary education, with limited academic and vocational training to vulnerable teenagers.[24]

## Christian Education

This department of the Diocese offered workshops and a vacation Bible school. A 73rd Convention Report submitted by the Director of Christian Education, Father Emmanuel Hodges noted a number of education pamphlets produced such as "The Ember Season," "What Every Episcopalian should know," and "Listening in Lent." Others contemplated were "Organizations in the Episcopal Church," "Instructions for Confirmation," "The Episcopal Diocese of Liberia," "The Seasons of the Church," "The Sacraments," "The Ministry of our Church," "Forgiving and Forgetting," and "Steps to entering the ordained Ministry."[25]

Theological Education was carried out under the auspices of three institutions—the Seth C. Edwards Theological Institute, the Division of Theology at CU, and the university's graduate school in Monrovia. The then Dean of the Cathedral Jonathan B. B. Hart coordinated the institute in 1998, which had an enrollment of 44. Father Edward Thompson who was the first administrative assistant to the Bishop began work on a plan to revive Cuttington's Division of Theology. Father Augustine Tamba subsequently became Director of Theological Education and Chaplain of CU. As well, a graduate program leading to a master's degree in theology is offered at the institution's facility in Monrovia.

## Cuttington: Transition from Dr. Mason to Dr. Henrique Tokpa's Presidency

At the 69th Diocesan Convention in 1997, Bishop Neufville said the following about Cuttington: "In chapter 48 sec. 6 of the Act incorporating the 'Cuttington College Protestant Mission, Liberia' in 1923, it is stated: 'The purpose of the College shall be to disseminate and promote Christianity in accordance with the form of worship and doctrine of the Protestant Episcopal Church, personal piety and virtue, the knowledge of languages and of the liberal and useful arts and sciences as shall from time to time be laid out in its curriculum rules.' We are in no position to compromise this objective," Neufville asserted. Such sentiments are also expressed in the school's motto "Sancte et Sapiente," meaning "holy and wise."[26]

Civil war and related circumstances had taken Cuttington into exile where it sought to serve a few students while attempting to lay the basis for its return home at war's end. With the death in February 1993 of Bishop George Browne a leadership interregnum in the church ensued, ending with the election in 1995 of Bishop Neufville and his installation as Diocesan Bishop the year following. Dr. Melvin Mason was president as Neufville took office, having succeeded Dr. Stephen Yekeson in 1988 following the interim presidencies between January 1987 and February 1988 of Father Samuel Yanquoi Reed and Dr. Christian E. Baker. The Cuttington-in-Exile saga greeted Neufville and he worked along with the arrangement.

A few months in office, Neufville in August 1996 appointed a "strategic planning committee" to develop a plan for the reopening of Cuttington College." Chaired by Seth C. Edwards Jr. (son of the first president of the new Cuttington at Suakoko) and dubbed the Committee for the Third Cuttington (First Cuttington started 1889 in Cape Palmas while the second started 1949 in Suakoko), the nine-member committee submitted its thirty-three-page report to the Bishop in July 1997. In a covering letter the committee wrote: "Our committee has spent many hours studying Cuttington's past and present and discussing its future. In postwar Liberia, Cuttington must take a leadership role in the rebuilding of the country. It must develop a cohesive and harmonious learning, teaching and research environment that will focus upon national reconciliation and international understanding and peace. The university must respond to local development needs in terms of health, education and agriculture. Cuttington must work with former combatants in order to prepare them to make a legitimate contribution to society." The statement added: "As it has in its proud history, Cuttington must prepare new leaders for careers in the areas of education, government, medicine, law and the ministry for Liberia. Cuttington is needed now more than ever. We see Cuttington of the future with strong ties to the Episcopal Church and the Diocese of Liberia."[27]

Dr. Mason thus took over the university from Dr. Baker (interim October 1987–February 1988). He reports that the turnover was abrupt as Baker refused to stay on a minute longer despite Mason's request. This may have been a consequence of old distrust between the two men of early 1970s vintage. Mason's expressed vision was to restore Cuttington to its former enviable status and carry it beyond that as well. The political context of the day was the regime of President Samuel K. Doe, a former military leader. The historian Dr. Joseph Guannu characterized Mason's willingness, even eagerness to work with Doe as acceptance of General Doe "with three hands." Mason's relations with President Charles Taylor seemed tailored to ensure that Cuttington would be kept alive.[28]

A first graduation took place December 1988. Exactly a year later civil war broke out, and the CU was forced to close in May 1990. The horrors of war ensued and Mason eventually departed for the United States where he found Vice President Henrique Tokpa and other administrators. There they attempted to regroup, eventually establishing a Cuttington In Exile (CIE) scheme with the slogan of "keeping hope alive." CIE would last from March 1991 through March 1996. Accomplishments included preparation for "the third Cuttington," service to some students, including graduation for those in the pipeline to complete their degrees.

Mason gingerly returned to Liberia in September 1992 and attempted contact with each of the two rival governments in place—Charles Taylor's National Patriotic Reconstruction Assembly Government (NPRAG) and Amos Sawyer's Interim Government of National Unity (IGNU). A West African peace force, Economic Community Monitoring Group (ECOMOG) was then trying to keep the peace. He presented identical assistance packages to the self-style President Taylor and Interim President Amos Sawyer, with no response from either, though Taylor give him a new vehicle reportedly to facilitate his mobility amid a depressed economy.[29]

The collaboration with Taylor continued as he was elected president of Liberia in 1997. Getting on with the building of the third Cuttington, an American architect/planner was granted $50,000 by TEC to conduct a damage assessment of CU. Restoration and innovation plans were estimated at

$4.5 million for short, intermediate, and long term plans. The university had seventy-two buildings on its sixty-five-acre inner campus with a total value of over $70 million. Student and faculty growth increased steadily. In 1998–1999, there were 333 students to twenty-five faculty. In 1999–2000, it had increased to 435 students and forty-one faculty. In 2000–2001, the numbers were 507 students to fifty-six faculty, and in 2001–2002, there were 558 students to sixty-nine faculty.

Reflecting some of the work of CIE, funding was encouraging. TEC provided $21,500, while Executive Council of TEC resolved the withdrawal of $450,000 from CU's Endowment Funds (Trust Fund no. 844) to remit "over a period of three years to enable the College to meet its operating expenses." The American Schools and Hospitals Abroad (ASHA) granted $882,000. Donations came from the Maytag Foundation ($35,000), International Foundation ($45,000), University of the South/Sewanee ($10,000), Government of Liberia ($10,000), and ECL ($25,000).

But there was a concerning note struck by Mason at the 74th Diocesan Convention in 2002. While ECL owned CU, Episcopal student enrollment ranked sixth or ten percent of the enrollment, the lowest percentage, even below the Baptists with twelve percent. Echoing Bishop Neufville, Mason attributed the low enrollment to "the closure of four of the senior high schools of the Diocese: Ferguson in Cape Palmas, Episcopal High in Cape Mount, St. Augustine in Kakata and Bolahun in Lofa," though the real reasons were multi-factored, mostly related to the dislocations of war.[30]

Then only a few years from retirement, Mason presided over two more commencements, February 1999 and February 2000.

Then came the movement into closing mode with thanksgiving and recognition convocation of 2001 at which a number of Americans and Liberians were honored for service to CU. Each American was awarded the doctorate of Humane Letters, honoris causa. Dr. Linda Chisholm, former President of the Association of Episcopal Colleges, was the guest speaker. The visiting Americans departed Liberia in February 2001. Their departure marked the formal and symbolic ending of the CIE experiment and the effective installation of the third Cuttington.

President Mason presided over the third millennium graduation in July 2002, retiring at the 74th Diocesan Convention held at Cuttington's Suakoko campus. He was thus ending almost half-a-century in service to ECL, beginning as a science instructor at St. John's Episcopal High School in Cape Mount County in the early 1950s, and at CUC/CU as dean of men, registrar, instructor, 1956–1961, and dean of instructions, 1960–1971. There was a hiatus of seventeen years before his return to Cuttington as university president in 1988.

Mason's vice-president for administration and planning, Dr. Henrique Flomo Tokpa, succeeded him in August 2002. A CU alumnus, he became the sixth president and went on to serve for thirteen years of growth and expansion as Cuttington added to its mainstay undergraduate program at the Suakoko campus a community college in Kakata and a graduate school in Monrovia. Tokpa had earlier served as vice president for development and planning, and was the effective number two on the team that created CIE in the United States, shouldering responsibly for the fund-raising aspect of the program.

During Mason's presidency the university remained closed for almost eight years of war (1991–1998) as the facilities were used as a training base for rebels and then camp for some 30,000 displaced people. Students nearing the completion of their studies were serviced through arrangements made with the University of Liberia and institutions in the Ivory Coast and the United States, the latter two through the Cuttington-in-Exile scheme. Resumed war conditions forced closure again in 2002, this time the university reopened in Monrovia on at least two occasions.

Though appointed president in 2002, Tokpa was not formally inducted into office until three years later. The reasons were financial challenges and renewed hostilities in 2003. As peace was restored to a war-weary country with the intervention of international peace forces, Tokpa visited the United States to mobilize resources for a possible return to the Suakoko campus. There, he was able to secure some of the needed funds from the Episcopal Church, Trinity Episcopal Church Wall Street, and Friends of Cuttington. These funds enabled him to reopen the Suakoko campus and undertake needed renovation of the facilities. From a student body of 600 and faculty of seventy-five in 2003, the university had in excess of 4,000 students in all its campuses by 2012.

In reaction to the war environment within which he operated including his relations with President Taylor, Tokpa once wrote: "The govt. needs Cuttington. The govt supports about one-fifth of our students; it has a large amount of students there, mainly those who served in the military who decided to go back to school, and they are pretty good students. They have no intention of going back to the war front. They are on scholarship. In most cases they told us what was coming up and we were prepared to take the kind of safety measures that we needed. The govt supported our fundraising effort to appeal to the Tiawanese govt. to try to get some money to fix up the university."[31]

Though Tokpa assumed leadership of Cuttington in turbulent times, he came to the office with a wealth of experience. Upon acquiring his PhD degree from Florida State University in 1988, he returned home and served briefly at the government's Ministry of Education. Recruited by President Mason in 1988 as vice president for administration, he subsequently became vice president for development and planning. He played a critical role during the first phase of Liberia's civil crisis when the University College was forced to close and relocate, first to Monrovia, and then the Cuttington-in-Exile arrangements in the United States.

When Tokpa took over the leadership of the institution in his own right in 2002, he started by assembling a team to develop his first strategic plan. According to Dr. Charles Mulbah who also played important roles at the university during this period, Dr. Joseph Saye Guannu led the team whose members included Augustine Laveleh, David Kemkpan, and Yark Kolva. In time he came to describe that plan as focused on reconstruction, growth and versatility. Based on interview with Dr. Theodore Brown, a veteran administrator at Cuttington, Tokpa used his heritage as a son of Bong County to solicit assistance from local villages in some of the rehabilitation work of cleaning and rebuilding. He soon embarked upon building a socially engaged institution at the local, national and international levels. The school sought to be responsive to its environs so that as village elders asked what their benefits were after having donated the land on which Cuttington was located, the forthcoming response was President Tokpa's scholarship grants to leading student graduates from the high schools of Bong County.

Such an approach would soon be reflected in the ongoing development of the curriculum. His vision for the university was thusly expressed: "We are here to supply our students' minds with facts and images, then giving them the logical tools for organizing these facts, and the opportunity to reflect and present conclusions' to what they have learned to the betterment of the wider society."[32]

Translation of the vision came at least at two levels—faculty development and curriculum development. Acknowledging the difficulty of recruiting Liberian faculty from Monrovia and the Diaspora into Suakoko's rural setting, Tokpa first looked to neighboring West African states where he was able to recruit some faculty. Rutgers University chipped in with short-term lecturers while some junior faculty were in training in graduate schools in Africa, Asia, the Americas, and Britain. The university as well benefitted from the expertise of Fulbright scholars and others from the International Foundation for Education and Self-Help (IFESH), the Excellence in Higher Education for Liberian Development (EHELD), and lecturers from Peace Corps Response Volunteers.

He developed a curriculum that came to offer programs leading to a certificate, and associates, bachelors and masters degrees. From a prewar four of natural science, theology, humanities and social science, and agriculture, the new administration added education, business and public administration, nursing, and integrated rural development. A junior college was established in Kakata, Margibi County and a graduate school offered professional studies in Monrovia. An important feature of the curriculum was a service-learning course required of all upper class students and designed not only to link the university to neighboring communities as partners in education but also to make the students active participants in the development of their communities and their nation. As the university undertook a "minor shift toward excellence," there was also a program of remediation for students and junior faculty through a Center of Excellence in Teaching and Learning, designed to assist both students and junior faculty fill in the gaps in their education. CU accepted 500 of the 10,000 annual high school graduates in the country, offering then remedial opportunities.

Tokpa considered a number of areas as the university looked to the future. They included: making CU accessible to all qualified students and shedding an "elitist exclusionary image;" continuously raising "the bar of intellectual excitement and challenge, finding new ways to educate the whole person," a notion compatible with the thinking of Bishop Neufville; and strengthening "support for graduate programs and investing in intellectual infrastructure that facilitates great scholarship." Above all, he concluded: "We must commit to moving forward as one university, one community of faculty from various disciplines, of staff with diverse strengths, of students with many goals, and of alumni, donors, and friends with many interests—but all sharing a singular focus, an unrelenting focus: the success of the CU. We must work together to demonstrate our value to the citizens of Liberia through the education of our students, through the opportunities we provide, and through the improvements we bring to the quality of life in our country."[33]

## EXTERNAL TIES: CHURCH OF THE PROVINCE OF WEST AFRICA AND THE EPISCOPAL CHURCH (USA)

At least since 1982, the Episcopal Church (ECL) has added to its historic American ties a relationship with the CPWA. But the Province has itself been fragmenting, first with the withdrawal of the Nigerian Anglican Church and imminently the Anglican Dioceses of Ghana which carved out their own province in 2003. So, with the impending departure of Ghana, CPWA will be left with the Anglican churches of Liberia, Guinea, Gambia, Bo, and Freetown (Sierra Leone). There the situation stood as Neufville's episcopacy ended in 2007.

Ever since the episcopacy of Bishop Browne the relationship between the American and Liberian Episcopal churches has been perceived in terms of the changing agendas of the two historic Christian bodies. Both bodies have faced the increasing challenge of relating to complex social issues. Perhaps the challenge has been greater on the Liberian side given cultural and financial pressures. Browne led the church to its natural social and cultural habitat without renouncing its catholicity. His successors have struggled with that position given the exigencies of their times and their personal dispositions. A Covenant Agreement of 1979 vintage has framed the relationship, the first iteration under Neufville coming in 1997 when a revision was effected calling on ECL to become a part of, and to give leadership to CPWA. In the same year Neufville was elected Dean of the Province. One year earlier Archbishop Okine of the Province attended a meeting in New York of the Joint Covenant Committee where the idea of reviewing the Covenant was discussed "in a Provincial context," while at the same time reaffirming the "special relationship" between the American and Liberian churches. What was not made clear was the place, if any, of CPWA in the TEC relationship with ECL.[34]

At any rate, a 2001 expression of aspirations as to TEC/ECL relations may be suggestive: While praying for each other to be guided by the Holy Spirit, the partners pledged:

1. The Episcopal Church of the United States (ECUSA) will assist ECL in the renovations of church-related buildings, including such facilities as schools, clinics, and hospitals.
2. ECUSA will continue to give moral and financial assistance to ECL in its support of CUC.
3. ECUSA will collaborate with ECL in the recruitment and training of appropriate candidates for ordination, to serve in Liberia.
4. ECUSA and ECL will work together to develop and operate outreach programs to assist Liberians who have lost their homes, possessions and means of livelihood as a result of civil conflict.
5. ECUSA will continue to support the annual operating budget of ECL, with the understanding that the amount of support may decline each year until ECL has eventually achieved full financial independence.
6. ECUSA and ECL will develop strategies to work together in partnership to accomplish these goals. Of great importance is the exchange of people to share the ministry of Christ through different spirituality, churches, and skills. We see parish to companionships to be beneficial for both Churches.
7. ECUSA will render assistance to ECL in the review and updating of its Pension Plan for Clergy and qualified church workers.
8. The Bishop of Liberia shall continue to be a collegial member of the House of Bishops of ECUSA. Representatives of ECL shall continue to be provided, through the Rules of a "Seat and Voice" in the House of Deputies of ECUSA, when that body meets.

9. A Joint Committee of Consultation (the Covenant Committee), including members of ECUSA and ECL, will continue to consult, cooperate, and offer advice on a regular basis.
10. This Covenant shall be subject to review and modification as may become necessary and will continue in effect until agreement by both parties to terminate.

Against the backdrop of these aspirations and understandings the ECL-ECUSA relationship proceeded during the Neufville episcopacy. Such defining features as an annual block grant from ECUSA to ECL and the establishment of companion diocese arrangements between ECL and American dioceses marked the relationship. But an instance of hiccup in the relationship emerged in April 2004 as Neufville attended a meeting of the House of Bishops and the American issue of the ordination of gay Bishops emerged. The candidate was Gene Robinson of New Hampshire, a practicing homosexual. Neufville subsequently reported to his flock: "For your information, Anglicans from Africa decided that they would not accept donations from any diocese that recognizes gay clergy. Africans are half of the 77 million Anglicans. Archbishops declared refusal of cooperation with any missionary who supports ordaining gay priests."[35]

ECL membership in CPWA has often been marked by ambivalence on part of some Liberian Episcopalians, some of them prominent. One easily recalls the issue of reluctance in 1970 of Liberian Episcopalians deciding to forego missionary Bishops and elect their own Bishops for fear of loosing TEC financial support. And then the less than unanimous, indeed controversial, decision a decade later to sever ties with the American church and join the CPWA. Many Liberian Episcopalians have wondered aloud about the tangible benefits Liberia derives from the relationship especially in the aftermath of national political instability and civil war. Some bluntly see fellow African partners struggling like themselves with all looking in the direction of the Western world for assistance. They ignore the powerful intangibles of history and culture, which formed the basis of Bishop Browne's leadership on this matter.

In more practical terms, Liberian Episcopalians and other observers see the role of CPWA in the Browne to Neufville transition saga, including the role of CPWA in the 1995 election of Neufville as Diocesan Bishop, as giving shape to the relationship going forward. These were occasions of tension where Neufville was uncomfortable with the decisions of Bishop Dadson in 1993 following the funeral of Bishop Browne when the Ghanaian prelate appeared to support the administrative arrangements put in place by the late Liberian Bishop to the consternation of Suffragan Bishop Neufville. A similar sentiment of foreboding marked the divisive politics of the 1995 election as Provincial officials witnessed Liberian Episcopalians display in public their disagreements. The issues stemmed from the Browne-Neufville differences and included matters of the legitimacy of the Browne-created team ministry and vicar general, constitutional and canonical provisions for interim Diocesan succession such as Browne's sudden death created. All of the foregoing raised issues about Browne's legacy and Neufville's rightful entitlements during the interim and pending the election. Such developments left unsettled the Liberian Diocese and its Diocesan Bishop.

Neufville inherited relations with the Province. He seemed perfunctory in his approach to his West African colleagues. The American ties seemed more important for a whole host of reasons, the principal of which being tangibly real and potential support that America offered. Though he was elected Dean of the Province in October 1997 and served through 2002 with the election of Bishop S. Telewa Johnson of The Gambia as successor, there is little accounting of his stewardship during his five-year tenure. One mines in vain his annual addresses for such accounting. In the minutes of the provincial standing committee held in Guinea in September 2000 one finds Bishop Neufville sharing routine information on his Diocese in common with the other dioceses represented.

Did he not take seriously the relationship? Was the title "Dean" more for status enhancement purposes, considering that he often laughed it off when asked by some of his priests in lighter moments? The only instance recalled of Neufville's interest in being in solidarity with his fellow African Bishops was a common opposition by conservative elements to the perceived American issue of homosexuality.

## NEUFVILLE'S EPISCOPACY ASSESSED

As he has himself indicated, Neufville's journey to the priesthood was a "personal and inward and a prolonged journey." He wrestled with doubt before surrendering to "God's agenda for me." In time he became a priest, then a Bishop Suffragan, and then Diocesan Bishop of ECL in which capacity he served until attaining the canonical age of 70 years when he retired. Again, as he has said in his last Charge in 2007, his retirement was history-making in the ECL as he was the first "indigenous Liberian Bishop" ever to end "his term of office and is still around relatively strong and active. This heralds a new era in the creation of a line of active retired Bishops by divine Providence." But it was precisely because of this happy event that institutional arrangements were necessary for Bishops emeriti going forward.

Rather than thinking in institutional terms, it appears that the Diocesan Council of ECL thought narrowly and consequently had to reverse a critical decision as to appropriate retirement benefits for bishops. On October 5, 2006, several month's to Neufville's retirement, the Council decided that the retiring Bishop would be provided with $35,000 to purchase a vehicle for his private use. In addition, the Council agreed that the retiring Bishop be provided a monthly stipend of $1,500. Institutional considerations such as a set retirement package for retiring bishops came into the picture after these decisions were taken, so that a few weeks following the Bishop's retirement in February 2008, it became necessary for the Council to reverse itself.

A special committee was mandated by the Council to meet with the Bishop and Mrs. Neufville. The meeting was held on February 9, 2008. The Bishop and his spouse were politely persuaded to accept a reversal of the decision of October 4, 2006 for the following reasons: serious budgetary implications of the ordination of twenty-two priests on November 15, 2007 in terms of payroll and other budgetary constraints; in view of a report by Canon Bruce Woodcock of the Church Pension Fund that the retiring Bishop was generously provided for under the Church Pension scheme "and there is no reason for ECL to use its meager resources to provide additional monetary support"; and heavy toll inflicted on the Dioceses' finances for Bromley Mission support . The Committee informed the Bishop and his spouse that the Council proposed the offer of the vehicle currently used by the retired Bishop as a "one –time gift" from ECL. In sympathy with the Church the Neufvilles' response was cordial as they thanked the committee for visiting with them and for the Council's offer of the vehicle. They accepted the offer in good faith and prayed that the cordial relationship with the Church would continue beyond that visit.[36]

Before this gracious exit of retirement, Neufville had carried out his almost four decades of ministry in ECL. The road was rugged, exacerbated by war and strife of all sorts. But Neufville no doubt felt that he had a charge to keep as he pressed forward. I once sat in his family home in South Carolina and watched a video of one of his sermons. When it was done I said to his wife and one of his daughters who wondered earlier in conversation why her dad had not simply quit going to Liberia: "Where would he unload all that spiritual energy?" I inquired. He was a man on a mission, a mission made difficult by strife and war and all the attending consequences.

Though he was not able to heal fully the divided church he inherited, he did make his mark in the areas of education and evangelism. CU, the flagship institution of ECL made strides under the administrations of both President Mason and President Tokpa. Many Episcopal schools were reopened and revived, some with the critical assistance of alumni associations in the Diaspora.

Above all was the symbolism of revival at Bromley Mission where Neufville's vision for the education of orphan and other disadvantaged girls was to bear fruit. Consider the testimony of an alumni of Neufville's Bromley, Kpana Nnadia Gaygay: "In Dec. 2003, wretched, hungry little girl was given the greatest opportunity by the late Rt. Rev. Edward Wea Neufville, II through the ECL to go to school here (the Julia C. Emery Hall, Bromley Mission), one of the greatest gifts I've ever received yet in my life. I am a product of the generosity of strangers through the ECL and I remain forever grateful. Our dearest ma, mother Louise Morais Neufville, thank you there ohhhh. See us behind her down waterside buying shoes, gari, sugar, milk, etc." Gaygay, now author of *Daunting Years: The Liberian Civil War in the Eyes of a Child*[37] was even more expansive:

> The recruitment of girls for the reopening of Bromley was the idea of . . . Bishop Neufville of ECL. I was fortunate to be among the initial 54 girls selected from among thousands of displaced girls. . . . When the news first reached Mama, she abruptly replied, 'No, you are going nowhere. . . . Mama refused because she did not know the people who wanted to take me and did not wish to give me to any stranger. The war was just over and many individuals were into human trafficking. Many people took other people's children with the impression of helping but once the child was given to them, it was another story. This she feared. Luckily for me, Papa heard the news and came rushing to the camp to have me prepared to leave for Bromley. . . . Mama was madly against his acceptance of this offer but Papa was firm in his decision. He said I was going since in fact, he was a member of the Episcopal Church and thought this was a worthy cause undertaken by his Church. In the end, Papa won.[38]

Bishop Neufville's passion for education was matched only by his zeal for evangelism. A shy, perhaps introverted personality with a gifted mind, many recall his evangelistic fervor. A highly spiritual person, he used every opportunity for prayers, Bible study and reflection. When I made my first and only visit to his office at Trinity Cathedral in 2004, he greeted me holding my hands and suggested a word of prayer before we sat to reminisce on our time together as students at Cuttington, as well as the state of our country and our church. He remained, as Fr. Edward Thompson has indicated, the "deeply spiritual bishop," the "spiritually-grounded leader," focused on moral restoration "starting with strict family fidelity."

Clearly influenced by his spouse, he gravitated toward education of girls, as well as encouraging females into the priesthood of the church. In this way he ordained the largest number of women priests. Those ordained were: The Rev. Abeoseh M. Flemister, The Rev. Josephine H. Davies, The Rev. Shirley M. M. Diggs, The Rev. Elizabeth K. W. W. Hina, The Rev. Rachel Bornynor

Davies Jarebo, The Rev. Naime K. Kpoto Garley, the Rev. Theresa Hawa Saah, and The Rev. Wyman F. Davies.

In retirement, Neufville was learning Hebrew through a correspondence course as he contemplated some day teaching at the theology division at CU. Health and family circumstances decided otherwise as he settled in Sumter, South Carolina where he expressed gratitude to God that at Good Shepherd Episcopal Church in that city he could "serve my Lord at an altar today."

In the end, what Bishop Neufville was able to restore—the tangibles of buildings and other physical plants of the church, as well as the intangibles of moral and spiritual upliftment—were now left to his successors to enlarge upon, adding dimensions of their own.

The Bishop died peacefully at the Medical University of South Carolina. Services over his remains were held January 27, 2011 at the Cathedral of St. Luke and St. Paul in Charleston. The body was flown to Liberia where Services were also held at Trinity Cathedral on February 5, 2011. Interment followed on the premises of Bromley Mission.

## NOTES

1. Neufville Family, "Draft Life Sketch, The Rt. Rev. Edward Wea Neufville, BA, M.Th. DD, 11th Diocesan Bishop of the Episcopal Church of Liberia, Second Suffragan Bishop of the Episcopal Church of Liberia, courtesy of Mrs. Louise Morais Neufville, n.d., 8 pages, located in Dunn Archives, Silver Springs, Maryland, USA, and Monrovia, Liberia (Author's files and archives of original documents of church collections and letters.) (hereafter cited Dunn Archives).

2. Seth C. Edwards, quoted in *The Canon Missioner's Report* (1969), 6 pages (Archives of the Episcopal Church, Austin, Texas, Domestic and Foreign Missionary Society [hereafter cited DFMS Papers]).

3. D. Elwood Dunn, *A History of the Episcopal Church of Liberia, 1821–1980* (Metuchen, NJ: American Theological Library Association and the Scarecrow Press, 1992), 176; Dean Arthur Holt, "Change Strategies Initiated by the Protestant Episcopal Church in Liberia from 1836 to 1950 and Their Differential Effects" (EdD diss., Boston University, 1970), 276.

4. George D. Browne, "Are Bishops Essential to the Church? What can we expect from our Suffragan?" Sermon by Archbishop George D. Browne on the occasion of the Ordination and Consecration of The Ven. Edward W. Neufville as Suffragan Bishop, Trinity Cathedral, May 6, 1984, 6 pages (Dunn Archives).

5. Bishop Browne's Sermon at consecration of Bp. Neuffville, in Browne, "Are Bishops Essential to the Church?"

6. Letter, Bishop Edmond L. Browning to The Rt. Revd. Edward Wea Neufville II, May 24, 1995 (Dunn Archives).

7. Excerpts from message printed in Episcopal Church of Liberia (ECL), "Souvenir Programme, Installation and Enthronement of The Rt. Rev. Edward Wea Neufville II, BA, MTS, DD, the 11th Bishop of Liberia." Trinity Cathedral, Broad Street, Monrovia. January 6, 1996. Feast of The Epiphany.

8. Partial text of Edward W. Neufville II, "My Episcopacy," draft autobiography, courtesy of Mrs. Louise Morais Neufville, 35 handwritten pages (Dunn Archives).

9. Bishop Neufville, 68th Diocesan Convention, February 1966, quoted in *Journal of the Diocesan Conventions of the EC* (DFMS Papers).

10. Fr. Edward Thompson, interview by email with author, July 5, 2018.

11. Episcopal Church of Liberia (ECL), "A Concept Paper for the Post War Development Program of the Episcopal Church of Liberia," March 7, 2005, 9 pages (Dunn Archives).

12. *Journal of the 74th Diocesan Convention*, February 2002 (DFMS Papers).

13. Fr. Thompson, interview, July 5, 2018.

14. Bishop Neufville's Address at the 76th Diocesan Convention, in *Journal of the Diocesan Conventions of the EC* (2005): 52 (DFMS Papers).

15. Bishop Neufville's Address at 2007 Convention, *Journal of the Diocesan Conventions of the EC* (2007): 20 (DFMS Papers).

16. Brother Lawrence, OHC, interview with author, September 8, 2010, West Park, New York.

17. "History of the Leprosy Ministry" (Mbalotahun, Liberia, 2009); Report on the Holy Cross Mission, Bolahun, Lofa County submitted by the Committee on the State of the Church, by A.E. Nyema Jones, Melvin J. Mason & Clavenda Bright, Monrovia, June 11, 1971, 22 pages (Dunn Archives); Lawrence, interview, September 8, 2010; John Gay, "The 50th Anniversary of the Holy Cross Mission at Bolahun," Cuttington College, February 22, 1972, 9 pages (Dunn Archives).

18. "History of Leprosy Ministry" (Dunn Archives).

19. *Journal of the 71st Diocesan Convention* (1999).

20. Resolutions of the 78th Diocesan Convention (Dunn Archives).

21. "Tribute to the Late Retired Bishop Edward W. Neufville II, . . . Eleventh Bishop of the Episcopal Church of Liberia," delivered by The Rt. Rev. Jonathan B. B. Hart on Behalf of the Episcopal Diocese of Liberia, February 4–5, 2011; and Hart's Tribute of February 2011 (Dunn Archives)

22. 69th Diocesan Convention (1997) (Dunn Archives).

23. Hart, "Tribute"; See also notes from Bishop's Addresses re: Rafiki (Dunn Archives).

24. Rafiki Agreement between ECL and Rafiki Foundation, Inc. February 28, 2006 (Dunn Archives).

25. See pages 133–34 of *Journal of the 73rd Convention* (Dunn Archives).

26. Robert Fulton Cutting, June 27, 1852–September 21, 1935, 82 years old. See *Who's Who in the World* (1912).

27. Endnote Letter Edwards to Neufville, July 14, 1997. Committee members: Dr. Linda Chisholm, Mr. Seth C. Edwards, Jr. Dr. J. Rudolph Grimes, Dr. Stephen Kaifa, Ms. Margaret Larom, Dr. Melvin Mason, Rev. John Powers, Dr. Henrique Tokpa and Mr. Tonneh Tokpah.

28. Melvin J. Mason, *Savoring Education: An Autobiography* (Columbus, GA: Brentwood Christian Press, 2007), 308–9.

29. Mason, *Savoring Education*, 302.

30. Mason, *Savoring Education*.

31. Henrique Flomo Tokpa, interview by the *Episcopal News Service*, July 2, 2003 (Dunn Archives).

32. Romelle A. Horton, supplied in email message to author, November 19, 2018.

33. Henrique Flomo Tokpa, "The Challenges of Building the New Cuttington," *Cuttington Review*, Special Retrospective (2011–2012): 7–9.

34. 69th Convention (1997), Reviewing the Covenant in a Provincial Context (Dunn Archives). See also Charges of Bishop Neufville, "The Covenant Plan" (Dunn Archives).

35. 76th Diocesan Convention (2005) (Dunn Archives); and the Bishop's Charge regarding ordination of Gay priests, as he gleaned from meeting of the House of Bishops in Houston, Texas, March 2004 (Dunn Archives).

36. Episcopal Church of Liberia (ECL), "Report of The Committee Appointed by the Diocesan Council to meet with Retired Bishop Edward W. Neufville II. Subject: Special Committee meeting with Bishop and Mother Neufville," February 9, 2008, 3 pages, submitted by Juanita E. Neal (Chairman, Diocesan Board of Trustees), Wilbert Clarke (Member, Diocesan Board of Trustees), Ida B. Ajavon (Chairman, Diocesan Board of Education), Sandei A. Cooper (Diocesan Treasurer), and the Rev. Roberta A. Phillips (President, Diocesan Standing Committee).

37. Kpana N. Gaygay, *Daunting Years: The Liberian Civil War In the Eyes of a Child* (Alexandria, VA: Forte Publishing, 2017).

38. Dunn, *History of the Episcopal Church*, 108–9.

*Chapter Four*

# Episcopacy of Bishop Jonathan Bau-Bau Bonaparte Hart (2008–)

In the twelfth year of his episcopacy, Bishop Hart was enthroned as the 11th Primate and Metropolitan Archbishop of the Church of the Province of West Africa (CPWA). At an elaborate Thanksgiving Service marking the transfer of the Primatial Cross to Hart from Ghanaian Archbishop Daniel Yinkah Sarfo, the Liberian Prelate wrote:

> On the blessed occasion of the transfer of the Primatial Staff of the Church of the Province of West Africa (CPWA), it seems my ministry has come full circle. As a young priest and seminary student in 1982, I had returned home from the United States for the funeral of my father when Bishop George D. Browne, then only a few days to his enthronement as the first Liberian Archbishop and Primate of CPWA asked that I delay my return trip in order to be a part of that historic ceremony. I was thus recruited to serve as chaplain on that occasion.
>
> An account of the enthronement replete with historic photographs, in Vol. II, No. 2 issue of the CHRISTIAN HERALD refreshed our memory of that memorable event. There I was in the vestment of a priest as Bishop Browne was resplendent in the vestment of Archbishop and Primate of our Church.
>
> Little did I know that 37 years later, amid the turmoil and vicissitudes of life, I would stand in that identical spot at Trinity Cathedral to become the 11th Chief Pastor and Primate of the Church of the Province of West Africa. God moves in a mysterious way, and I today rejoice and offer him praise and adoration for bringing me and my ministry to this level in the one Holy, Catholic and Apostolic Church. Rejoice with me, dear sisters and brothers, as this new dimension of service to West Africa comes again to the Episcopal Church of Liberia and to the Republic if Liberia.[1]

It was on March 3, 2019 at Trinity Cathedral in Monrovia where in addition to Archbishop Sarfo, the following other bishops of CPWA were in attendance: Bishop Alexander Asmah of Sekendi, Bishop Abraham Ackah of Wiawso, Bishop Daniel S. M. Tortu of Accra, Bishop Festus Yeboah-Asuamah of Sunyani, Bishop Dibo Elango of Cameroon, Bishop Victor Atta-Baffoe of Cape Coast, Bishop Thomas A. I, Wilson of Freetown, Bishop James Y. Odico of Gambia, Bishop Jacques Boston of Guinea, Bishop Felix Annancy of Kofordua, Bishop Cyril Ben-Smith of Asante Mampong, Bishop Matthias Metadues-Madohu of Ho, Bishop Emmanuel A. Arongo of Tamale, and Bishop John K. Otto of Dunkwa-on-Offin.

The Episcopal Church of the United States was represented by The Rev. David Copley, Director of Global Partnership at headquarters of The Episcopal Church (USA) (TEC) in New York.

The impressive occasion was also witnessed by many Liberian church leaders, other dignitaries, and Episcopalians from across the country.

In transfer remarks Archbishop Sarfo said that having served his full term as Primate of the CPWA in accordance with the constitution of the Province, it was his distinguished honor to turn over the Cross of office to Archbishop Hart. "I hand over the Primatial Cross to you, the Most Rev. Jonathan Bonaparte Bau Bau Hart, the incoming 11th Primate and Metropolitan Archbishop of the CPWA, in the name of the Father, the Son and the Holy Spirit, Amen," Sarfo intoned as he pledged his support to the new Primate, adding that he would do everything possible to support Archbishop Hart because when he had headed the Province, Hart was fully supportive.[2]

In response, Archbishop Hart characterized the task ahead as "a challenge, overseeing several dioceses and requires the support of all its members."[3] He called on everyone to support the work of the church in order to achieve the goal. Hart's term of office is five years.

Hart's ministry had indeed come full circle for he had risen through the ranks from a humble priest ordained in 1980 to become the 12th Diocesan Bishop of ECL in 2008, the second Liberian Dean of CPWA in 2009, the 2nd Archbishop of the Internal Province of West Africa (IPWA) within CPWA in 2014, and then, the apex of them all, the Primate of CPWA in 2019—a multi-layered ministry indeed.

But first, on the verge of attaining the canonical requirement of age 70 years in 2007, Bishop Edward W. Neufville II had set in motion the process for the election of his successor. Chaired by Layperson and Acting Diocesan Chancellor, Comfort Natt, other members of the Bishop nominating committee were: Joanna M. Hill, Negbalee Warner, Clemenceau B. Urey, Rev. Fr. Sayonkon Jarteh (deceased), Samuel Ngaima, Rev. Fr. Thomas Williams, Rev. Fr. Victor King, and Rev. Fr. Elijah Harris.

A Bishop was to be nominated and then elected from among more than sixty Clergy. Amid the politicking that ensued, the name of the Rev. Fr.

Emmanuel D. Hodges, former Vicar General of the Diocese (1991–1996) resurfaced as it had done in the Browne to Neufville succession contest. Hodges had managed the affairs of the Diocese during the period of illness of Bishop Browne, including the controversial interim period between Browne and Neufville. One church publication put it this way: "For a while, it seems that the Rev. Fr. Emmanuel D. Hodges would be the likely choice to succeed Neufville until a stroke left him partially paralyzed. Fr. Hodges remained a very popular priest with both clergy and laity, and it seemed, in spite of his ailment, his chances of becoming the next Diocesan did not diminish until his untimely death right after the 77th Diocesan Convention" in 2006.[4]

With the late Fr. Hodges now out of the running, the process, as reported by the Bishop nominating committee, produced the following three clergy as candidates qualified for the twelfth bishopric of the church—The Rev. Canon Dr. Herman B. Browne, vicar, St. George's Episcopal Church; The Very Rev. Jonathan B. B. Hart, dean, Trinity Cathedral; and The Rev. Fr. Dr. James B. Sellee, rector, St. Thomas Parish.

Who were these men? Browne, a chip off the old bark, is the son of the late Bishop Browne who upon graduating from Cuttington University (CU) with a Bachelor of Arts degree in theology pursued graduate studies in Britain leading to a doctorate in theology. He was ordained deacon in 1987 and priest in 1997. Following a stint in the office of the Archbishop of Canterbury, Browne returned home to service in the church. Hart is also a CU graduate with a Bachelor of Arts in theology and a Masters of Divinity (MDiv) from the Episcopal Divinity School in Cambridge, Massachusetts. Ordained to the diaconate in 1979 and to the priesthood in 1980, he served many largely rural congregations before becoming Dean of Trinity Cathedral in 2001. Sellee graduated as well from CU with a Bachelor of Arts in theology. Like Browne he too pursued graduate studies in Britain leading to a doctorate in theology. He was ordained deacon in 1987 and priest in 1989. Sellee served the CPWA in Banjul, The Gambia, and led many congregations in Liberia before being elected rector of St. Thomas Episcopal Church Camp Johnson Road.

As Neufville contemplated retirement and called for the election of a Bishop Coadjutor, he called the event of his retirement unique in that this was the first time "an indigenous Liberian Bishop had ever ended his term of office and is still around relatively strong and active." He quoted William Shakespeare: "All the world is a stage and all the men and women mere players. They have their entrances and their exits." He invoked as well Ecclesiastes and a time for everything refrain. "The year has come for me to retire and God willing we will do so with joy, gracefulness and thanksgiving."[5]

## ELECTION OF BISHOP COADJUTOR

The first special session of the 78th Diocesan Convention for the election of a Bishop Coadjutor convened at the Epiphany Chapel, CU, November 16–18, 2007 under the theme "Praising God should be life long and not seasonal," Text Psalm 146 with theme song "The Church's One Foundation." Bishop Neufville was celebrant and preacher on the second day of the Convention. He was thankful for a "huge turn out at the Convention." He gave a two-fold purpose to the special seating of the 78th Convention: (1) to praise God for bringing us safe thus far as a church, and (2) to elect a Bishop Coadjutor. He cautioned carefulness and prayerfulness, commending all to the guidance of the Holy Spirit.

With Neufville presiding, in attendance were sixty Clergy (96% of clerical force), thirty-seven officers (62%), and 345 lay delegates (86%). The nominating committee presented three priests in competition for the post of Diocesan Bishop. They were The Very Rev. Jonathan B. B. Hart, Dean of Trinity Cathedral, The Rev. Fr. Dr. James B. Sellee, Rector of St. Thomas Parish, and the Rev. Canon Dr. Herman B. Browne, Vicar, St. George's Episcopal. In all, there were 475 registered delegates—sixty clergy, thirty-seven officers, and 378 lay delegates. A first round of voting produced the following results:

Hart: 211 votes
Selle: 181 votes
Browne: 71 votes
Discarded: 9
Blank: 3
Total: 475

Because no candidate received the canonical requirement of two thirds of the vote, a second balloting ensued, involving the two top vote getters, and those results were as follows:

Hart: 296 votes
Sellee: 157 votes
Total: 453 votes

Though this outcome did not give Hart the required two thirds to win outright, and as delegates were both exhausted and de-spirited at the late hour of 3:00 a.m., Fr. Sellee decided to take the podium and concede defeat, pledging his full support to Hart. Bishop Neufville then spoke, commending the nominating committee for a job well done, and glowingly calling Sellee "a man of strong heart and love for the church," and "a true man of God." Neufville concluded: "We now have a new Bishop Coadjutor" and that it was important to rally around him and give him our full support. Hart then spoke, praising God and thanking all for the outcome. The Doxology was sung and Bishop Neufville, who brought the Convention to a close at 3:30 a.m., dismissed the gathering with Benediction.

It did not take long before the self-congratulating conventioneers discovered that there was something amiss. Upon being duly informed about the proceedings of the Convention, the Archbishop of the Province of West Africa, The Most Rev. Justice Akrofi, informed the Diocese of Liberia that the just ended election was irregular with regard to the Constitution and Canons of both the Province and the Diocese of Liberia as Hart did not receive the two thirds required even in the second round of voting. The Province accordingly annulled the election and a new election was ordered. Since the term of Bishop Neufville had ended, Archbishop Akrofi appointed as Vicar General of the Diocese of Liberia the Rev. Fr. A-Too Williams, rector of St. Stephen's Episcopal Church. It then became the responsibility of Williams to arrange a fresh election, which he promptly proceeded to do.

A second Special Convention of the 78th Diocesan Convention convened at St. Thomas Chapel New Kru Town January 19, 2008 under the theme: "With God above, we can make the impossible, possible" (Matthew 17:20), with theme song "The Church's One Foundation." The presiding Fr. Williams preached, speaking to the theme of the Convention. He told the gathering that they had assembled to complete what they thought they had completed at the last special session, adding: "when the news of the nullification of the last result reached the Diocese, the church was disturbed, but God wanted us to do it right."[6] He then concluded that if they did the right thing, God would make the impossible, possible.

In attendance at this Convention were sixty-two Clergy (93% of clerical force), thirty-two officers (64%), 441 lay delegates (97%), and representatives of 128 congregations (99% of congregations of the Diocese). The nomination committee presented the same three candidates, Hart, Sellee and Browne. The balloting produced the following result:

Hart: 376 votes
Sellee: 80 votes
Browne: 41 votes
Discarded: 2 voites
Total: 499 votes

Hart, having this time exceeded the two-thirds requirement of 333 votes in a single round had now won decisively. A more subdued Convention ended with retired Bishop Neufville advising Episcopalians to refrain from media publication pending approval of the result by the Archbishop of the Province. Fr. Hart then took the podium and thanked the Convention for the confidence reposed in him, and re-echoed Bishop Neufville's warning about awaiting final approval of the Province. Hart expressed thanks to Dr. Sellee and Dr. Browne for a good process, adding thanks to his wife for her standing by him, thanking as well everyone for their support. The day's activities ended at 6:30 p.m. The church now had a Bishop Coadjutor.

## EVENTS LEADING TO CONSECRATION OF TWELFTH DIOCESAN BISHOP

The Vicar General, Fr. Williams soon communicated the outcome of the elections to the Archbishop of the Province, Archbishop Akrofi. Receipt of the communication was acknowledged in short order with a "mandate for the consecration of the Very Reverend Jonathan Bau-Bau Bonaparte Hart as Bishop of the Episcopal Church of Liberia." The Mandate said, inter alia, "Whereas, testimony has been given of the piety, sobriety and honesty of life of the said Very Reverend Jonathan Bau-Bau Bonaparte Hart to be Bishop of the Episcopal Church of Liberia, and, of his sound doctrine and faithfulness to the discipline of the Church of Christ, and of worthiness of his moral conduct." "Now therefore, we by Divine Providence, Archbishop and Primate of the Province of West Africa, do, by this our mandate, direct that due order be taken for the Consecration by US of the said Very Reverend Jonathan Bau-Bau Bonaparte Hart to the office of Bishop in the Church of God, in accordance with the manner and form prescribed and used by the Episcopal Church of Liberia and the CPWA, their being to assist and take part in that Consecration such Bishops of this and of other parts of the Anglican Communion as shall be convenient. Signed by Archbishop Akrofi and dated February 5, 2008.

With the date of March 2, 2008 set for the consecration and enthronement Fr. Williams coordinated with the office of the Archbishop of the Province in preparing for the grand occasion, the American church was duly informed, all of this in close collaboration with the relevant committees and councils of ECL.

As the Primate of the CPWA, Archbishop Akrofi contemplated the consecration, he penned words of admonition to the Liberian church:

> For good or ill, you have made your choice of a leader. Now, be focused on the task of prosecuting God's mission through the Diocese of Liberia. Be done with power games and struggles. Be done with rivalries and jealousness. Be done with the works (desires) of the flesh (Gal. 5:16–21). By contrast, let me set before you the powerful words of Scripture that changed Augustine of Hippo

from the philanderer and scoundrel to become a great African Saint, scholar and churchman.... It is the hour now for you to awake from sleep. Let us then throw off the works of darkness and put on the armor of light, let us conduct ourselves properly as in the day, not in orgies and drunkenness, not in promiscuity and licentiousness, not in rivalry and jealousy. But put on the Lord Jesus Christ, and make no provision for the desires of the flesh (Rom. 13:11–14).[7]

The Archbishop continued:

Allow me one more comment on the Province as a vehicle of solidarity. This idea is on the model of the Church as family of the people of God. But if you are Anglican/Episcopalian, there is a particular twist: rooted in the core Christian message of the Incarnation (Jn. 1:14). Anglicans officially go further to articulate it in Articles XXIV of the Articles of Religion, styled the vernacular principle or paradigm. Just as Christ in the fullness of time was born a Jew (Gal. 4: 4) so too, does he desire to take flesh in the West African context and reality. The new bishop is called to lead the search for a vital, vibrant, and viable Episcopal Church/diocese of Liberia in West Africa, not as an American or any other Caucasian clone. How will the Episcopal Church of Liberia propose to become truly African Christian Church in West Africa alongside the siblings in CPWA? It means receiving and giving.[8]

And then the Chief Consecrator welcomed Jonathan Bau-Bau Bonaparte Hart to the Episcopal bench of CPWA, adding: "This rite will welcome you to the CPWA as a bishop. But it is more than just a rite of consecration and enthronement. It is a call from Christ to lead God's people on a God-given task of mission according to the African genius and use. What will be your memorial and legacy? Will posterity smile when your name is mentioned? Or will they spit and curse?"[9]

The consecration took place at Trinity Cathedral on March 2, 2008 with President Ellen Johnson Sirleaf of Liberia leading an array of government and civic personalities. The Most Rev. Dr. Justice O. Akrofi, Archbishop of CPWA was the principal consecrator, with coconsecrators and celebrants being the Bishops of the Province. The preacher was the Bishop of Tamale (Ghana), The Rt. Rev. Emmanuel A. Arongo. Presenters were: The Rt Rev. Julius O. P. Lynch, The Rt. Rev. Daniel S.A. Allotey, The Rev. Fr. James B. Sellee, The Rev. Roberta A. Phillips, Bro. Wilbert Clarke, and Sis. D. Sheba Brown. The Old Testament was read my Mother Frances A. Hart, Epistoler, The Rt. Rev. Abraham Ackah, Gospeller, The Rt. Rev. Samuel S. Gbonda, Litanist, and The Rt Rev. Edward W. Neufville II.

Jonathan B. B. Hart was born in Crozierville, Montserrado County, Liberia on January 9, 1953. His father was Albert Hart Sr. and his mother was Victoria Thorpe.

A gifted student, he went from exploring a career in electrical engineering (even poised to go abroad for study before a diversion happened) to the sacred ministry. When spotted by Bishop Browne he was taken under the wings of the church and nurtured through the church's educational institutions, subsequently sent off to graduate school in the United States.

The late Bishop George Daniel Browne ordained him a deacon on November 11, 1979 and to the priesthood on August 10, 1980. He was one of a relatively small number of young clergy trained and deployed during Browne's twenty-two year episcopacy. Hart has been married to Frances Amanda Logan Hart for almost forty years and they are parents to four children.

Among the congregations in which Hart served are the historic St. Mark's Episcopal Church in Harper and concurrently as Archdeacon of the Southeastern Archdeaconry covering Maryland, Grand Kru, Sinoe, and Grand Gedeh Counties (1984–1996), and Trinity Cathedral, which he served both as priest-in-charge and subsequently as dean (1996–2008). He holds a MDiv degree from the Episcopal Divinity School in Cambridge, Massachusetts, United States, and a Bachelor of Arts degree in theology. One of the hallmarks of his earlier ministry is that he is among the few priests who remained with their flock throughout the fourteen years of civil war. When war conditions forced him to briefly leave Maryland County, it was across the Cavalla river in the Ivorien town of Tabu that he went to continue his ministry among Liberian war refugees.

Six years into his episcopacy, and having served as the second Liberian dean of the CPWA (2009–2014), Bishop Hart on May 1, 2014 was elected the second Archbishop of the IPWA. Plans were afoot in 2003 to have Ghana made an autonomous Province by 2004 but war conditions in Liberia and Sierra Leone led the Anglican Consultative Council (ACC) not to approve the move. At Synod in Guinea in 2011 a decision was taken to meet in Liberia in September 2012 to initiate the process of creating two administrative provinces within the CPWA—IPWA comprising all the Dioceses outside Ghana, and the Internal Province of Ghana. Final decision to go separate ways was attempted at Synod in Gambia in 2016 but decision by the Synod was to allow another five years before taking the plunge. The vision of separation finally saw the light of day in 2019 with the completion of a process that led to Bishop Hart becoming on March 3 the Primate of the CPWA. All of this was possible because of a change in the constitution of CPWA limiting the term of Provincial Primate to five years.[10]

Five years earlier, however, Bishop Hart was enthroned as Archbishop of the IPWA in the CPWA at a colorful service at Trinity Cathedral in Monrovia on July 6, 2014. The Primate and Metropolitan Archbishop of the Province of

West Africa, The Most Revd Daniel Y. Sarfo officiated. He enjoined the new Archbishop to be "guided by the legacies of His Grace, Most Rev. Dr. George Browne, our late Primate and Metropolitan Archbishop of the Church of the Province of West Africa. He was one of our finest Primates."[11]

Hart would himself utter these words on the occasion of his enthronement: "I choose you before I gave you life, and before you were born I selected you to be a prophet to the nations (Jer. 1:5). "These were the exact words of our Lord to the Prophet Jeremiah when He commissioned him to be a prophet to the nations. Today, I can say with faith in the midst of disbeliefs and anxieties that the Lord who has called me to His service some thirty plus years ago is saying these same words to me as I assume this new ministry. Our God is good. His doings are marvelous in our eyes and beyond our comprehension."[12]

High hopes were expressed by Cathedral Dean Herman Browne as Bishop Hart was being enthroned Archbishop of IPWA: "The soon-to-be Archbishop has been offered a platform—one he rightly deserves—that will enable him take the Province beyond evangelism and education, into the realm of health and medicine." Browne added: "Title bestows responsibility, and Bishop Hart is now better positioned to bring more to the challenges ahead, now that he finds himself less hindered by earlier hindrances—and limitations."[13]

Even higher hopes were entertained as Hart had reached the pinnacle in ecclesiastical aspirations, or that God had lifted him up and planted his feet on higher grounds. What would now be his words and actions expressive of a renewed vision?

There was a smooth transition from Neufville to Hart on March 2, 2008, from the 11th to the 12th Diocesan Bishop of ECL. The Primate and Metropolitan of CPWA officiated at Hart's consecration and installation. Now, it was the turn of Bishop Jonathan Hart to shepherd the Episcopal flock.

There was no shortage of both challenges and opportunities. Evangelism and education continued to loom large on the diocesan agenda, as did the nature of external ties with both TEC and CPWA. Issues of sustainability of the whole mission of the church soon forced themselves to center stage—the pension plan for clergy, decreasing subsidy from TEC, dwindling income from the church's real estate, poor stewardship in a country still recovering from civil war. In short, sustainability concerned the financial difficulties facing the diocese and what needed to be done to remedy the situation.

Because he is the sitting Diocesan Bishop, in addition to the other charges from CPWA, this study will be limited to introducing Hart's episcopacy while highlighting the state of the church in the beginning years of his leadership of the Diocese. Only a tentative conclusion will be attempted.

## HIGHLIGHTS OF FIRST TWELVE YEARS

### State of the Church and Hart's Vision

Shortly following his consecration and installation as the 12th Diocesan Bishop of the Episcopal Church of Liberia (ECL), Bishop Hart was asked what vision he had for the Diocese. "The number one problem which we have to deal with," he replied "is that of uniting our Clergy, and as a result of the unity of our Clergy, I would be able to unite Episcopalians." Hart was in these words signaling his sense of the state of the church that he had inherited, namely, that without a united clerical force and concomitantly, his flock, a successful bishopric could be in peril.[14]

Consequently, he wasted no time in inviting a two-day clergy retreat at St. Stephen's Episcopal Church under the theme: "That they may all be one" (Jn. 17:21). Conducted by the late Canon Marilyn K. Robertson, Honorary Canon of Trinity Cathedral, former missionary-educator at the once famous House of Bethany in Cape Mount, and widow of the venerable missionary-educator E. Bolling Robertson, the idea seems to have been borrowed from Hart's mentor, the late Bishop George Browne who sensed the need in his time for clergy unity and thus invited his own inherited clergy to a retreat at St. Thomas Camp Johnson Road in 1970.

Further, well into his episcopacy, Bishop Hart acknowledged that the church had fallen on hard times, that it was clearly not what it used to be. Might the reason be his inheritance including the long shadow of a war-devastated Liberia? He did not want to travel that road, for the "blame game leads nowhere." Instead, being fully cognizant of all the impacting environmental circumstances, he admonished that "no matter what the vicissitudes of life may be, 'we must rise up and walk' (Acts 3:6)." He continued: "Let us [clergy and lay Episcopalians] embrace one another and develop a shared vision regarding the things we must do." Such a shared vision "must be buttressed in the framework of encouraging a self-sustenance of our church where our members are actively participating in the Christ-centered ministries of preaching, teaching and healing (loving, caring, supporting)." Such sentiments would feed into his strategy for "growing more Episcopalians" which entailed both that "our priests and lay leaders are adequately schooled," but also that Episcopal schools become anew the avenue to "growing church membership" and evangelism. To this end, he called on Episcopalians to "work to strengthen those schools that are still breathing; work to resurrect those that lie in ruins; and work to develop more schools from bottom to top."[15]

## Sustainability Challenges

From the inception of Bishop Hart's episcopacy and given the state of the church he inherited, the issue of funds to conduct effective ministry has dogged the Episcopal Church.

Operational funds for ECL emanate from three basic sources as follows:

1. Real Estate: The church's properties such as the ECL Plaza building, the Jean Travis building, and the 15th Street buildings.
2. Block Grant from TEC to ECL (See Neufville's "Stewardship" section)
3. Trust or custodial funds "which wise people of God, many years ago so graciously set aside for such a time as this."[16]

A Trust fund consists of more than one hundred individual funds with aggregate book value at April 30, 2018 of $740,333. An ECL endowment fund managed by TEC had a book value at June 30, 2018 of $190,696, while a separate endowment for CU had a book value at September 30, 2018 of $937,938.

TEC's Church Pension Fund administers a Liberia Plan and manages investment of the assets of the Liberia Plan. Pension for Clergy under the Church Pension Fund has been firmly institutionalized.

The problem with funding sources is three-fold: diminishing block grant based on Covenant agreement between TEC and ECL; radically reduced intake from the church's real estate because of downturn in a post-war national economy; and the absence of any productive economic activity of the church. "The only option we find viable, if we are to meet the ever increasing demands of the Diocese and sustain our pension plan over the years (and not lose it)," wrote sustainability committee chairman Clemenceau Urey, "is to develop the ways and means to generate our own internal resources on a large scale." For one could hardly carry out the mission of the church regarding evangelism, education, healing without the requisite funds. Convention after Convention had grappled with the issue, passing resolution after resolution to address the issue. The 81st Convention in 2011 endorsed "the holding of an economic symposium with the objective of bringing together experts in the field of financial investment and management in order to diversify and optimize returns on our financial portfolio."[17]

To this end, a Sustainability Committee emerged and was chaired by churchman Clemenceau B. Urey, Sr., a prominent businessman. Other equally prominent Episcopalians who were members included Wilbert Clarke,

Roosevelt Jayjay, D. Sheba Brown, Cora Peabody, and Gerald Cooper, a Liberian Episcopal Community in the United States (LECUSA) representative.

One document probably produced by this committee offered thoughts on how to achieve economic sustainability for ECL. It set forth an analysis of the current economic situation of the diocese by first laying out some basic facts. It proposed an investment or economic development unit in the diocese inclusive of a functional administrative structure that would incorporate the Boards of Trustees, Planning and Development, Education, and Health. Seed money to carry forward the plan was proposed as $250,000 to be funded both locally and from abroad. Local funding would start with a scheme whereby one hundred Episcopalians with means would contribute $500 each, and thus raise the first $50,000. A "decent professional brochure" would set forth and contextualize the plan. This brochure would then be presented to potential donors to include in the first instance all Liberian Episcopalians at home and in the Diaspora. Other support from abroad was specified as TEC-Trust Fund, companion relationship with American dioceses, etc.

Professional brochures were in fact prepared, one to coincide with a visit to Liberia in January 2010 of the American Presiding Bishop Katherine Jefferts Schori, and the other a year later for the "ECL Economic Summit for Achieving Economic Sustainability." Dubbed the "first economic sustainability symposium of the Episcopal Church of Liberia," it was convened on April 13, 2011, but there is little record of its operational accomplishments. Subsequently, a sustainability committee, which emerged from past forums, held a joint meeting with LECUSA, the Church Pension Group, and TEC, and came up with a number of critical recommendations to Bishop Hart (Hire Diocesan administrator, hire full-time treasurer, and be more collaborative with Trustees and Diocesan Council). The symposium chairman, Clemenceau Urey, confirmed this much to me.[18] It reviewed such matters as the church's assets and liabilities, including its dwindling operational funds to conduct ministry.

Other subsequent efforts included: carrying forward Convention mandate to establish a business or economic development unit for the diocese; and to identify church assets and fund-raise to make assets income generating to make up for chronic budget shortfalls. Executing the Plan going forward included approaches to TEC and LECUSA abroad for seed money amounting to $400,000, with $150,000 to be locally raised.

Efforts seemed stalled at one point despite the many representations at home and abroad on the part of the sustainability committee. Thus, at a meeting of the Diocesan Council of ECL on November 28, 2012, Chairman Urey reported that despite the sympathetic hearing abroad, the momentum at home seemed lost. He frankly pleaded with Bishop Hart in an effort to regain the momentum: "We need your inspiration. We need you to inspire the Sustainability Committee, the Board of Trustees, all auxiliary groups of the Diocese, the Diocesan Council and individual members of the Diocese. Your inspiration will mobilize the entire Diocese to rally behind you and the Committee to achieve what we have set out to do." Urey continued" "You can inspire us, Bishop, not only with your verbal support but also with active support. We need you to show more concern and interest in what the Sustainability Committee has set out to do. We need your guidance, and motivation, Bishop. Finally, Bishop, we need you to demonstrate that what we are trying to achieve is a part of your vision and your legacy you have for the Diocese of Liberia."

Some specific suggestions then followed to the Bishop from the Sustainability Committee:

1. That in order to strengthen the administration of the Diocese a professional full-time General Administrator be contracted;
2. That accountability and transparency become the hallmark of the Diocese's financial management team;
3. That the resolution passed at the 82nd Convention authorizing that a balanced budget for the year 2012 be prepared be immediately implemented;
4. That a full-time treasurer be employed
5. That the committee to engage the GOL relative to the outstanding rent due for the Jean Travis building be established;
6. That the Sustainability Committee be expanded to include at least two members of LECUSA; and
7. That the Sustainability Committee in consultation with you, Bishop, ensure that these suggestions are appropriately and speedily addressed.

It is unclear whether responses to these suggestions were forthcoming.

## RE-LAUNCHING SUSTAINABILITY EFFORTS: EPISCOPAL CHURCH OF LIBERIA STRATEGIC PLAN OF 2019

The ECL held a one-day Special Diocesan Convention on February 15, 2019 at Episcopal Church of the Good Shepherd in Paynesville. I was in attendance as an observer. Its purpose was contained in a Preamble provided by Bishop Hart. He saw the exercise as "a guide to the ministry of the church, reflecting all elements of our work in advancement of God's kingdom in the Liberian vineyard. Though approached with renewed vigor, the idea has been reflected upon in a variety of ways in the past few years." The Bishop continued:

> We feel the need today, perhaps more than ever before, to infuse the ministry of this Diocese with a renewed thrust. This thrust is occasioned by the need to expand the base and meet the needs of the Church in Liberia. There exists an urgent need to spread the Gospel throughout Liberia and impact the unfinished work of reconciliation and healing in our country and the need comprehensively to engage our people in all areas of our common life as a Christian community. This can be done when Episcopalians have a commonly agreed vision and are resolved on a mission to pursue that vision in a targeted manner. The Strategic Plan, once agreed by this Special Convention, will guide the development decisions of the Diocese.

He then concluded: "The Church is being challenged at all its institutional levels to drive this revival and renewal, indeed this new agenda for action. No one is a spectator. All our human and material resources must now be marshaled to expand mission, development work and advocacy, ecumenism, healing ministry, and enhanced economic activity." He rallied his flock to "respond to the demands of our times and circumstances" and "re-calibrate" to carry forward the work of the Church today and in the years ahead.

At an early morning opening Eucharist, Bishop Hart set the tone of the Special Convention in a sermon based on the Gospel of Luke 5:1–11. His title was "Re-direct our Efforts for a Catch." He referenced the symbolism of a boat as a preaching post to teach. From the boat Jesus re-directed the heretofore disappointed fishermen, and a large catch of fish resulted. Jesus then says, follow me and I will make you fishers of men.

The whole purpose of the Church is evangelism, and this enterprise is directed to winning souls for Christ. The missionaries initiated the work in Liberia, and as they left to us the challenge of continuing to win souls became ours. Their immediate successors right down to us, the most remote of them, must assume our responsibilities and become fishers of men in our own contexts, amid our own circumstances and challenges.

Catching fish, or keeping the few we have already caught? Winning souls? Building congregations?

We meet one day to redirect our efforts about how to catch more fish, about how to win more souls, about how better to do ministry!

"Go ye into all the world and make disciples!" An "Amen" was in order.

The draft Strategic Plan was thoroughly vetted by the delegates, some making incisive and critical comments reflective of the lethargy of years past. Contents of the Plan include: improving and expanding mission areas; maintaining, improving and expanding education institutions of the Diocese; improving and expanding existing advocacy and development work beyond its current scope; developing a Diocesan health service program; improving and expanding programs on ecumenism; and enhancing economic activities to support the vision/mission of the Diocese with focused attention to agriculture, real estate, securities, and special Diocesan fund drive. With substantive comments incorporated, the edited draft Plan was almost unanimously adopted. The challenge of implementation now looms as a first review is mandated at the church's 2020 Convention.

**Sustainability and State of External Relations**

The two major features of the ECL's external relations are the historic ties with TEC as expressed in a Covenant Agreement since 1979, and membership in the CPWA since 1982. Like his predecessors, Bishop Hart faced the challenge of further developing these two primary relationships and perhaps adding to them new dimensions.

*ECL and TEC*

Several joint meetings of the respective committees of TEC and ECL served as occasions for assessment and evaluation of the relationship. In 2009, the Covenant document endorsed and supported "the special relationship between our Churches and reaffirms our need for each other as members of the body of Christ." The 2010 visit to ECL of the Presiding Bishop of TEC was occasion for expressions of hope and of renewal, but hardly any material change in the nature of the relationship. What change of substance there was came months later as the relationship found expression and expansion through parish-to-parish, and/or diocese-to-diocese companion relationships. So that going beyond the Covenant agreement, a series of partnerships- in- mission was being realized involving the following American dioceses and ECL.

Diocese of Western Massachusetts (gifts of Prayer Book and other worship objects)
Diocese of Maine (Funds for teachers salaries)
Diocese of North Carolina (support to Bromley Mission)
Diocese of Virginia (support to Bromley Mission)
Diocese of Ohio (support to Bromley Mission). ECL also has a Partner-in-Mission scholarship program for Liberian students from primary to college level.

There were other material benefits for ECL from TEC within the framework of the Covenant agreement. Missioner Finley Middleton facilitation of a loan to ECL resulted in the latter's securing grants of up to $4.5 million for the growth and expansion of CU in the areas of agriculture and reconstruction. Through partnership relations with United Thank Offering (UTO) a grant was realized that contributed to the construction and staffing of the Diocesan education secretariat building, its furnishing, as well as a vehicle for rural travels. The first year salary for the director of the secretariat was paid from UTO funds to which ECL made some contribution. As well, UTO with matching grant from the Diocese of Virginia supplemented by ECL-sponsored, led to construction of new staff housing at Bromley Mission.[19]

These developments notwithstanding, the circumstances that led Bishop George Browne to temper ECL's relationship with TEC and lead the Liberian church into CPWA seem to resurrect every so often. And so it was that ECL in its companion relationship with the Diocese of Western Massachusetts wanted to know about that diocese's policy of allowing same sex blessings. Bishop Gordon Scruton sought to make clear the matter in a letter to Juanita Neal, chair of ECL's Board of Trustee. An attached memo stated:

> In obedience to the guidance of the Archbishop of Canterbury, our Presiding Bishop and the official guiding documents of our church, all the Bishops of the New England dioceses have agreed that we cannot permit same sex marriage to be performed in our churches. At the same time, we want to walk pastorally with the gay and lesbian couples within our dioceses that will choose to be legally married. Each diocese in New England will formulate its own pastoral response.[20]

Despite the modest tenor of this statement, its message remained disquieting for ECL, and was amplified in this exchange among Liberian clergy: "The issue of Companion Relationship in the Diocese of Southern Ohio, which recognizes gay rights was hotly debated in individual groups with a general consensus that we do not need the relationship." In fact, earlier efforts at establishing a working companion relationship with the Diocese of Southern Ohio came to grief on the issue of same sex relations.[21]

In my conversations with Bishop Hart he pointed out how incensed retired Bishop Neufville was when informed about developments regarding companion relations that possibly involved gay clergy serving in ECL. Neufville threatened to go to "his people" in Cape Palmas to warn them about unwholesome developments in the church. When pressed to express his own views about the matter Bishop Hart indicated that his episcopacy was welcoming to all from TEC and the wider Anglican Communion, hoping that gay individuals would show restrain as to their lifestyles while serving in the diocese of Liberia—a sort of "Don't ask, don't tell" stance.

At any rate, the "mutual sharing of resources, information and exchange" which had become a hallmark of the ECL/TEC relationship was expected to endure even when authentic autonomy inclusive of economic self-sufficiency was attained, for a new Covenant is contemplated " which does not include specific financial support will be developed to express our ongoing commitment to partnership in the Gospel of Christ."[22] In an earlier forward-looking exchange between Bishop Hart and Bishop Gordon Scruton of Western Massachusetts, the American cleric suggested that it might be helpful were Hart's ECL to consider the covenant model of Brazil and the Philippines "since they have covenants without money involved. That can help you and the committee see the kind of covenant which might evolve after 10 years."[23]

Perhaps the time is at hand when ECL should go beyond the old model of covenant relations and embrace a new model of companion relationship. The old model of covenant was unequal partnership where one side gave things of value and the other did not reciprocate with anything more than acts of gesture. So ECL receives block grants, admittedly diminishing, with no clear relational model to replace it.

There is a new model of companion diocese relations between equals as developed by the Diocese of Southern Ohio and reportedly gaining currency in TEC. The model stipulates:

1. That both dioceses contribute things of equal value (though value-loaded, there are practical considerations about how to offset things). Issue becomes how to offset financial advantage of American dioceses? Things valuable to cover or offset might include in the Liberian case: preaching/teaching tour by leading cleric or lay parishioners; prison ministry visits; Liberia to share reconciliation experience and seek to apply them to U.S. race relations; Cuttington University to accept exchange U.S. students free of charge; and any other program that U.S. companions would find spiritually meaningful.
2. A bottom up approach, rather than the traditional bishop to bishop arrangements;
3. Term limits of five years maximum, open to renewal;
4. Focus not to be on money;
5. Each diocese should respect the other regarding canon and tradition. Where there are issues, Christian charity should frame the discussion; and
6. The relationship should be heavy on person-to-person contacts and parish-to-parish relationships.[24]

## LECUSA, ECL, and TEC

The LECUSA is a developing partner in the Episcopal Church's relationship with the American church. A draft Memorandum of Understanding (MOU) set forth the purpose and objectives of the relationship, but the MOU was still being discussed in 2019.

Prior to LECUSA's establishment, an ad hoc group calling itself "The Liberian Episcopal Community in America," addressed a letter to Presiding Bishop Edmond L. Browning in 1990. The letter was signed by Harry A. Greaves, Sr., chair Budget & Finance Committee of ECL, and Dr. Christian E. Baker, Senior Warden St. Stephen's Church, Monrovia, and former president of CU), and a very long list of Episcopalians resident in the United States or who had recently fled the Liberian civil war, including the Rev. Dr. Emmanuel W. Johnson, himself a former president of CU. It implored Bishop Browning to come to the rescue of Liberian Episcopalians in peril and distress, including bishops and clergy, some of whose whereabouts was unknown. "We believe yours would be a voice of conscience for the American people to its leadership to bring about a new order and an end to the conflict among our countrymen," the letter underscored.

Individual Liberian Episcopalians had earlier sought to engage the American Church and U.S. President George H. W, Bush as conflict clouds hung over Liberia. Then Presiding Bishop John M. Allin was instrumental in effecting the release from political prison of the Chancellor of ECL, J. Rudolph Grimes, who was also a former Secretary of State of Liberia.

It was no doubt the planted seed of the 1990 approach to TEC officials by Liberian Episcopalians in the United States, that Fr. Johnson then partly drew upon to inspire the first assembly on August 26, 2006 of Liberian clergy in exile in the United States. He partnered with The Rev. James N. Wilson, former rector of St. Thomas Camp Johnson Road, and The Rev. H. Budu Shannon, former Curate at Trinity Cathedral, in hosting twenty-two Liberian clergy at St. Anne's Episcopal Church in Reston, Virginia. At this first gathering an organization of Liberian Episcopal Clergy in the United States was established.

Fr. Johnson saw the effort as African or Liberian converts engaged in a reverse missionary enterprise, considering the much earlier American missionary efforts in Liberia. These reverse missionaries are ministering to Episcopalian Americans, teaching in American schools and colleges, and serving as physicians and health care workers, thus engaged in evangelizing, educating, and healing ministries in America. At least the Liberian clergy were to be seen in America as missionaries, focused on spreading the Gospel in their new land, developing fellowship among themselves, as well as engaging in outreach ministry to the ECL. To the assembled clergy Johnson spoke: "We are Josephs in this land, perhaps the Lord has placed us here so that we can look back and help improve our native land and better the livelihoods of our people."[25]

Soon it became evident that the clergy could not alone carry out this ministry. Lay Liberian Episcopalians had to be engaged as well. Thus, it was that at the fourth gathering of LECUSA at the Virginia Theological Seminary in April 2009, Lay Episcopalians were welcomed to membership of LECUSA, the "c" for clergy was simply changed to mean community.

LECUSA is organized under the laws of the State of North Carolina as a non-profit Corporation with objective to liaise between TEC and ECL with a view to gathering resources for ECL, as well as to serve the needs of member Episcopalians in the Diaspora. Specific role and responsibilities to be carried out in partnership are spelt out in the draft MOU.[26] The organization is growing and developing into an important arm in the United States of the ECL. LECUSA engages meaningfully with ECL, attending ECL Conventions and contributing holistically to the ministry of the Liberian church. At the same time, LECUSA members are clergy in various American dioceses and lay communicants in scores of American Episcopal churches. They are also becoming an important part of the structures of TEC. In 2019, The Rev. Canon Wilmot Merchant was named by the Presiding Bishop of TEC as chairman of TEC's counterpart of the joint Covenant Committee that manages the Covenant Agreement between TEC and ECL. Before Merchant, the late Rev. Canon Burgess Carr once served first as director of Episcopal Migration Ministries of TEC and subsequently as TEC Partnership Officer for Africa at the Church's headquarters in New York City. Liberian-born Episcopal priests serve in a number of parishes across the United States; at least three of them ran unsuccessfully so far for Bishop in American Dioceses. Developing research may lead us to questions regarding how things may have fared in his time for Canon Carr, and how Canon Merchant's work might serve simultaneously the ECUSA and the ECL.

## ECL/CPWA (Liberia & West Africa)

In an interview with Bishop Hart, he intimated to me that there are those in ECL who would like to "close down" relations with CPWA and return fully to TEC, repudiating thus the work of Bishop George Browne and returning to the status quo ante. Hart was firm in asserting that this would *not* happen under his watch. One might also add the impracticality of returning, as it were, to TEC when TEC has removed itself from the old missionary model of the Domestic and Foreign Missionary Society (DFMS) and embraced mutual partnerships of shared ministries worldwide.

The ties of ECL with CPWA and its permutations were being pursued as inherited when circumstances thrust leadership upon Bishop Hart, first as Dean of CPWA, then Archbishop of the IPWA since 2012, and now as Primate of

CPWA since March 2019. In this way ECL is integrating, willy nilly, into CPWA. Not so clear is the issue of mutuality of benefits and responsibilities. One ECL official when asked stated that "the Diocese [of Liberia] has not netted any real benefit apart from the moral linkage to the Anglican Communion" in West Africa. He added: "At the moment, the IPWA depends on various Anglican and Episcopal groupings in the UK and the USA for support to small programs. The inability to generate its own support framework remains a source of frustration."[27]

There seems a certain eroding of the rationale that led Bishop Browne to gravitate toward West Africa where Liberia is obviously geographically, culturally and historically located. Yet many Liberian Episcopalians seem more enamored of the American as opposed to the CPWA ties. As the ECL prepared for Presiding Bishop Katherine Jefferts Schori's 2010 visit to Liberia, an ECL document contained the following: The Episcopal Church [of Liberia] "is still basically an American Church trying its best to be African under enormous strains."[28] The question now is whether Bishop Hart's ecclesiastical elevation in the CPWA will result in ECL returning to the George Browne basics, namely, deeper commonalities and thus ties with West Africa. How will the Province and with it the ECL grow otherwise?

## TENTATIVE ASSESSMENT

Bishop Hart is the most credentialed of all his Liberian predecessors, having become in succession Diocesan Bishop, Dean of the Province, Archbishop of the Internal Province, and Metropolitan Archbishop and Primate of CPWA. These achievements were made possible for a variety of reasons, including the confidence of his peers in his leadership abilities, and being in the right place at the right time. All such positions, however, are enablers or opportunities to do ministry in the Church of God. No doubt this remains the Bishop's focus while he is on the stage of action.

And precisely because he is a sitting Bishop and we thus see through a glass only dimly, we offer only tentative conclusions. As did his immediate predecessor, Hart came to the episcopacy when Liberia was still struggling to recover from decades of political instability and civil war. The Episcopal Church was itself far from whole following the unhappy divisions that surfaced after the death in 1993 of Bishop George Browne. Both State and Church circumstances provided the backdrop to Hart's episcopacy. We have highlighted the Bishop's major actions and those of the many stakeholders of ECL.

These actions cumulatively point to a church that is spiritually alive but struggling to make functional and grow its many institutions. The 2019 Strategic Plan now provides a credible roadmap for addressing critical sustainability issues. These actions also raise identity issues both internally with regard to ECL, and externally with regard to ECL's external relations. Is there still commitment to a church that self-governs, self-propagates, and self-supports? What are the real challenges facing the ministries of evangelism, education, and healing (perhaps the weakest of the links)? Have Liberian Episcopalians allowed themselves serious conversations about these things, seeking to know where the church really now stands and where it wishes to go as it moves forward?

The external ties are no less daunting. Clearly, it is not a matter of choice between America and West Africa for the circumstances of history and culture have placed Liberia squarely in both camps. The question is how Liberia perceives and thus conducts its relations with the two in a way that serves the interest of ECL, while at the same time advancing the Kingdom of God.

## NOTES

1. Daniel Yinkah Sarfo, Program at Trinity Cathedral marking transfer from Sarfo to Hart (Dunn Archives).
2. Sarfo, Program at Trinity Cathedral (Dunn Archives).
3. Hart, Program at Trinity Cathedral (Dunn Archives).
4. Roberts, H. Augustus Jr. Diocesan Information Officer, in Episcopal Church of Liberia (ECL), "The Episcopal Church In The New Millennium: Challenges and Opportunities, H. Augustus Roberts, Information Officer, Diocese of Liberia," June 2008, 27 pages.
5. Edward Wea Neufville II, "The Official Charges (Pastoral Letters) of The Rt. Rev. Edward Wea Neufville, 11th Diocesan Bishop of the Episcopal Church of Liberia," January 1996 to March 2007, unpublished manuscript with Foreword by D. Elwood Dunn. 284 pages (permission of Neufville family).
6. A-Too Williams, Personal notes from Fr. Williams to author.
7. Church of the Province of West Africa (CPWA), "Mandate for the Consecration of the Very Rev. Jonathan B. B. Hart as Bishop of the Episcopal Church of Liberia, from the Most Rev. Justice O. Akrofi, Archbishop and Primate," N.d., 1 page.
8. CPWA, "Mandate for the Consecration of the Very Rev. Jonathan B. B. Hart."
9. Episcopal Church of Liberia (ECL), "Souvenir Programme, Consecration and Enthronement of the Very Rev. Jonathan B. B. Hart, BA, Th., M.Div. The Twelfth Bishop of Liberia," Trinity Cathedral, Monrovia, Liberia. March 2, 2008.
10. From Rev. Canon Anthony Eiwuley, Provincial Secretary, CPWA, email communication with author, October 27, 2017.
11. Episcopal Church of Liberia (ECL), (Anglican Communion), "The Enthronement Service of The Rt. Rev. Dr. Jonathan B. B. Hart As Second Archbishop of The Internal Province of West Africa (IPWA)," Church of the Province of West Africa, Trinity Cathedral, Monrovia, Liberia. July 6, 2014.

12. "Message of the Most Rev. Dr. Jonathan B. B. Hart, Bishop of the ECL/Archbishop-IPWA," August 24, 2018, St. Stephen's Church, Monrovia.

13. Herman Browne, quoted in *Observer*, July 4, 2014, 10.

14. Bishop Hart at St. Stephen's Church, August 24, 2018; See also "Profile of the Rt. Rev. Jonathan B. B. Hart, Bishop of the Episcopal Church of Liberia," by Kenneth Y. Best Lay Episcopalian, in "The Episcopal Church of Liberia Entering a New Millennium From Bishop Payne to Bishop Hart," 1851–2008, ECL document (Dunn Archives).

15. Memo from Board of Trustees to Presiding Bishop, January 8, 2009; See also "Status Report.

16. Memo from Board of Trustees to Presiding Bishop, January 8, 2009; See also "Status Report."

17. Clemenceau Urey, quoted in document (Dunn's Archives).

18. Clemenceau Urey, personal communication with author by telephone, April 2018, Monrovia.

19. ECL, "The Covenant Agreement: A Follow-up. Office of the Bishop," February 21–27, 2011, 5 pages (Dunn Archives).

20. Scruton to Juanita Neal, February 22, 2008 (Dunn Archives); Memo from the Bishop to Clergy of the Diocese, May 7, 2004 (Dunn Archives).

21. Email chain Howe to Harding w/17/12 regarding the 2012 Liberian Diocesan Convention, and Harding to James Yarsiah. References made to 81st Diocesan Convention at Cuttington University in 2011 (Dunn Archives).

22. Bishop Jonathan B. B Hart, personal conversations with author, October 13, 2016 and October 21, 2016, Monrovia.

23. See Draft Covenant Document, January 21, 2009 (Dunn Archives); Scruton to Hart, October 23, 2008 (Dunn Archives).

24. Clifton Flemister (Diocese of Southern Ohio), personal communication with author by email exchange, December 26, 2018, on "ECL's Ties with Diocese of Southern Ohio," December 20, 2018. See also "Report on Liberian Discernment from the Diocese of Southern Ohio" (2003) (Dunn Archives).

25. Fr. Johnson, quoted in document (Dunn Archives).

26. See "Memorandum of Understanding Between The Episcopal Church of Liberia And Liberian Episcopal Community USA (LECUSA)," Draft, February 2019 (Dunn Archives). See also Letter to Presiding Bishop Edmund Browning from "The Liberian Episcopal Community in America," (n.d., but possibly 1990 as civil war began) (Dunn Archives).

27. Roosevelt Jayjay, personal communication with author, by email, October 31, 2018, Monrovia.

28. "ECL Readies for Historic Visit from TEC," a memo from H. Augustus Roberts, Jr., December 18, 2009 (Dunn Archives).

*George Daniel Browne, Diocesan Bishop, 1970–1993*
Courtesy of the Bishop's family.

*Edward Wea Neufville, II, Diocesan Bishop, 1996–2007*
Courtesy of the Bishop's family.

*Jonathan B. B. Hart, Diocesan Bishop, 2008*
Courtesy of Bishop Hart.

*Joseph K, Dadson, CPWA/Interim Bishop, 1993–1996*
Courtesy of the CPWA.

*Bishop and Mrs. Clavender Railey Browne*
Courtesy of Bishop Browne's family.

*Bishop and Mrs. Louise Morais Neufville*
Courtesy of Bishop Neufville's family.

*The Rev. Emmanuel Douglas Hodges (1952–2006)*
Courtesy of D. Elwood Dunn Archives.

*The Rev. Theodora N. Brooks*
Courtesy of Rev. Brooks.

*Bishop Neufville exits Cavalla River after Baptism*
Courtesy of Bishop Neufville.'s family

*The Rev. Samuel Lloyd (left) (Chaplain, Sewanee: The University of the South), Bishop Browne (center), and author D. Elwood Dunn (right).*
Courtesy of D. Elwood Dunn Archives.

*The Rev. Seth C. Edwards, President, CU, 1949–1960*
Courtesy of D. Elwood Dunn Archives.

*Dr. Christian E. Baker, President, CU, 1960–1972*
Courtesy of Dr. Yede Baker Dennis.

*The Rev. E. Bolling Robertson, Interim President, 1972–1973*
Courtesy of D. Elwood Dunn Archives.

*The Rev. Emmanuel W. Johnson, President, CU, 1974–1980*
Courtesy of Rev. Johnson's family.

*Dr. Stephen M. Yekeson, President, CU, 1981–1986*
Courtesy of Mrs. Janet Yekeson.

*The Rev. Samuel Y. Reed, Interim President. 1987*
Courtesy of D. Elwood Dunn Archives.

*Dr. Melvin J. Mason, President, CU, 1988–2002*
Courtesy of Dr. Mason.

*Dr. Henrique F. Tokpa, President, CU, 2002–2015*
Courtesy of Dr. Tokpa.

*Dr. D. Evelyn Kandakai, Interim President, 2015–2016*
Courtesy of Dr. Kandakai.

*The Rev. Dr. Herman B. Browne, President, CU, 2016–*
Courtesy of Dr. Browne.

# Conclusion

As we bring to a close this remarkable story of the Episcopal Church as embedded in Liberian society, we first summarize briefly the episcopacies of the three diocesan bishops. We then provide an epilogue or reflections on the church that was, the church that is, and the church of the future.

The preceding pages attempted to contextualize the ministry of the Episcopal Church of Liberia (ECL) through the lenses of three episcopates—George Daniel Browne's (1970–1993), Edward Wea Neufville's II (1997–2007), and to a lesser extent, that of the incumbent, Jonathan Bau-Bau Bonaparte Hart's (2008–).

Bishop Browne succeeded the last American missionary bishop and thus became the first indigenous bishop elected by Liberian Episcopalians. In the course of his twenty-two-year episcopacy, his ministry impacted the church and society in significant ways. He left his mark in at least two areas, namely, an irreversible Africanization of the Episcopal Church, and critical training of a clerical force including setting a pace with the ordination of the first woman priest in the person of the Rev. Theodora N. Brooks.

Browne seemed proud of the number, diversity, and quality of the relatively large number of clergy trained during his episcopate. He pointed out that of the more than fifty ordained, twelve held the MDiv or its equivalent, ten held the bachelor of theology degree from Cuttington; ten held diplomas from the Gbarnga School of Theology. There were two theologians in training when Bishop Browne died in 1993—The Rev. Canon Dr. James B. Sellee (PhD/theology and current Dean, Trinity Cathedral), and The Rev. Canon Dr. Herman B. Browne (PhD/systematic theology former dean, Trinity Cathedral, and current President, Cuttington University). Eight clergy already had bachelor's or master's degrees in other disciplines and were given a crash training in theology. Browne also set the pace in women's ordination, ordaining the first woman priest. In recent times, more than a dozen women have served or are serving as ordained ministers in the Church. The deployment of these individuals seemed strategic, both before and after Browne's death. A pattern emerged that absent the intervening national insurrection and civil war, the church had acquired such clerical capacity that it was well placed for significant work going forward. But even amid the negative social forces the Browne-trained clergy are leading in the church today, as well as abroad in their self-imposed exile.

The impact of Neufville's ministry on the church was arguably in the two primary areas—education and evangelism. Seeking to conflate the two, he harkened back to nineteenth-century circumstances when education was viewed as an effective, even indispensable, tool of evangelism. He was emphatic: "For the church, our schools over the years have always been an arm of evangelism, a crucible through which we have instilled sound moral education necessary to the formation of a wholesome well-rounded citizen."

Neufville also sought to respond to what he considered Liberia's greatest challenge in the post-war period. He was also keenly aware of sharp criticism leveled at his predecessor in the 1970s when financial and ancillary challenges led to educational retrenchment. Perhaps in direct reaction to Browne's critics who accused him of "presiding over the demise of Episcopal schools," Neufville prevailed on the Diocesan Convention to "lift the ban on the closure of schools" and thus "give us a free hand to do education." Education thus became a centerpiece of his ministry.

He wanted restoration as reflected in the education thrust of Bishop B. W. Harris (1945–1964). He wanted brought back such Episcopal schools of note and high academic standards as Bishop Ferguson high school in Cape Palmas, St. John's/House of Bethany of Cape Mount, and the Order of the Holy Cross (OHC's) St. Augustine's high school of Bolahun. Browne retrenched for reasons of finance, but also because of Browne's belief that the business of educating its citizens is primarily the government's. Neufville took the opposite tact. Given the needs of post-war Liberia, he saw the need for partnership between the church and the state in advancing a common education agenda. He appealed to government for subsidy to private schools while scouting abroad for funds to renovate schools and expand education opportunities through Episcopal schools.

He sought specifically to focus on orphan and other disadvantaged young girls, even with the meager resources at his disposal. The Bromley Girls School became a special focus, which rescued and educated many disadvantaged young girls. Many other Episcopal schools were restored, even if some again fell victim to Liberia's seemingly unending political violence. Neufville kept rebuilding, as resources were available. The dent in his efforts may not have been large, but there was a dent. It would be left to his successors to enlarge upon what he was able to accomplish.

Bishop Neufville had an uncommon zeal for evangelism. He tried to bring back the "old time religion" with moral restoration starting with the family. Though not universally appreciated in the Episcopal Church of his time, many fondly remember him as a spiritually grounded religious leader. In this way he brought a measure of spiritual vitality to the church. His persona was at the center of his faith propagation. He encouraged and led retreats to inculcate the faith. Bible study remainded an important feature at Diocesan conventions. He carried forward the church's ministry of ordination of women, himself ordaining the largest number to date. So with a critical mass of female component to the clerical force, one could conclude that Neufville has also left a clergy likely to sustain the thrust of his ministry.

Bishop Hart, the incumbent, who has also become the Primate of the Church of the Province of West Africa (CPWA), is leading a church that is spiritually alive but struggling to grow and make fully functional its many institutions.

Adequate funds to conduct ministry seemed elusive for a variety of reasons. Labeled "sustainability issues," the Episcopal Church seemed challenged for many years in wrapping its mind around this one. Then the church seemingly got serious, prepared for, and launched a one-day special diocesan convention to vet a well-prepared Strategic Plan. Held February 15, 2019, the convention, many observers agreed, infused "the ministry of the church with a renewed thrust." Now looming is the challenge of implementation.

There is as well a heightened challenge regarding identity issues, both internally with regard to the Episcopal Church, but also externally with regard to the church's dual external ties with the American church and the CPWA. Is there still commitment to a church that self-governs, self-propagates, and self-sustains? What are the real challenges facing the ministries of evangelism, education, and healing, the latter being perhaps the weakest of the three, though now taken up in the new Strategic Plan?

# Epilogue
## *Church That Was, Church That Is, Church of the Future*

### CHURCH THAT WAS

More fully covered in the first iteration of the history of the Episcopal Church, though touched upon in this volume, the Episcopal Church of Liberia *that was*, is a fascinating story of a transplanted church and mission from the United States into nineteenth-century Liberia. The early church was critical to the shaping of modern Liberia, and over time, this church came to be shaped by the peoples and cultures of the land. At a time when the government could not afford to educate its citizens, the Christian church led the way, and the Episcopal Church proffered a triple ministry of evangelism, education, and healing. From Cape Palmas and adjacent parts the church expanded to Cape Mount, the Monrovia area, and deep into northern regions of Bolahun and Kolahun, as the Order of the Holy Cross set up shop in the early 1920s.

With evangelization linked to modern education, the church's institutions produced the first cadre of highly educated indigenous and immigrant (also mixed) Liberians. Over time, these men and women came to lead in church and the wider society. Martin Parks Keda Valentine became the first principal of the 1889–established Cuttington Collegiate and Divinity School, Samuel David Ferguson became the iconic first Bishop of Liberian nationality to lead the church, Henry Too-Wesley became the first Liberian of indigenous background to become Vice President of the country, Theophilus Momolu Fikah Gardiner became the first Bishop Suffragan of the church, and Samuel W. Tobe Kade Seton was among the first indigenous Liberians elected to the House of Representatives, and serving 1887–1893. At least two Liberian presidents were educated in Episcopal schools and became priests in the church. President G. W. Gibson was a rector of Trinity Church (now Cathedral), and President Alfred Russell was an Episcopal priest, serving at Grace in Clay Ashland.

Rose D. Gibson was a female deacon of the church at the turn of the twentieth century, and Annie E. Harmon was made a deacon in 1946. Victoria Elizabeth Jellemoh Grimes, born Jellemoh Fahnbulleh, raised by President and Mrs. Cheeseman and married to Louis Arthur Grimes, was educated at the Episcopal Brierly School for girls. Bromley Mission trained scores of female Liberians, among them veteran University of Liberia Biology professor Mary Tedi Bryant.

The old Cuttington College in Cape Palmas also produced men closer to our time such as Nete Sie Brownell (jurist and statesman), Francis W. M. Morais (early advocate of civil rights for indigenous Liberians). And before 1980, Cuttington produced a number of strong social gospel advocates that came to lead not only the Episcopal Church, but the Methodist (such as Bishop Stephen Trowen Nagbe, Bishop Bennie Dee Warner, Bishop Arthur Flomo Kulah), the Lutheran (Bishop Ronald Diggs), and other denominations as well. Medical doctors such as Festus Halay, Kanda Golafala, Zolu Traub, Joseph Diggs, Vuyu Golakai, Walter Gwenegale, Kate Bryant, Vanii Freeman, to name but a few, were all products of the new Cuttington College in Bong County. The Episcopal Church pioneered in the establishment of hospitals in Liberia, such as St. Mark's in 1859 (converted today as the J. J. Dossen Hospital in Cape Palmas), St. Timothy's in Cape Mount, St. Joseph's in Bolahun, and Phebe in Bong County (joint venture with Lutherans and Methodists).

Far out of sync with its number, among Liberian Christians, Episcopalians were 2% in the 1970s. There were twelve Episcopalians for every one hundred students in Episcopal schools. The church, to the tune of $1,500 annually, subsidized each student at Cuttington College in the second half of the twentieth century. The story was similar for the leading Episcopal high schools.

Other dimensions of the *church that was*, include strategic shifts from a church espousing a Christianizing/civilizing ethos to the three selves of self-governing, self-propagating, and self-sustaining. It shifted as well from a church enamored of its social standing and elitist moorings, toward a more inclusive church. This soon raised an issue of identity as the church furthered its expansion into rural Liberia, and joined Anglicanism in its West African region. There was more. Bishop Browne and his Roman Catholic counterpart, Bishop Michael K. Francis, were prescient as they undertook in the 1980s a study designed to understand the rapid changes in the Liberian Christian landscape (the rise of Pentecostalism) and how best to address the consequent challenges.

## CHURCH THAT IS

The Church that is: Much that was still lingers, though overlaid by new material givens. Consider the state of Christianity in today's Liberia as told by the national census. In the 1984 census, the third following those of 1962 and 1974, Christians were 67.7% of the population, Muslims 13.8%, and 18.5% claimed no religious affiliation. The total population was 2.101 million. The fourth census in 2008 had Christians at 85.6%; Muslims at 12.2%, African Traditional Religions at 0.6%, and 1.4% reported no religious affiliation. The population was 3.476 million.

Though the current percentage of Episcopalians in relation to the Christian population is not available to me, one can extrapolate from the past and present trends that the number is not large. But that is hardly the point. What needs uncovering is the current state of the Episcopal Church of Liberia. It seems to be developing more steadily from below rather than at the diocesan level—its ecumenical ministry needs recalibrating; its external ties could benefit from a sharpening of focus. These are not the only areas that could benefit from reviews. We limit ourselves to these because, in the grand scheme of things, the 2019–endorsed Strategic Plan captures adequately the state of the church and how the church intends systematically to address its contemporary challenges, particularly the generation of funds to conduct ministry including the enhancement of a robust stewardship.

Research directs us to the three areas highlighted—the development from below phenomenon, ecumenical ministry, and external ties issues. Few parishes of the church seem well organized and doing well their various ministries, while at the diocesan level, a strategic plan has only recently been formulated. Thus while some parishes are growing and developing, the diocese has itself largely been muddling through. The hope is that the new strategic plan will spur balanced growth and development—from below at the parish level, but also from above at the diocesan level. Growth at the diocesan level is critical because only nine of the more than 100 parishes and congregations are today self-supporting or autonomous, and this is quite apart from the other requirements of diocesan leadership.

Where does the Christian church, and with it the Episcopal Church stand today regarding ecumenicalism? In a conversation with retired Methodist Bishop Arthur Kulah, I was reminded that Episcopalians, Lutherans, and Methodists worked together to build a strong and vibrant Cuttington University at Suakoko, including the jointly operated and strategically-located Phebe Hospital in Bong County. Each of these mainline denominations has now gone its separate way with strength and vibrancy in short supply. Once the Liberian Council of Churches worked together to advance evangelism, to unify the Christian church in the country to speak prophetically with one voice on national issues, and to protect human rights. The story today is, as The Rev. Dr. Jerry Kulah of the United Methodist Church underscores in conversations with me, wholly otherwise with a proliferation of the Pentecostal "prosperity gospel," and a Christian church that otherwise seems to have lost its prophetic voice.

Movement away from mainline churches seems on the upsurge since 1980. Some prominent Episcopalians left the church early in the 1980s when the church did not minister to their needs as they were under siege by the government of Head of State Samuel Doe, one year following the public execution of thirteen former officials of the deposed government of President William R. Tolbert Jr. It was the first anniversary of the executions. A religious event was planned for Trinity Cathedral. Doe defied the church to host the event and proceeded to surround the Cathedral with armed soldiers. Cathedral Dean Emmanuel W. Johnson, according to many accounts, including that of the current Dean, Canon James B. Sellee, did not take a Christian stand. Instead, Dean Johnson locked the building and disappeared with the keys. At least two prominent female Episcopalians left the church for this reason and never returned. They subsequently followed the Pentecostal path.

Retired Methodist Bishop Authur F. Kulah informed me that both the current president and vice president of Liberia were Methodists and Lutherans, respectively, but each has also taken the Pentecostal path. Thus officialdom and a sizeable portion, if not the majority, of Christians in the country, apparently find the Pentecostal churches more attractive for a variety of reasons.

There are two dimensions to the historic ties—those between ECL and TEC, and ECL's membership in CPWA. A covenant agreement defines the relationship between the American and Liberian churches. The arrangement is likely to last to 2030 and is based on the American church's partnership in mission thrust of "mutual responsibility and interdependence in the Body of Christ." Though renewed periodically by the parties and fostering as a subset of companion relationships between dioceses of TEC and those of ECL, the model that predominates is one of unequal partnership in practice. One side largely gives and the other side largely receives. The companion relationship at diocesan level has itself fallen prey to this model though there are often discussions tending toward some form of reciprocity.

Challenge remains to overcome this practice and to return to genuine partnership such as mutual contribution of things of equal value. This may mean offsetting the financial advantage of the American church. Things deemed valuable enough to cover the offset might include preaching/teaching visits by leading cleric and lay Episcopalians from Liberia, prison ministry visits, students' exchange between Cuttington University and Episcopal universities where in-kind contribution of Cuttington is significant; a bottom-up as opposed to bishop-to-bishop understanding—rather heavy on person-to-person and parish-to-parish. In short, the focus might be a companion relationship of grassroots sharing of human, spiritual and material resources.

As heirs of the teaching, doctrine, history, and tradition of the One Holy Catholic and Apostolic Church of the United States, the time seems at hand for the Episcopal Church of Liberia to affirm that inheritance in the diverse cultures, linguistic and ethnic richness of the West African region to which it belongs, taking ownership in the process of the burning issues impacting the lives of the Liberian people. Might this be an opportunity to explore an Africanized theology or thought pattern, or the development of "authentic structures, orders and programmes based upon African values and priorities?" Might this be the opportunity the late Canon Burgess Carr had in mind when, as Secretary General of the All-Africa Conference of Churches in the 1970s, he called for a Moratorium on Western missionary activity on the Continent?[1]

Bishop George Daniel Browne was elected Primate of the CPWA shortly upon Liberia acquiring membership. He was both thoughtful and active during his eleven years as Primate and Bishop of Liberia. Division in the ECL upon Browne's death in 1993, soon claimed the attention of the Province as the dean of the Province assumed oversight for ECL pending the election of a successor diocesan bishop. Bishop Joseph Dadson's many mediations and other interventions did not go down well with some, including then Suffragan Bishop Edward Wea Neufville II. But all storms were weathered. The last Provincial action of note regarding ECL was to annul the first attempt by ECL to elect a successor bishop to Neufville. The Primate of the Province annulled the irregular process and a new reconvened Convention was required to elect a bishop in keeping with constitution and canon.

Bishop Jonathan B. B. Hart served the Province as Dean (2009–2014), and Archbishop of the Internal Province (2014–2019). Since March 3, 2019, Hart began a five-year tenure as the Eleventh Primate of the Church of the Province of West Africa. A pertinent question is how the joining of provincial and diocesan responsibilities will impact both the West African province and the diocese of Liberia. The diocese was seen to be putting its house in order at the February 15, 2019 Special Convention when a strategic plan was adopted. Implementation issues will no doubt claim the attention of the scheduled regular Convention of the diocese in 2020. Such issues will, of necessity, relate as much to the diocese itself as to Liberia's relationship to the Province brought front and center with Bishop Hart's leadership of the Province.

The Bishop's leadership will be severely tested with the withdrawal of Ghana from the Province. Back in the 1960s, Nigeria decided to leave the Province in order to bring to bear its prophetic Anglicanism on national Nigerian issues. Might Ghana be leaving for the same reason? Are we witnessing a regression in the church from regional arrangements toward nationalism? A number of other pertinent questions impose themselves: Can one still call an Anglican/Episcopal association of Liberia, Sierra Leone, Gambia, Cameroon, and Guinea. the church of the province of West Africa? What will be the financial implications of Ghana's departure from an already struggling Province? For answers to these and related questions the church awaits with baited breadth.

## THE CHURCH OF THE FUTURE

Unlike the first volume which narrated the role of the Missionary District of the Episcopal Church of the United States in the creation and early shaping of the Liberian national character, this sequel volume has attempted a narrative embedded in a social mindset linked to national challenges in the closing decades of the twentieth century and the beginning of the twenty-first. As such it sought to interrogate issues of social vision and future scenarios. In the case of the former the question is whether the Christian church in Liberia has been able to work out a common social vision through debate, study and cooperation. Are the lead Christian organizations such as the Liberian Council of Churches, the World Evangelical Fellowship, the Association of Evangelicals of Liberia, the Pentecostal Union of Liberia, and etc. vehicles for such an undertaking? Still the church can contribute to the hope of society aware of its past "but seeking a future which is qualitatively better." In the case of future scenarios, a number of questions have surfaced: How is the church thinking of its future?—Rebuilding the past? Restoring the years the locusts have eaten? "Making all things new"? (Rev. 21:5).

More specifically, will the Episcopal Church remain faithful to sociohistorical trends, such as the shift from the American church to the Church of the Province of West Africa and the redefining of the church's mission and ministry that would entail? Furthermore, will the building of a more inclusive church go forward unburdened by institutions and practices of the past such as the myth of Liberian society resting on three pillars—an exclusivist state, an elitist church, and free masonry? For some, these may seem moot questions with the power shift in Liberia since the 1980 coup d'état. The current state of the nation may suggest otherwise as the quest for "one people, one nation united for sustainable peace and development" remains elusive. The future of the church then, cannot be disassociated from developments in the national social space.

Continuing the theme about how the church is thinking about its future, is the path of genuine reconciliation contemplated with urgency and as a critical task? Are we thinking of a perspective that sees conflict as a social phenomenon, an inevitable part of life that must be comprehended and managed? There are too many tragic examples of ethnic conflict in which religion has been part of the fuel igniting the fires of mutual hatred. Consider the Irish Catholic/Protestant divide or fault line. Though waxed and waned, that conflict still holds potency and a license to hate one another. Do we have in Liberia our Irish problem, our divide, our fault line that gives license to spurt out hate and distrust?

As Liberia emerges from the nightmare of fratricide, will religion become a way to perpetuate anger between and among ethno-regional and religious groups? Will the demographic shifts in religious adherents be occasion increasingly for religious tolerance, inter-faith dialogue and ecumenical engagements? Will the waves of Pentecostalism sweeping the nation be viewed as "opportunities for diversified leadership and different forms of ministry," rather than "endless denominationalization and fragmentation" of the Body of Christ? It is my hope that this account of the history of the Episcopal Church since 1980 will be read and understood against the backdrop of these challenges and issues.[2]

## NOTES

1. See Burgess Carr, "The Mission of the Moratorium," *Occasional Bulletin of the Missionary Research Library* 25, no. 2 (March-April 1975): 1–9. New York.

2. See Mkunga Mtingele, *Leadership and Conflict in African Churches: The Anglican Experience* (New York: Peter Lang, 2017). See also Herman B. Browne, *Appreciating Pentecostalism* (National Printers. September 2011), 1–25.

*Appendix 1*

# Bishops of the Episcopal Church of Liberia

John Payne—1851–1871
Johann Gottlieb Auer –1873–1874
Charles Clifton Penick—1877–1884
Samuel David Ferguson –1884–1916
Arthur Seldon Lloyd (interim)—1918–1919
Walter Henry Overs—1919–1925
(Theophilus Momolu Fikah Gardiner-Suffragan)—1921–1941
Robert Erskine Campbell, OHC—1925–1936
Leopold Kroll—1936–1945
Bravid Washington Harris—1945–1964
Dillard Houston Brown—1964–1969
Charles Alfred Voegeli (interim)—December 1969–August 1970
George Daniel Browne—1970–1993
(Edward Wea Neufville II-Suffragan)—1984–1996
Joseph K. Dadson (interim-CPWA)—1993–1996
Edward Wea Neufville II—1996–2007
Jonathan B. B. Hart—2008–

*Appendix 2*

# Biographical Data of Episcopal Church of Liberia and Diaspora Clergy

Clergy of the Episcopal Church of Liberia and Liberian-born clergy in the Diaspora (USA) are listed separately in this appendix. The following abbreviations are used. The sign + designates Bishop.

| | |
|---|---|
| AA | Associate of Arts |
| AACC | All Africa Conference of Churches |
| AMEU | African Methodist Episcopal Univ. |
| B | Bishop |
| b. | born |
| CU | Cuttington University |
| BD | Bachelor of Divinity |
| CDSP | Church Divinity School of the Pacific |
| CJR | Camp Johnson Road |
| CPWA | Church of Province of West Africa |
| D | ordained Deacon |
| d. | died |
| dio | diocese |
| EDS | Episcopal Divinity School |
| ETS | Episcopal Theological Seminary |
| GTS | General Theological Seminary |
| GST | Gbarnga School of Theology |
| Inst. | Institute |
| KRTTI | Kakata Rural Teachers Training Institute |
| LOBONI | Lofa, Bong and Nimba region of ECL |
| MDiv. | Master of Divinity |
| Mis. | Missionary |
| MTS | Master of Sacred Theology |
| Par | Parish |

153

| | |
|---|---|
| P | ordained Priest |
| R | Rector |
| S | Saint |
| Sch | School |
| SNT | Smell No Taste |
| STD | Doctor of sacred Theology |
| PhD | Doctor of Philosophy |
| STM | Master of Sacred Theology |
| SWTS | Theological Seminary of the Southwest |
| U | University |
| UL | University of Liberia |
| UMU | United Methodist University |
| V | Vicar |
| VTS | Virginia Theological Seminary |
| ZRTTI | Zorzor Rural Teachers Training Institute |

## CLERGY OF THE EPISCOPAL CHURCH OF LIBERIA SINCE 1980

Anthony, Paul S., b. November 15, 1985. BA Theo. CU 2016; D. 2017, P. 2019 by Bishop Hart. St. Teresa/Voinjama, Epiphany/Cuttington, Good Samaritan/Ganta, Good Shepherd, Paynesville.

Bainda, Lawrence Moses, b. May 3, 1950; BA Theo. CU; D. 1980, P. 1982 by Bishop Browne, retired.

Bazzie, Wozeyan, b. August 23, 1974; UL (BSc. Biology 2007), SC Edwards Dipl. D. 2015 P. 2016. St. Stephens/Sinkor, Curate, St. Stephen's, Sinkor.

Bondoe, Philip Saa, b. January 29, 1963; Evangelist 1980 with OHC; educated SC Edwards Dipl. 2007. D. P. 2007 by Bishop Neufville.

Bonner, Olaf Libi, b. Aug 1, 1969; Liberty Theo. Seminary (Monrovia), SC Edwards Dipl.; D. 2011, P. 2012 by Bishop Hart. Annunciation, St. Mark's/Harper, Priest, Trinity Cathedral.

Browne, Herman Beseah, b. March 11, 1965; CU (BA Theo.),King's College London (BD) and University London (PhD Theo.). D. 1987 by Bishop Browne, P. 1997 at Canterbury Cathedral/London; Bromley Mission, Simon of Cyrene Theo, Institute (London), Archbishop of Canterbury's senior advisor on Anglican Communion Affairs, Grace/Clay Ashland, Dean Trinity Cathedral, President CU since 2016.

Brownell Jackson Flade, b. November 29, 1980. Dipl. SC. Edward, D. 2019, Bishop Hart, St. Stephen, Pleebo.

Cooper Frederick, Anne Kaziah, b. May 5, 1951 at Cavalla, Maryland County; UL (BBA), VTS (MA Christian Education & DMin. Edu. Leadership); D. 2012 P2014 by Bishop Hart. Episcopal/Anglican Diocese of Egypt with North Africa and the Horn of Africa, non-Stipendiary Priest at Trinity Cathedral.

Crabbe, Richard Kojo, b. May 22, 1978; Dipl, SC Edwards, BA Theo, CU 1994; D. P. 2019. St. Augustine's/Kakata.

Davies, Andy B. K., b. March 2, 1974 in Monrovia; Monrovia Bible Training Center, S. C. Edwards Dipl. 1998. D. 2007, P. 2008 by Bishop Neufville. Rector, Grace/Clay Ashland

Davies, Josephine H., b. October 19, 1936; professional administrator before call to priesthood; SC Edwards (Dipl. Theo.), D. 1989 by Bishop Browne; rector St Thomas CJR, retired.

Dennis, Samuel Ford, b. Harper, Maryland County August 14, 1918 Dipl Hartzell Acad; BD CU 1952, VTS 1954–1955; D, 1952, P. 1953; R St Paul's Greenville; Chapl CU 1973, Good Shepherd Paynesville. d. 1996.

Diggs, Shirley Monger, b. Sinoe Decembr 25, 1948; SC Edwards, CUC (BA Theo); D. 2007, P. 2008; Dean Women at CUC, Doctrine Instructor BW Harris. d. 2013.

Dormu, Alfonso, b. April 14, 1968; Dipl SC Edwards D. 1989, P. 1992; St Augustine Gardnersville, St John's Buchanan, St Mark's Harper. Deceased.

Dunor, Emmanuel M., b. November 6, 1964; St. Augustine's/Kolahun ; Novice at Umariya Umama Wethemba Monastry, Graham Town, South Africa; Professed Monk 2002 (vow under Bishop Neufville); Superior, Community of the Love of Jesus Monastry at Bolahun under Fr. Benedict Vannie D. 2012, P. 2014 by Bishop Hart, The Church of Advent, Sangailo.

Essah, Moses Tamba, b. December 12, 1978; St. Augustine's/ Kolahun, SC Edwards Dipl. D. 2017 by Bishop Hart. St. Peter's Episcopal Church/Konjolloe/Lofa County.

Fahnbulleh, Momo T. Duke, b. 20 Aug, 1968; SC Edwards, Dipl 2001; BSc AME Zion Univ; 14 years teaching; D. 2017, P. 2019 by Bishop Hart; St. John's Lower Buchanan, St. Thomas, CJR.

Fakoli, Lawrence, Pelema, II b. November 6, 1950., Dipl. Theo, S C. Edwards, retired.

Floe, Albert B., b. November 29, 1965., SC Edwards Dipl., CU (BA. Theo). D. 2007, P. 2008 by Bishop Neufville. Priest, St. Martin -on -the Mount, Yekepa, Nimba County.

Foday, Joseph Fayia, b. February 1, 1974, Bryant Seminary, AMEU, B.Theo, SC Edwards Cert; D. 2007, P. 2008 by Bishop Neufville. St. Anthony/Lofa County.

Freeman, Macdonald B., b. December 15, 1963; Dipl in Theo—S C. Edwards B.Theo. UMU., MSc. Edu. Adm CU. D. 2014, P. 2015 by Bishop Hart. rector, St. Augustine's/Gardnersville.

Freeman, Roosevelt S. Jr., November 11, 1976. Dipl. SC. Edward. D. 2019, Bishop Hart. Deacon St. Stephen's Sinkor.

Freeman, Sie Sunday, b. June 9, 1968 Takoradi, Ghana; S C. Edwards, Dipl Theo, CU, B.Theo. D. 2004, P 2007. St. Augustine's Kakata, Achdeacon, Southwestern Archdeaconry.

Garley, Naime K., b. November 29, 1977. Dipl Theo, S C. Edwards. BA. Theo, CU, M. Ed, CU Graduate School, D. 2007, Bishop Neufville P. 2008, Bishop Hart. Priest, St. Agnes Bromley.

Gaye I, Allen Vahton, b. 23 Feb 1977; SC Edwards (Dipl. Theo); BA Theo. CU, M.Ed. CU 2018; D. 2007 by Bishop Neufville, P. 2019 by Bishop Hart. Trinity Cathedral, Monrovia, St. Stephen's Sinkor.

Gbe, Edward K., b. September 19, 1958; UL (BSc.), MTS, VTS, Seamen's Church Institute, New York and New Jersey (Certificate) B. Theo, GST; D. 1998, P. 2001 by Bishop Neufville. Rector, St. Peter's Caldwell.

Gborkie, Harrison G., b. February 9, 1984, B.A. Theo, CU. D. 2019, Bishop Hart. Deacon, St. Mark's, Harper.

Gbusseh, Wilfred, b. May 6, 1962; All Souls' Episcopal Church in the Buduboram Refugee camp in Ghana. D Ghana August 2, 1997, buried Liberia August 22, 1997.

Gooding, Thomas Jonathan Odunto, b. Freetown, Sierra Leone October 10, 1906; CUC 1954 1 D. 1954, P. 1955; S Peter's Gbarnga, Trinity Cathedral, founder S Augustine's Kakata; retired 1970s; d. November 16, 1997.

Griffiths, John B., b. July 9, 1949; Dipl SC Edwards;D. 1981 by Bishop Browne, P. 1983 by Bishop Browne, retired.

Hammond, Christian G., b. June 14, 1958; SC Edwards Dipl. D. 2014, P. 2015 by Bishop Hart; Emmanuel Chapel, Marshall.

Handsford, Joshua, b. July 17, 1959; GST BA Theo; D. 1998, P. 2001; Episcopal Refugee Outreach Ministry, Ivory Coast, St. Timothy's New Georgia, St. John's Robertsport, St. Peter's Caldwell, deceased.

Harmon, G. Nyema, b. February 28, 1965; D 2004, Dipl Theo, SC Edwards, B.Th, CU. M.Th, CU D. 2004, P. 2007 Bishop Neufville; Curate, Trinity Cathedral.

Harris, Daniel Giakquee, b. Grand Bassa June 21, 1917; D. 1973, P. 1975; Priest in Charge St. Mary's Buchanan; retired 1988; d. 1999.

Harris, Elijah, G. b. December 24, 1960; Dipl, GST. B.Th, GST, D. 1990, Bishop Browne, P. 1992, Bishop Neufville; St. John's Lower Buchanan, St. Mary's Lower Buchanan. Archdeacon, Bassa Archdeaconry.

Hart, Jonathan B. B., b. Sept 1, 1953; CU (BA, Theo.), Episcopal Divinity School, (M.Div); St. Mark's Cape Palmas and Archdeacon Southeast; Trinity Cathedral; D. 1979, P. 1980; consecrated Diocesan Bishop 2008; Archbishop of the Internal Province of West Africa 2012; and Primate CPWA since March 3, 2019.

Hina, David Sayndee, b. July 7, 1966 ; SC Edwards Dipl ; AMEU; D. 2007, P. 2008 Priest, St. Thomas, New Kru Town.

Hina, Elizabeth W. W., b. May 27, 1957 in Cape Mount; Monrovia College (Accounting), GST (BA Theo). D.2007 Bishop Neufville, P. 2008 Bishop Hart. Priest St. Augustine's Gardnersville.

Hne Sr., Macarthy S., b. November 10, 1960; educated KRTTI, SC Edwards,, BA Theo. CU 2012; D. 2014 by Bishop Hart; Priest St. Philip's, Grand Gedeh County.

Hodges, Emmanuel Douglas. b. November 1, 1952; CU, Sem of Southwest (MDiv) D. 1978, P. 1979;BW Harris, St. Mary's Bolahun, Trinity Cathedral, Dir. Christian Edu, ECL, Chapl Bromley Mission, Vicar General ECL 1991-1996; Grace Clay-Ashland, d. 2006.

Howard, Richard T., b. March 14, 1973; SC Edwards Dipl., B. Theo CU D. 2017 Bishop Hart; St. John's, Lr Buchanan, Grand Bassa County.

Inuah, Peter, M., b. November 25, 1976. Certificate, YWAM, Dipl, Music, Dipl. Theo, BTh. MTh. CU; D. 2002, P. 2003. Rector, Good Shepherd, Paynesville.

Jarbo, Richael Bornynor, b. January 24, 1961 in Freetown Sierra Leone; C. Certificate, AA. School Adm, LACOSESS Teacher College. dipl.S C Edwards; D. 2007 P. 2008 by Bishop Neufville; Priesr Good Shepherd Paynesville.

Jarteh, Say-Younkon Amos, b. January 1, 1944; GST, S Philip's Ecumenical Sch 1975-1978; D. 1981, P. 1983; St, Thomas Chapel NKT, St Mark's Harper. Deceased.

Johnson, Ernesty, T. b. May 2, 1973 in Monrovia; SC Edwards (Dipl.), BA. Theo., CU), Dipl, Luther Seminary, Minnesota, USA; D. 2004, P. by Bishop Neufville.

Jurey, Francis K., b. Grand Kru February 11, 1938; KRTTI, SC Edwards Dipl. D. 1999, P. 2001; St Stephen's Pleebo; d. 2013.

Kahn, Isaac S. W., b. May 3, 1972. AA Rural Development), ZRTTI (Certificate in Education), and B.Theo, CU. D. 2010 by Bishop Hart P. 2012; St. Stephen's, Mambo, Grand Cape Mount County.

Kandakai, Christopher Kei, Sr., b. Village of Mbaloma, Dei Chiefdom near Roysville, Bomi County July 15, 1916; sem at St. Cyril Bolahun, theo tutelage with Frs. SC Edwards and Paul M. Washington at Bromley prior to establishment of CU/Suakoko; D. 1949, P. 1951; 10 yrs. Church dev & preaching Cape Mount (1949-59), 11 yrs (1959-70) at St. Andrew's Church of Our Lord & St. Michael & All Saints krural Cape Mount; priest in charge Bromley (1971-1973); St Peter's Caldwell & Grace Clay Ashland; language work (Gola & Vai) as he translated portions of New Testament into Vai, part of Book of Common Prayer and Hymnal into Vai; produced some six manuscripts including "The Christian & Moslem Religions in Liberia," "The Relationship between Church & State." (See Liberian Collections Project at Indiana University, USA); retired 1981; d. 2010

Kanneh, William, b. April 15, 1969, Dipl. SC. Edward. D. 2019, Bishop Hart. Deacon St. Mary's Bolahun.

Karmorh, J. Tutus, b. June 6, 1984, Certificate, Food Security, African League, Accra, Ghana, AA Agriculture CU, Dipl Theo, SC Edwards, MA Edu.; D.2007 P.2008 Priest –in- charge, St. Michael's All Angel, Suakoko, Bong County.

Karr, Jonathan, b. January 1, 1969 in Suakoko, Bong County; Theo Edu by Extension (TEE) 1990; D. 2015 P. 2016, Priest St. Peter's, Little Liberia, Rivercess.

Kimber, Joshua Dwalu, b. Kparwoo Cape Mount November 18, 1924; CUC (BA 1954, BD 1957); D. 1958, P. 1959; St. John's Cape Mount, rector St. Thomas CJR, 1965-1989, coordinator SC Edwards Inst, d September 12, 1989.

Kollie, Isaac, b. February 15, 1969, Dipl. SC. Edward. D. 2019, Bishop Hart, Deacon St. Thomas, Wohomba.

Korpu, William, b. September 28, 1968; St. Aug's Bolahun. SC Edwards Dipl. 2005; BA Theo. CU, D. 2012; P. 2014 Bishop Neufville, Priest, St. Mary's Bolahun.

Kparlue, Andrew, b. February 2, 1959 ; Dipl. SC Edwards; D. 2014, P. 2015 by Bishop Hart, Priest, Holy Name, Foyah, Lofa County.

Kpartor, Momo B., b. June 22, 1955;BA Theo. CU, M.Div; D. 1980 Bishop Browne, P. 1981 Bishop Browne; Missionary Vicar General, Anglican Church of Cameroon, retired.

Kpehe, Richard B., b. August 11, 1978, B.Theo,, M. Theo, CU; D. 2007; P. 2010 by Bishop Hart; Priest St. John's Irving Mem., Cape Mount.

Lewis, Slewion P., b. March 14, 1976 in New Kru Town; Dipl. SC Edwards, BA. Theo CU, Luther Seminary, Minnesota, USA; D. 2007, Bishop Neufville P. 2008, Bishop Hart; study leave USA.

Mason, Tamba Songor, b. September 8, 1965 Bolahun, Lofa County; St. Aug. Bolahun, Lofa County, 1982, SC Edwards. D 2007 by Bishop Neufville. P 2008.

Matthew, G. Nyankan, b. April 13, 1960 at Barclayville, Grand Kru; SC Edwards. D. 2004, P 2007, Bishop Neufville, Priest St. Thomas, Barclayville, Grand Kru County.

Merrian, J. Nye-Nyema, b. December 15, 1952; SC Edwards (Dipl. Theo.); D. 1989 Bishop Browne, P. 1992 Bishop Neufville; Church of Annunciation, Springhill, retired.

Mitchell, Lee Oliver Dia, b. Harrisburg, Mont. County 10 Sept, 1931; CU (BA 1956, BD, 1959); D. May 1962, P. December 1962; Bp Ferguson, St James Hoffman Station, Annunciation Apringhill, Epiphany Cavalla, St Paul's Sinoe, St. Aug. Kakata, St. Philip & St James When Town & Jarr Tiowb, St Mary the Virgin Charlesville, Margibi, St. Aug. Gardnersville, St Wade Harris S A Tolbert Estate, St James Chocolate City. d. October 8, 2013.

Momo, William Sele, b. October 8, 1969 in Yekepa, Nimba County; Dipl SC Edwards ; D 2007 Bishop Neufville P. 2008, Bishop Hart ; Priest. St. Monica, Ganta.

Neh, J. Simbo, b. March 19, 1971 in Ylatwen Wedabo, Grand Kru County; SC Edwards, Dipl. D. 2007 by Bishop Neufville, P. 2010, Priest. St. Paul's Sinoe.

Nemah, Frank K. W., b. Sept 20, 1978, B.Theo; MA Edu. CU; D. 2010. P. 2012 . Bishop Hart Priest, Christ Church, Crozierville .

Nimley, Edwin B. T., b. Lr Buchanan, Grand Bassa; Elyskon College (Delaware, USAS) (BA & MA), SC Edwards Dipl; D. 1999, P. 2004; St Augustine Gardnersville, St. John"s Buchanan, Trinity Cathedral, retired 2017, d. 2019.

Nyenmoh, Tebeh, Kofa, b. 1954, BA. Theo. CU; D. 1999, P. 2001, Bishop Neufville, retired

Passewe, C. Letomber, b. May 21, 1957; SC Edwards dipl theo; D. 1989, P. 1992; r Good Shepherd Paynesville, d. 2017.

Phillips, Roberta A., b. January 13, 1944; A.A. Dipl. Theo. Seth C. Edwards. MA. Edu. UL;. D. 1989, P. 1990 Bishop Browne; special assistant to the Bishop, retired.

Quoi, Augustus, b. June 9, 1966; BA Theo. GST, MA. Edu., UL; D 1999, P 2001 by Bishop Neufville; Rector, St. John's, Buchanan.

Quoi, Terry M., b. December 26, 1967; GST. MA, Theo, Sewanee: Univ. of the South, USA. D 2004, P 2007, Bishop Neufville,, Priest, St. Barnabas, SNT, Margibi.

Roberts, Stanley Yonkon, b. Montserrado County, May 18, 1982; CU B.Theo 2016; D P. 2017 by Bishop Hart, Deacon St. Thomas CJR.

Sackie, John, b. September 6, 1968; SC Edwards; D. 2014; P. 2015, Bishop Hart; St. Paul's, Sinoe.

Sengbeh, Emmanuel J., b. December 28, 1965 Dipl. SC. Edward. D. 2019, Bishop Hart; Deacon, St. Peter's, Caldwell.

Seimavula, David M., b. March 17, 1961; Dipl. GST. D. 2007, Bishop Neufville, P. 2008, Bishop Hart.
Sellee, James B., b. Lofa County March 3, 1961; BA Theo. CU, MA Theo. Middlesex Univ. UK, PhD, Biblical Studies, Gloucestereshire University, UK. D. 1987, P. 1989 Bishop Browne; Missionary Anglican Church of Gambia, Rector, St, Thomas, CJR, Dean Trinity Cathedral, Monrovia.
Sie, Michael Tuan, b. April 21, 1978;, UL (BBA Management), MBA. CU, M.Div. VTS. D. 2011 P. 2012, Rector St. Thomas, CJR.
Siebo, Gbutu Kla, b. September 25, 1963. B. Theo, GST; D 2004, P 2007, Bishop Neufville.
Smith Jerry N.: b. August 9, 1976, Dipl. SC. Edward, D. 2019, Bishop Hart, Deacon,St. Stephen's, Pleebo.
Sonpon, D. Boniface, b. July 26, 1966 ; Dipl. SC Edwards, B.Theo. Baptist Theo Seminary; D. 2007. P. 2008 ; Priest, St. Stephen's, Pleebo.
Sulloe, John T., b. September 28, 1961; Evangelist Foya District; Kissi Literacy School 1981' D. 2017 P. 2019, Bishop Hart.
Talmon, Wilmot B., b. February 29, 1964 Grand Bassa County; B.Theo CU D 2010, P 2012 Bishop Hart; Priest, St. Peter's Gbarnga.
Tamba, James, M., b. Lofa County 1960; BA Theo. CU; DMin. Sewanee: Univ. of the South; D. 1989, Bishop Browne, P. 1992, Bishop Neufville; Chaplain, CU.
Tamba, Stephen N., b. November 20, 1992. Dipl. SC. Edward. D. 2019, Bishop Hart. Deacon, St. Peters, Gbarnga.
Targbe, Joseph Wargee, b. December 29, 1966; SC Edwards, dipl, D. 2007 P. 2010, Priest, St. Stephen's, Pleebo
Togba, D. Mark, b. August 12, 1960; BTh, GST, M.A, VTS, D. 1990, P. 2001, Bishop Neufville. Priest in charge, St. Timothy's Episcopal Church.
Togba, Jonah Nagbe, b. Sasstown November 10, 1931; CUC 1958-59 SC Edwards, 1966; D. 1968., P 1972; Vicar St. Augustine's Kakata, d. May 5, 1994.
Tomah-Fallah, John., b. June 19, 1965 ; St. Nicholas Theological College Cape Coast, Ghana (Licentiate in Theology). D. 1996 P. 2000, Bishop Neufville; Vicar, St. Theresa's Voinjama, Lofa County.
Ware, George O. B., b. February 9, 1972; Dipl. SC Edwards; D.2017 P.2019, Bishop Hart, Priest, St. John's Irving Mem, Robertsport.
Williams, A-Too, b. July 18, 1966; BA Biblical Studies, African Bible College, Malawi; S C Edward (Cert.), MTh, CU. MA, Peace Studies, Koffi Annan Institute of Conflict Transformation, UL ; D. 1999, P. 2001, Bishop Neufville; Trinity Cathedral, Rector St. Stephen's Sinkor.
Williams, Siede A., b. Aug 30, 1976 in Montserrado County; CU (BA. Theo),CU Graduade School (Pastoral Theology) D. 2015 P. 2017; Bishop Hart. Archdeacon, South Eastern Archdeaconry.
Williams, Thomas H., b. March 15, 1964 ; SC Edwards (Dipl. Theo.), CU B.Theo., D. 2004, P 2007, Archdeacon, LIBONI Archdeaconry.
Woart, Harris W., b. October 29, 1984 ; B.Theo., MA. Edu, CU D 2010 P 2012
Wreh, Prince T., b. December 24, 1957 BTh. CU, MA. EDS,. D, 1987, P. 1987 Priest, St. Wade Harris Episcopal Church, Stephen Tolbert Estate. Monrovia.

## Appendix 2

## LIBERIAN-BORN EPISCOPAL CLERGY
## IN THE DIASPORA (USA)

Afolabi, Andrew O., b. Nigeria June 10, 1938; D 1994, P 1995; BWH Sch., Trinity Cathedral, Mon., Lib., St. Aug. Gardnersville, Chaplain to Bishop Edward W. Neufville II; d. November 26, 2016

Bright, Dee Wellington, b. Rivercess, Bassa January 13, 1961; CU, ETS, Hartford Sem.; D.1986, P.1987; S John's Buchanan, BWH Sch. Mon., C-t-K Fort Worth, S Philip's San Antonio TX, S Peter's Springfield MA, Grace Ponca City OK, Ch of Our Savior Palm Bay FL

Bright, John Jellico, b. Rivercess 15 Nov 1931; UL, Liberia, Lafayette Col, PA, ETS, MA; D.1976, P.1977, chaplaincy, Bird S. Coler Hosp NY; Trinity Cathedral (curate & canon) Mon., S Stephen's Mon., Emmanuel Lib., Chapl JFK Hosp. Mon., S Peter's Richmond, Calvary Hanover, Trinity Highland Springs, VA

Bright, Wheigar Jefferson, b. Zorzor, Lofa 22 Apr 1958; CU, Nashotah House Sem. WI; D.1986, P.1987; S John's Irving Mem. Cape Mt, Trinity Cathedral, S Gabriel's Queens NY, S Barnabas Newark NJ, Grace Utica NY, Redeemer Greensboro NC, S. Luke's, Yanceyville NC, S Luke's Eden, NC

Brooks, Theodora Nmade, b. Grassfield, Nimba February 2, 1963; CU, VTS, VA, GTS, NY; D.1987, P.1989; Asst to Bp of Lib, St. Margaret's, Bronx NY

Carr, Burgess Alpha, b. Crozierville, Lib. July 8, 1935; CUC (BSc 1958, BD 1961) Harvard (MTh) D 1961, P 1962; Trinity Cathedral, Lib, Mass. WCC/Geneva, AACC Nairobi, Kenya; St. Cyprian, Prof. pastoral theo. Yale Univ, TEC Africa Desk, S Timothy's, Decatur, GA; d. May 14, 2012.

Cole-Bright, Enid Omodale, b. Monrovia, Liberia June 30, 1950; Bennett College, Univ. of MI (MBA), Edu for Ministry Program, Deacon prep Diocese of Wash. DC & National Cathedral; D (Vocational) Sept 22, 2018; Ascension (Gaithersburg, MD) St. Nicholas (Darnestown, MD), St. Peter's (Poolesville, MD).

Collins, Amos Bani Collins, b. Rocktown October 26, 1926; UL, CUC, GTS; D.1958, P.1959; S John's, Lower Buchanan, S John's Irving Mem. Cape Mt, S James, Hoffman Station, Bp Ferguson Sch., Ch of the Good Shepherd Paynesville, Trinity Cathedral, Bromley Girls Sch, Mon., S Mary's Cathedral, S Paul's Fajardo Banjul, The Gambia—d. March 2, 2013

Cummings, Alexander Benedict, b. Harper January 20, 1922; BA Liberia Coll 51; BA AMU Beruit. D 1973, P. 1974; St Thomas CJR, Grace Clay-Ashland, Supply Priest Diocese of NJ early 1980s; d. July 28, 2002.

Dennis-Boyd, Maggie, b. Harper, Lib, May 3, 19 40; UL Lib., SCEdwards, CU; D.1990, P.1992; Bromley Sch., CREDO Mon, Trinity Cathedral Mon., S Michael's & All Angels Baton Rouge LA.

Dunn-Greene, Matilda Eeleen. b. Greenville, Sinoe, June 13, 1952; CU, Bloomfield; College, U of Illinois Edwardsville, Sewanee Univ. of the South (MDiv & DMin) D.1994, P.1995; All Saint's Chapel Sewanee, St. Peter's Chatt, Grace Chatt. UTC Chaplaincy, St. Mark's Copperhill, TN, St, Barnabas, Triune, GA, Emmanuel, Potosí, MI; Episcopal. Community of the Cross-of-Nails, Assoc. St. Mary's Convent, Women Church History Project.

Flemister, Abeoseh M., b. Robertsport Cape Mt July 9, 1939; CU, CDSP (MA, 1965); first director Christian education, ECL; D.1997, P.1998; Asst to Bp of Lib, St. Matthew's Church Westerville OH; prior services in Dioceses of NY and NJ.

Flemister-Cassell, Ernestine, b. Monrovia, Lib April 8, 1952; Franklin Univ OH, Law School UL, Xavier Univ OH, Bexley Hall Sem Columbus, OH (DMin); D. 2006, P. 2007; Grace Cincinnati, OH, St. James House of Prayer, Tampa FL, St, Luke's Grant Staff, Oregon

Freeman, John Edgar, b. Robertsport, Cape Mt December 9, 1956; UL Lib., Freetown SL; D.1999, P.2004; BWH Sch., S Thomas, St. Stephen's, S Thomas NKT, Mon., S Stephen's Pleebo, Epiphany Cavalla, Lib., S John's Irving Mem. Cape Mt, Missioner to African Comm., S Luke's, St. Matthew's, Dio WM

George, Allen S. W., b. Harper May 26, 1963; CU, Southern U., D.1989, P.1990; Baton Rouge LA; S John's Irving Mem Cape Mt, S Michael's & All Angels Baton Rouge LA, St. Andrew's, Bronx, Nativity Brooklyn, Epiphany St. Simon, Bronx

Greene, Joseph L., b. Rivercess June 5, 1950; SCE Mem. Inst. Mon., CU Theo (Special Student); D.1990, P.1992; St. Stephen's Monrovia, St. Mary's Bolahun, St. Thomas Chapel, Monrovia, St. Andrews's Anglican Mission (Charleston, SC), St. Paul's Anglican Church, Orangeburg, SC, retired.

Hanson, John H., b. Cape Palmas, Lib. Sept 8, 1946; UL, Syracuse Univ,, Florida State Univ (PhD), Diocese of NJ School for Deacons; Liberian Star newspaper; Vocational Deacon. 2002; Archdeacon Pastoral Care, Diocese of NJ,, St Thomas Glassboro & Chaplain Rowan Univ.

Harding, Christian Charles, b. Sierra Leone December 25, 1933; BS, Fourah Bay, SC Edwards . D.1981, P. 1982; Trinity Cathedral, B.W Harris School, Monrovia V. Prin. S John's Irving Mem. Cape Mt., S John's Buchanan, Bassa; S Augustine's, Oakland, CA.

Harmon, John T. W., b. Harper 16 November, 1964; S Paul's Col VA, VTS (MDiv); D.1991, P.1992; S Stephen's, Hampton VA, Trinity, DC

Howard, David Zayana., b. Liberia Sept 15, 1937, U of Lib (BSc, 1960), Pittsburgh Theo Sem. (BD), D 1979, P 1981; Trinity Cathedral, S Thomas CJR Mon., Cincinnati, OH

Johnson, Emmanuel Dabe-Wea, b. Fishtown, May 24, 1924; Langston Univ., Roosevelt Univ, SC Edwards ; LLD & DD (honorary);' D.1968, P.1970; S. John's Irving Mem. Cape Mount, Trinity Cathedral, Monrovia; Pres. CU, Dean Trinity Cathedral, Monrovia to 1990, St. David's, Ashburn, VA, USA, d. March 2, 2018.

King, Edward George Wilmot, Jr.. b Harper, Cape Palmas March 10, 1927. UL BS 1951, FiskU BA 1954, Boston U MS 1959.SC Edwards; D. 1969, P. 1970. S. Thomas, Monrovia, Dean Trinity Cathedral 1972-1980, Grace NY 1980-83, Vicar St, Michael & All Saints Charlotte, NC to 1993. d September 1993

King, Victor Moses, b. Monrovia February 4, 1961; CU Theo, 2000, Cert, Church Leadership CPWA, Trauma Training UNMIL, 1996. D. 1996, P 1997, S Timothy New GA, St John's Buchanan, Trinity Cathedral, Grace Clay Ashland, St. Aug. Kakata, SW Archdeacon, Calvary Andover VA

Kowbeidu, Anthony, b. Monrovia, Liberia February 18, 1964; Voorhees College (BSc), Sewanee: Univ. of the South (M.Div, DMin); D,2000, P.2000; St, Andrew's

Mission, Charleston SC, St. Andrew's Parish, Mt. Pleasant,SC (Assoc rector for Missions)

Merchant II, Wilmot T., b. Gbarnga December 28, 1961; CU, EDS, Weston Jesuit Sch of Theol MA, Drew U. NJ; D.1986, P.1987; S Stephen's Mon., S Bartholomew Cambridge, MA, S Paul's Patterson NJ, Trinity Bronx NY, S Stephen's NMB SC

Mitchell, John Worjloh. b. Monrovia October 1, 1975; UNU (BA), M.Div (Luther Seminary); D, 2004, P. 2007, Bishop Neufville; St. Augustine Gardnerville, Good Shepherd, Grace Clay Ashland, Trinity Cathedral Monrovia, S Andrew's Minneapolis, MN

Shannon, Himie-Budu, b. Monrovia, March 26, 1954; S Aug. Raleigh, NC, VTS (MDiv); Trinity Cathedral, Good Shepherd Paynesville, S Monica's Hartford CT, CTK Charlotte NC, S Andrew's Cleveland, OH, d. February 2, 2015

Speare-Hardy, Benjamin E. K., b. Monrovia May 31, 1958; S Aug, Raleigh NC, VTS (MDiv); D. June 1992, P. December 1992; Holy Comforter, Wash.DC, Christ Church, VA, A Mary Magdalene, rector, S Margaret's Trotwood, OH

Thompson, Edward Hnebe, b. Fishtown Lib Mar 21, 1962; WVST Tech Col, CU Lib., Int'l Sch. of Ev Nig., Nashotah House Sem. WI; D.1989, P.1990; Adm Asst to Bp of Lib, Trinity Cathedral, S Timothy Mon., S Paul's Bomi Lib., S Matthias Waukesha, S Andrew's S Martin's, Milwaukee, WI, S Paul's St. Croix USVI, All Souls S Luke's New Orleans LA, Trinity Galveston, TX

Vani, Benedict Silee., b. Loifa County, Lib. Sept 14, 1932; CUC, ETS (Kentucky) D 1976, P 1977; S Peter's Gbarnga Lib., S Michael's & All Angels SKT Lib., OHC Mission, Bolahun, GST, Ch of Our Savior Palm Bay FL

Walker, Frederick W., b. Mon. November 21, 1961; Lic. Th. MA Theol; D.2007, P.2009; S Mark Suffolk, S James, Portsmouth, VA

Williams, Desmond Akpata, b. Mon. Sept 17, 1960; Dipl Th, BA Th, Lib; D.1987, P.1989; S Peter's Caldwell, Holy Name, Foya & Lofa Region, S Paul's, Sinoe, Lib; affiliate, Diocese of Delaware.

Wilson II, James Nyebe, b. Hoffman Station Lib Feb 28, 1961; CU, VTS, Luther Sem; S Thomas CJR, S Thomas NKT Mon., S Andrew's, S Philip's & S Thomas Minneapolis, Holy Trinity Minneapolis, MN

Yarsiah, James T., b. Mano River, Cape Mt, October 9, 1965; CU, Sewanee (DMin); D.1996, P.1997; St Stephen's, Trinity Cathedral, Mon., S Andrew's, Charleston, Voorhees Col, S Philip's Denmark, SC.

*Appendix 3*

# Chancellors of the Diocese Since 1976

J. Rudolph Grimes—1976–1993
Joseph P. H. Findley (Acting)—1993–1996
C. L. Simpson Jr.—1996–2001
Emmanuel S. Koroma—2002–2007
Comfort Natt—2007–2009
James E. Pierre—2009–2018
Seward M. Cooper—2018–

*Appendix 4*

# Presidents of Cuttington College/University, 1949–2019

The Rev. Seth C. Edwards, BA, BD, MSc.—1949–1960
Christian E.W. Baker, BA, MSc., DVM—1960–1972
The Rev. E. Bolling Robertson, BA, BD, DMin. (interim)—1972–1973
The Rev. Emmanuel W. Johnson, BA, MEd.—1974–1980
Stephen M. Yekeson, BSc., MSc., PhD—1981–1986
The Rev. Samuel Y. Reed, BA, MTh. (interim)—1987
Christian E.W. Baker (interim)—October 1987-February 1988
Melvin J. Mason, BA, MAT, EdD—1988–2002
Henrique F. Tokpa, BA, MA, PhD—2002–2015
D. Evelyn Kandakai, BA, MA, EdD (interim)—2015–2016
The Rev. Herman B. Browne, BA, BD, PhD—2016–

*Appendix 5*

# Brief Historical Sketch of St. John's Episcopal Church, Lower Buchanan, Grand Bassa County

One of the early churches in the Diocese, St. John's Episcopal Church inherited earlier ventures in mission of the Domestic and Foreign Missionary Society of the American Church in what became the Buchanan area in the 1830s. As the Missionary District of Cape Palmas and Parts Adjacent expanded beyond its base in Cape Palmas, The Rev. and Mrs. Jacob Rambo arrived as missionaries from Philadelphia in 1849 and were sent in 1853 to supervise the new mission station in Bassa Cove. (Later named Buchanan after the American Colonizationist Thomas Buchanan). The Rambos labored there through 1861.

Predating St. John's were St. Luke's in Edina, and St. Andrew's in Upper Buchanan. Bishop Samuel David Ferguson offered this account of the work in Grand Bassa County in his first Report in 1885 as head of the Church. "There were two functioning stations in the County, one in Upper Buchanan and the other in Lower Buchanan. The Church was mourning the loss in 1884 of the Rev. L. L. Montgomery. He had build perhaps the first chapel in Lower Buchanan and was completing St. Andrew's in Upper Buchanan, which the Rev. Paulus Moort was placed in charge of in March 1885. A Day School was begun by L. L. Herring, There were 18 communicants at St. John's and St. Andrew's combined."

By 1905 the Bishop reported continued healthy conditions in the sub-district now under the superintendence of the Rev. R. C. Cooper. St. Luke's chapel, Edina, had been completed and consecrated. "It is said to have cost $3,000 to build and furnish it; three-fourths of which was contributed by the people themselves. The Rev. J. S. Smith is in charge. I spent Passion Week and Easter there last year, when interesting services were held. A day school has been opened in Edina, a Vestryman pledging the teachers' salary for two years. The tower of St. Andrew's church has been completed at last. Both there and in St. John's Lower Buchanan, the work is vigorously prosecuted."

There was much activity in the Bassa sub-district, including Lower Buchanan, prior to the erection of the first church edifice of St. John's. A small community of communicants of the Episcopal Church met in the homes of parishioners before a small chapel was constructed. The first General Convocation of the Missionary District of Cape Palmas and Parts Adjacent was held at St. Andrew's, Upper Buchanan February 1–5, 1888. Two other General Convocations convened at St. Andrew's, the fifth in 1899 and the ninth in 1907. On February 25, 1912, Bishop Samuel David Ferguson consecrated the new and first edifice of St. John's Episcopal Church, Lower Buchanan, and the following year St. John's hosted its first General Convocation, the thirteenth, from April 14–23, 1913. On that occasion a change in nomenclature of the missionary district occurred, from the Missionary District of Cape Palmas and Parts Adjacent to the Missionary District of Liberia.

Following the death in 1916 of Bishop Ferguson who had provided effective leadership to the Church for some three decades, a leadership crisis developed. In response, the American Church sent a Commission headed by Bishop Arthur S. Lloyd to review the work in the entire missionary district and submit recommendations for consideration of the American Church. Here is what the Lloyd Commission said about the work in Grand Bassa County:

> Grand Bassa is one of the four important points on the coast from the viewpoint of industrial development. Once Liberia is eased from the machinations of those who would defraud her and becomes able to develop her resources, Grand Bassa will be a centre of influence and development and will be the point of contact with a large and rich territory thickly settled by people capable of development in every direction. Happily the Church is well established here. The people being prosperous have been generous in their gifts to the work of the Church. Their buildings are good and in good repair and besides the gifts which are regularly made, they are planning to assume support of their rectory. Because of the importance of this work as well as on account of its being rather difficult, Dr. Dunbar has been asked to be responsible for it, resigning the superintendency of Cuttington which he has filled with credit for fourteen years. There are four other important stations in the neighborhood of Grand Bassa—Hartford, Upper Buchanan and Tobacconnee. The men in charge are all doing good work, but it is probable that when a Bishop is appointed for Liberia he will arrange this work so as to release perhaps two of these men for work in the interior. The School at Grand Bassa is good and doing useful work, but it should be self-supporting and no doubt will become so as soon as Dr. Dunbar has had time to show the people the strength that cordial cooperation will develop.

The significance of the work of the Church in Grand Bassa County, particularly St. John's, Lower Buchanan, was reflected in the hosting of General Convocations spanning the episcopacy of most of the Bishops of the period—Bishop Ferguson (1913), Bishop Campbell (1929), Bishop Harris (1947, 1955), Bishop Dillard Brown (1964), Bishop George Daniel Browne (1975), and Bishop Edward W. Neufville (2000). There was no Convocation during the episcopacy of Bishop Leopold Kroll.

In his first Report in 1945 on the Missionary District of Liberia, Bishop Harris wrote the following about the Grand Bassa District of the Church:

> The work in this District is under the active leadership of Archdeacon F. A. K. Russell who is also the rector of St. John's Church, Lower Buchanan. Dr. Russell is one of the best-prepared men in the District and thoroughly capable of effective work. St. John's Church, Lower Buchanan, 175 communicants, is the strongest congregation in this area and the most active. The church building is galvanized iron and frame construction, but makes a good appearance and is kept in good condition. There is a school building of frame construction and in poor condition. The school has been closed for some time, but will reopen this year. This is a community that before the war depended upon exporting palm oil and piassava, and since this business was cut off during the war, has suffered. It is beginning to recover just now. It is also one of the communities where the Roman Catholic Church is making a strenuous effort and especially through its school. We have a large opportunity here.

A gem in St. John's education ministry is the Parish Day School that dates to at least a century. The school was refurbished in 1958, along with counterpart schools in Monrovia, Sinoe, and Maryland. Bishop Harris called them "decent modern schools" constructed with $200,000 from the Church School Missionary Offering of 1956, with contribution of $100,000 from the Government of Liberia.

St. John's was also instrumental in the establishment of St. Mary's Chapel, which for many years was lead by an industrious and energetic son of Buchanan, The Rev. Daniel G. Harris.

The Bishop reported on other churches in the District—St. Andrew's Upper Buchanan ("in a dying community"); St. Luke's Edina ("an old congregation and active," served by The Rev. J. T. Weaver); St. Philip's Fortsville (old but static community served by a retired priest, the Rev. William Alexander Greenfield); St. Michael and All Saints, Timbo, and St. James, River Cess, both served by the Rev. N.J. Jackson ("a most faithful and untiring worker.").

St. John's has enjoyed over the years the services of people of stature in the Episcopal Church of Liberia, clergy and laypeople alike. Among the clergy was The Rev. Dr. Joseph Fulton Dunbar who came to Buchanan following 14 years of service as principal of Cuttington College. Another clergy of prominence was The Rev. Dr. Fretus Africanus Kawi Russell, a product of the old Cuttington College in Cape Palmas, who with his brother, the late Chief Justice Martin Nimle Russell, settled in Buchanan and became prominent citizens. Rev. Russell was intimately involved in matters of State during the presidency of Edwin J. Barclay (1930–1944). Yet another was The Rev. Nathaniel Jethro Jackson who was a conscientious worker, serving St. John's diligently from 1947 through 1956 before his transfer to St. James, River Cess where he ended his career.

And then there are those hearty souls, many of them lay people who assumed the mantle of leadership in the construction of the second St. John's Church edifice, the present building. The cornerstone was laid December 2, 1962 and the building consecrated in 1964.

The cornerstone carries the following leaders:
The Right Rev. B. W. Harris, Bishop
The Right Rev. Dillard H. Brown, Bishop Coadjutor
The Rev. Fr. A. Bane Collins, Rector

Vestry:
Martin Nimle Russell, S.W.
Joseph P. H. Findley, J.W.
Samuel W. Payne
James G. Johnson
Edward L. Dunn
Philemon E. Harris, Sec.
Solomon H. Greaves, Treasurer
Edward L. Dunn, Building Chairman

A Succession of St. John's Clergy (partial):
The Rev. L. L. Montgomery (1878–)
The Rev. Paulus Moort, MD (1883–)
The Rev. James Skirving Smith (1902–)
The Rev. Josiah Randolph Davis (1903–)
Rev. Micaiah W. Goda Muhlenburg (1905–)
The Rev. Dr. John Wesley Pearson (1914–)
The Rev. Dr. Joseph Fulton Dunbar (1916–)
The Rev. J. Aladubi Johnson (1922–)
The Rev. James Pitman Harmon (1920s–)
The Rev. Henry Bagbo Wilson (1920s–)

The Rev. James David Kwee Baker (1929)
The Rev. Charles A. E. McIntosh (1930s–)
The Rev. Joseph T. Weaver (1930s–)
The Rev. Dr. Fretus Africanus Kawi Hemie Russell (–1947)
The Rev. John F. N. Brownell (1939–)
The Rev. Nathaniel Jethro Jackson (1947–1956)
The Rev. Lazarus Chike Okeke (1956–1962)
The Rev. Amos Bane Collins (1962–1968)
The Rev. Thomas S. Smith (1979–)
The Rev. Daniel Giakquee Harris (St. Mary's, 1974–)
The Rev. Philip Kpah Sherman (1972–1986)
The Rev. Momo B. Kpartor (2007–2008)
The Rev. Victor Moses King (2000–2005)
The Rev. Christian Charles Harding (1992–1997)
The Rev. Dee Wellington Bright (1987–1992)
The Rev. Edwin B. T. Nimley (2005–2007)
The Rev. Augustus G. Quoi (2008 to present)

# List of Interviews

Bright, John Jellico (2016, telephone and email)
Brooks, Theodora (May 14, 2018, email)
Browne, Clavender Railey (January 11, 2017, Milwaukee, WI)
Browne, Herman B. (October 18, 2016, Cuttington, Suakoko; and email)
Clarke, Charles A. (January 30, 2019, Monrovia)
Cooper, Seward M. (June 20, 2019, email).
Eiwuley, Anthony (The Rev. Canon, Provincial Secretary, CPWA, October 25, 2017, October 27, 2017, and July 2, 2019, email)
Fageol, Suzanne A. (June 27, 2018, telephone and email)
Flemister, Abeoseh B. (August 24, 2017 and February 8, 2019, email)
Flemister, Clifton (December 26, 2018, email)
Freeman, John Edgar (February 24, 2019, email and telephone)
Harding, Christian C. (January 6, 2017, email)
Harris, Elijah (February 2, 2019, Lr, Buchanan, Grand Bassa County, Liberia)
Hart, Bishop Jonathan B. B. (October 13, 2016 and October 21, 2016, Monrovia)
Hines, Deborah Harmon (January 19, 2019, email)
Horton, Romelle A. (November 19, 2018, email)
Howe, Emmanuel (2017, Monrovia)
Jayjay, Roosevelt G. (August 9, 2018 and October 31, 2018, Monrovia)
Jones, G. Alvin (August 8, 2016 in Silver Spring MD and December 26, 2018, telephone)
King, Victor (2018, telephone)
Lawrence, Brother OHC (September 8, 2010, West Park, NY)
Mason, Jonathan (August 28, 2018, Monrovia)
Mulbah, Charles K. (October 23, 2018, email)
Mulbah, Elizabeth S. (March 13, 2019, email)

Neufville, Louise Morias (March 1, 2016, telephone and Sumter, SC)
Quoi, Augustus (February 2, 2019, Lr. Buchanan, Grand Bassa County, Liberia)
Roberts, H. Augustus (January 26, 2019, Monrovia)
Sarfo, Archbishop Daniel (April 26, 2017, email)
Sellee, James B. (October 19, 2019, Monrovia)
Simpson, Alpha (2017, Monrovia)
Thompson, Edward (July 5, 2018, email)
Urey, Clemenceau (April 2018, telephone, Monrovia)
Ward, Amelia H. (February 2017, Monrovia)
Williams, A-Too (October 11, 2018 and April 23, 2019, Monrovia)
Yarseah, James (November 26, 2018, telephone)

# Bibliography

The bibliography includes primary archival as well as printed sources.

## PRIMARY ARCHIVES

Archives of the Episcopal Church, Austin, Texas. Domestic and Foreign Missionary Society (DFMS Papers). Boxes 2–18.
Preliminary inventory by the Archives produced a rough box listing which I viewed as follows:
Box 2: *Journals of the Diocese of Liberia* and other occasional reports, 1970–1988; Mixed Papers, c. 1994–1998, including newsletters, leaflets, service leaflets, events programs and announcements and occasional publications.
Box 3: Mixed Papers, c. 1978–1995.
Box 4: Mixed Papers, c,. 1968–1990.
Box 5: Mixed Papers, historical items, listed by folder; 1985, 1993; Bromley Mission School 1969–1988; Cuttington 1989–1990; 1985–1989; 1989–1993; 1979–1984.
Boxes 6–12: Mixed papers, very unorganized.
Boxes 14–18: Mixed papers, many loose in box.
My four visits to the archives in 2015 and 2016 drew considerably from this collection.
Archives of the Episcopal Church (USA). *Journal of the General Convention* and *Journal of the Special General Convention*, available online at https://www.episcopalarchives.org/governance-documents/journals-of-gc.
Dunn Archives. Silver Springs, Maryland, USA, and Monrovia, Liberia. (Author's files and archives of original documents of church collections and letters.)
*Journal of the Diocesan Conventions of the ECL*. 1863 to 2017.
Collection drawn from DFMS Papers and a number of individual collections, including D. Elwood Dunn and Bishop Jonathan B. B. Hart.

Liberia Papers of the Order of the Holy Cross. Holy Cross Library, West Park, New York. Reviewed September 2016.

Papers of Bishop Edward W. Neufville II. Sumter, South Carolina.

Through the kind courtesy of Mrs. Louise Morais Neufville, widow of the late Bishop Edward W. Neufville II, and their son, Edward W. Neufville III, I was able to access the private and as yet unorganized papers at their homes in Sumter, South Carolina, and Paynesville, Liberia over the years 2016 through 2019.

Papers of the Rt. Rev. George Browne and Records of the Diocese of Liberia. c. 1866–1998, 19 cubic feet. Located at Archives of the Episcopal Church, Austin, Texas.

This primary source is dominated by the papers as donated by The Rev. Herman Browne and his mother Mrs, Clavender Railey Browne. The Archives notes: "This is a collection of mixed files gathered and packed in early fall 2004 by Verlon Stone and Elwood Dunn from papers scattered throughout Bishop Browne's house in Virginia [Montserrado County, Liberia]. Many folders throughout were marked by the gatherers as 'disturbed by rebels.' Hanging files were replaced and loose papers were batched for boxes 6–19 as well. When no date is given for a box . . . the bulk of the material generally falls into the range 1972–1990."

## SOURCES

Berkeley, Bill. *Liberia: A Promise Betrayed: A Report on Human Rights*. New York: Lawyers' Committee For Human Rights, 1986.

Browne, George D. "Are Bishops Essential to the Church? What can we expect from our Suffragan?" Sermon by Archbishop George D. Browne on the occasion of the Ordination and Consecration of The Ven. Edward W. Neufville as Suffragan Bishop, Trinity Cathedral, May 6, 1984. 6 pages. Dunn Archives.

———. *The Autobiography of George D. Browne (1933–1993): Tenth Bishop of Liberia, Sixth Archbishop of the Province of West Africa*. Praha, Czech Republic: SÍŤ—Ecumenical Publishing, 1998.

———. "Christian Approach to the Adherents of The African Traditional Religions." Unpublished manuscript. 97 pages. (Complete with acknowledgment by author and dated Spring 1993, Milwaukee, WI. Author also acknowledges Bishop Dillard Brown for sending him to graduate school, and his VTS professors in Systematic Theology, and his children for sheltering him in Wisconsin. "To them is my acknowledgment and salute. God bless us all. GDB.").

———. "Dare To Be Different." Address to the Popolebo (Kru/Klao Organization), Monrovia, Liberia. August 11, 1989. 6 pages. DFMS Papers.

———. "Diaries and Log Books." 1970s, late-1970s-early-1980s, 1980, 1980–1982, 1982–1985; Log No. 4 (June–December 13, 1986), early 1980s to c. 1986, 1987, 1991–1992. Dunn Archives.

———. *The Episcopal Church of Liberia Under Indigenous Leadership: Reflections On a Twenty Year Episcopate*. Lithonia, GA: Third World Literature Publishing, 1994.

———. "New Structures for a New Day." Commencement Address, Baptist Theological Seminary, Schieffelin, Liberia. December 8, 1986. 6 pages. DFMS Papers.

———. "Our Responsibility For the Future Life and Character of Liberia." Inaugural Sermon. Delivered January 5, 1986. Monrovia, Liberia. DFMS Papers.

———. "The Philosophical and Structural Environment of the Liberian School System." Address to the 1983 Graduates of B. W. Harris Episcopal School. Monrovia, Liberia Dunn Archives.

———. "Religion and The Liberian Revolution." April 13, 1982. 5 pages. Dunn Archives

———. *Ten Years Episcopacy: A Reflection.* Sandpoint, ID: St. Agnes' Vicarage, 1980.

———. "The Theological Mindset of the Liberian Society." Commencement Address. Baptist Theological Seminary, Schieffelin, Liberia. Class of 1980. 7 pages. DFMS Papers.

———. "A Tribute To The Late President Tubman. July 26, 1971. 4 pages. DFMS Papers.

Browne, Herman B. *Appreciating Pentecostalism.* Monrovia: National Printers, September 2011. 25 pages.

Carr, Burgess. "The Mission of the Moratorium." *Occasional Bulletin of the Missionary Research Library* 25, no. 2 (March-April 1975): 1–9 (New York).

Cason, J. Walter. "The Christian Church in the Evolution of Liberian Society." Annual Meeting of the African Studies Association. Orlando, FL, November 1995. 11 pages.

Church of the Province of West Africa (CPWA). "Minutes of the Provincial Standing Committee. Novotel, Conakry, Guinea." September 11–13, 2000. Under the chairmanship of The Most Rev. Robert G. A. Okine, Archbishop and Primate CPWA. 19 pages.

———. *The Church of the Province of West Africa: Constitution And Canons.* Revised. Accra: Anglican Press, 1990.

———. "Memo from Archbishop Robert Okine to ECL Officials. Subject: Election of a Diocesan Bishop of Liberia." October 31, 1995. 5 pages.

———. "Mandate for the Consecration of the Very Rev. Jonathan B. B. Hart as Bishop of the Episcopal Church of Liberia, from the Most Rev. Justice O. Akrofi, Archbishop and Primate." N.d. 1 page.

Dunn, D. Elwood. *A History of the Episcopal Church of Liberia, 1821–1980.* Metuchen, NJ: American Theological Library Association and the Scarecrow Press, 1992.

Dunn, D. Elwood, Amos J. Beyan, and Carl Patrick Burrowes. *Historical Dictionary of Liberia*, 2nd ed. Lanham, MD: Scarecrow Press, 2001.

Edward, Vivian J. "History of Cuttington College: 1949–1960." Mimeographed. Raleigh, NC: St. Augustine's College, 1984.

Ellis, J. Robert, Jr. "Assessment and Recommendations on the Church of the Province of West Africa." Monrovia, Liberia. December 2, 1985. 105 pages. Dunn Archives.

Episcopal Church of Liberia (ECL). "Aide Memoire to Bishop Jonathan Hart from The Sustainability Committee, Subject: Issues Requiring Urgent Attention." N.d. 2 pages.

———. (Anglican Communion). "The Enthronement Service of The Rt. Rev. Dr. Jonathan B. B. Hart As Second Archbishop of The Internal Province of West Africa (IPWA)." Church of the Province of West Africa, Trinity Cathedral, Monrovia, Liberia. July 6, 2014.

———. "A Concept Paper For Post-War Development of the Episcopal Church of Liberia." March 7, 2005. 9 pages. Dunn Archives.

———. "Endowment Plan 1988–1992, Bishop George D. Browne." 4 pages.

———. "The Episcopal Church In The New Millennium: Challenges and Opportunities," H. Augustus Roberts, Information Officer, Diocese of Liberia." June 2008. 27 pages.

———. *The Episcopal Church of Liberia: Constitution and Canons*. Amended. Accra: Anglican Press, 1987. Revised 1990.

———. "Mbalotahun Leprosy Colony." Historical Background. 2010. 15 pages. Dunn Archives.

———. "Northern Archdeaconry, Nimba, Bong and Lofa, ECL. Report To The 66th Diocesan Convention." By The Rt. Rev. Edward W. Neufville II, Bishop (Suffragan). Trinity Cathedral, Monrovia, Liberia. February 1–5, 1989. 13 pages.

———. "Order of Service At the Ordination and Consecration of The Ven. Edward W. Neufville II, BA, MST, Archdeacon of the Northern Archdeaconry, As Suffragan Bishop of Liberia." Trinity Cathedral. May 5, 1984.

———. "Report of The Committee Appointed by the Diocesan Council to meet with Retired Bishop Edward W. Neufville II. Subject: Special Committee meeting with Bishop and Mother Neufville." February 9, 2008. 3 pages.

———. "77th Diocesan Convention and the Celebration of 170 Years of Mission in Liberia." Epiphany Church, Grand Cavalla, Maryland County, Liberia. March 15–26, 2006. Bishop's Charge.

———. "Souvenir Programme, Consecration and Enthronement of the Very Rev. Jonathan B. B. Hart, BA, Th., M.Div. The Twelfth Bishop of Liberia." Trinity Cathedral, Monrovia, Liberia. March 2, 2008.

———. "Souvenir Programme, Installation and Enthronement of The Rt. Rev. Edward Wea Neufville II, BA, MTS, DD, the 11th Bishop of Liberia." Trinity Cathedral, Broad Street, Monrovia. January 6, 1996. Feast of The Epiphany.

———. "Strategic Plan Adopted at the Special Convention at the Episcopal Church of the Good Shepherd." Paynesville. February 14, 2019, 24 pages.

———. "A Strategy For the Third Cuttington, A Plan For the Rebuilding of Cuttington University College." Suakoko, Liberia. July 14, 1997, 24 pages.

———. "A Survey of the Administrative Organization of the Episcopal Church of Liberia, CORAT (Africa)." P.O. Box 42493, Nairobi, Kenya. July 1977. 48 pages. DFMS Papers.

———. "Thanksgiving Service Marking the Transferring of the Primatial Cross to the Most Rev. Dr. Jonathan B. B. Hart as the 11th Primate and Metropolitan Archbishop of the Church of the Province of West Africa." Trinity Cathedral, Monrovia, Liberia. March 3, 2019.

———. "Third Partners-In-Mission Consultation, Church of the Province of West Africa, the Diocese of Liberia." Monrovia, Liberia. November 20–24, 1983. 27 pages.

———. "Toward A.D. 2000—A Plan For Evangelism" Draft submitted by the Diocesan Evangelism Committee. August 1992. 7 pages.

Gay, John. *A Letter To My Children, With Much Love.* Self-published, 1999.

———. "The 50th Anniversary of the Holy Cross Mission at Bolahun." Cuttington College. February 22, 1972, 9 pages. Dunn Archives.

Gaygay, Kpana N. *Daunting Years: The Liberian Civil War In the Eyes of a Child.* Alexandria, VA: Forte Publishing, 2017.

Grimes, J. Rudolph. "Memorandum To: The Team Ministry." Episcopal Church of Liberia. June 28, 1993. 3 pages.

———. "A Tribute to the Memory of THE MOST REVEREND GEORGE DANIEL BROWNE, BSc, BD, DD, KGB, BISHOP OF LIBERIA AND ARCHBISHOP AND PRIMATE of the ANGLICAN CHURCH OFK THE PROVINCE OF WEST AFRICA." Grimes as Chancellor of ECL and CPWA. New York. February 27, 1993. 5 pages.

Holmes, Edward A. "The Rural Development Institute at Cuttington University College: Its Founding," *Liberian Studies Journal* 13, no. 1 (1989): 67–75.

Holt, Dean Arthur. "Change Strategies Initiated by the Protestant Episcopal Church in Liberia from 1836 to 1950 and Their Differential Effects." Ed.D. diss., Boston University, 1970.

Liberia Institute of Statistics & Geo-Information Services (LISGIS). "Census." 2019. https://www.lisgis.net/ (accessed October 8, 2019).

Mason, Melvin J. *Savoring Education: An Autobiography.* Columbus, GA: Brentwood Christian Press, 2007.

Mtingele, Mkunga. *Leadership and Conflict in African Churches: The Anglican Experience.* New York: Peter Lang, 2017.

Neufville II, Edward W. "Handwritten Note from Bishop Neufville to Bishop Browne." Monrovia, Liberia. May 18, 1990. ("Due to recent developments in Gbarnga, I was constrained to bring my family down to Monrovia for security reasons."). DFMS Papers.

———. "In the Valley of the Shadow in Liberia." By the Rt. Rev. Edward W. Neufville II, Suffragan Bishop of Liberia. *Virginia Seminary Journal* (December 1991): 42–45.

———. "Memo from Suffragan Bishop Neufville to "All Clergy of the Diocese. Subject: As you know, the late Bishop Browne requested that I should have nothing to do with or at his burial ceremonies, as relayed by his widow and children." March 5, 1993. (Same message faxed to Bishop Edward L. Salmon and Bishop Allen L. Bartlett Jr.)

———. "My Episcopacy." Draft autobiography. Courtesy of Mrs. Louise Morais Neufville. 35 handwritten pages. Dunn Archives.

———. "The Official Charges (Pastoral Letters) of The Rt. Rev. Edward Wea Neufville, 11th Diocesan Bishop of the Episcopal Church of Liberia." January 1996 to March 2007. Unpublished manuscript with Foreword by D. Elwood Dunn. 284 pages.

———. "Welcome Statement at the Opening of the Joint Covenant Committee Consultation." Monrovia, Liberia. April 26–28, 1999. 5 pages.

Neufville Family. "Draft Life Sketch, The Rt. Rev. Edward Wea Neufville, BA, M.Th. DD, 11th Diocesan Bishop of the Episcopal Church of Liberia, Second Suffragan Bishop of the Episcopal Church of Liberia. Courtesy of Mrs. Louise Morais Neufville. N.d. 8 pages.

Oliver, Roland. *The Missionary Factor In East Africa*. London: Longmans Green, 1952.

Pew-Templeton. "Global Religious Futures Project." 2016. http://www.globalreligiousfutures.org/ (accessed October 8, 2019).

Tokpa, Henrique Flomo. "The Challenges of Building the New Cuttington." *Cuttington Review*, Special Retrospective (2011–2012): 7–9

# Index

Africa, 10, 20, 32, 45, 48, 51, 59n70, 106, 109, 135, 147, 153; Christianizing of, 26, 144; East, 1, 3, 6n9; faith customs, 2, 20–21, 55; fear of religion/clergy, 2, 46; modern, 1, 23, 27, 143, 169; religious views, 2; and the United States, 2–3, 48, 56n14, 137; West, 1, 7, 9, 21, 32, 41–45, 47–50, 62, 69–72, 81, 85, 99–106, 117–18, 121–23, 125, 135–36, 141, 153; and white missionaries, 14, 30. See also Liberia; organizations; Organization of African Unity; religion
African Traditional Religions (ATR), 2–3, 6n5, 25, 59n70, 145
Akrofi, Archbishop Justice, 121–23
All African Conference of Churches (AACC), 56n14, 153
Allin, Bishop John M., 50, 134
American Schools and Hospitals Abroad (ASHA), 36, 104
Anglican Church of the Province of West Africa (CPWA), 1, 3–5, 7, 9, 19–21, 24–25, 48–50, 55, 59n70, 69, 72–76, 77n11, 77n13, 81, 85, 107–9, 117–19, 122–25, 131–32, 135–36, 141, 145–47, 151, 153

Bachelor of Divinity (BD), 21, 30–31, 53, 153
Baker, Christian E., 32–36, 38–39, 102–3, 134, 165
Baker, Rev. Fr. James D. K., 33, 47, 171
Baker, Nathaniel H. S., 15,
Baker Plan, 17
baptism, 3, 20, 95; Cavalla River, 95
Baptist Theological Seminary, 1, 20–21
Bolahun Alumni Family and Friends Association (BAFFA), 96
Boys Town Institute, 90, 101
Bright, Rev. Dee Wellington, 160, 171
Bright, Rev. John Jellico, xvi, 15, 17, 52, 63–65, 68, 76, 81, 160, 173
Bromley Mission, 18–19, 27–29, 31, 100–101, 111–13, 131–32, 140, 144
Brooks, Rev. Theodora, 24, 41, 52, 160, 173
Brown, Bishop Dillard H., v, 10–13, 15, 34, 47, 80, 151, 169, 170; assassination of, 10–13, 34, 47
Browne, Clavender Railey, 69, 76n4, 173, 176
Browne, Bishop George Daniel, xiii, 1, 4, 124, 147, 169; death of and interim period, 61–74; episcopate of, 7–60

Browne, Rev. Dr. Herman B., x, xvi, 52–53, 69, 77nn4–5, 77n16, 119–20, 125, 139, 154, 165, 173, 176
Bryant, Gyude, 15
Bryant, Mary Tedi, 29, 144

Carr, Rev. Burgess, 10, 72, 135, 147
Christian (-ity), 25, 123, 146, 148; approach, 9; and charity, 14, 133; Christianization of Africa, 26, 48, 59n70, 95, 123, 144; clergy, 8; and community, 28, 44, 97, 130; denominations, 2–3, 14, 42–44; ecumenicalism, 54–55, 145; education/training, 15, 22–23, 25, 27–30, 40–41, 63–64, 101–2; and identity, 3; and interfaith, 42, 46; and the Liberian population, 3, 5, 6nn5–6, 18–19, 28, 42, 48, 107, 143–45, 148; and marriage, 97; and ministry, 32, 64; missions, 1, 11, 86, 102; non-, 42; and stewardship, 11; studies, 1–2; syncretism, 1–2. *See also* Episcopal Church entries; evangelicalism; religion
Christian Organizations Research and Advisory Trust (CORAT), 1–4, 5n2
Church of the Province of West Africa (CPWA), 1, 3–5, 7, 9, 19–21, 24–25, 48–55, 59n70, 69, 72–76, 77n13, 81, 85, 107–9, 117–19, 122–25, 131–32, 135–36, 141, 146–48, 151, 153
Clarke, Charles A., 173
clergy, 8, 19, 34, 52, 63–64, 73, 76, 82, 90, 98, 134; Christian, 8; and civil war of 1990s, 46, 134; conferences/conventions, 43, 120–21, 126; education and training of, 21–22, 26–29, 40–41, 53, 94, 124, 139–40; and evangelism, 21, 54; and exchanges, 51, 132; gay, 109, 132; and insurance, 22; Liberian, 9–10, 13, 18, 26, 28, 41, 49, 51, 53, 132–34, 153–62; and living moral lives, 99; pension plan and fund, 22, 63, 93, 108, 111, 125, 127–28, 93, 108, 125, 127; and retirement age, 53; salary, 22, 46, 53; shortage of, 98; and unity, 126; women as, 23–24, 141. *See also* diaspora; Masons
Collins, Rev. Amos Bane, 21, 49, 69, 81, 160, 170–71
The Community of the Love of Jesus Christ (CLJ), 94, 96–97, 99
Constitution and Canons of the Diocese, 53, 55, 66–71, 121, 133, 147; Board of Trustees, 40; for Ecclesiastical Authority, 66; Law, 44; provincial, 67–68; provisions, 65, 110, 118, 120
conventions (of the Church), 13, 22, 89, 92, 98, 128, 135, 140–41; of 1963, 47; of 1967, 12; of 1970, 13, 23; of 1971, 27; of 1972, 19, 28. 99; of 1974, 48; of 1976, 48; of 1978, 81, 83; of 1982, 49, 88; of 1987, 42; of 1988, 8, 46, 53; of 1989, 84; of 1990, 8, 62–63; of 1993, 147; of 1994, 72, 92; of 1995, 72–74; of 1996, 84, 87–88, 90; of 1997, 53, 93–94, 99–100, 102; of 2001, 101; of 2002, 104; of 2005, 90; of 2006, 94, 119; of 2007 (at Cavalla), 92–94, 96, 98–99, 120–21; of 2008, 94, 99, 121–22; of 2011, 127, 129; of 2019, 129–30, 147, 175; of 2020, 131; and Bible study, 141; districting of, 47
Cooper, Eugene, 15, 64
Cooper, Steward M., 66, 163, 173
covenant, 46–51, 85, 109, 131, 133; agreement, 1, 13, 56n9, 89, 91, 92, 108, 127, 131–33, 135, 146; committee, 48–49, 90, 108–9, 135; plan, 48–49
Cummings, Rev. Alexander B., 22, 29, 52, 160
Cuttington College/University (CU), 10, 15, 18, 22, 24, 27, 30, 34, 49, 53, 80, 100, 102, 111, 113, 119–20, 127, 132–34, 139, 144–46, 153, 170, 183; Presidents of, 165

Cuttington University College (CUC), 30, 36, 41, 45, 64, 100–105, 107–8
Cuttington In Exile (CIE), 39–40, 102–6

Dadson, Bishop Joseph K., 69–72, 81, 109, 147, 151
diaspora, 3, 26, 54, 97, 106, 111, 128, 135, 151–53, 160–62
Doe, Pres. Samuel K., 8, 35, 39, 42, 44–46, 103, 146
Domestic and Foreign Missionary Society (DFMS), 10–11, 26, 55n5, 135, 167
Dukuly, Mother Wilhelmina, 20, 55
Dunn, D. Elwood, xvi; *History of the Episcopal Church in Liberia, 1821–1980*, xi, xiii

Economic Community Monitoring Group (ECOMOG), 103
Economic Community of West African States (ECOWAS), 48, 51
ecumenicalism. *See* Christianity
education, xi, 4–5, 10, 25–41, 53, 87–88, 90, 97, 100–101, 103, 124–27, 132, 137, 140; absence of, 12; approach to, 37; avenue to church membership, 18; for clergy, 21, 83; committees/boards, 27, 29, 34, 63, 100, 105–6, 128; communities as partners, 107; faith-based/religious, 15, 22–23, 30, 40–41, 63, 91, 96, 101, 125, 140; funding/grants for, 16, 18, 100; interruption/effects of war, 40, 99, 100, 140; in Liberia, 28–30, 37, 96, 99, 107; and ministry, 26–27, 99–107, 140, 143, 169; Ministry of, 39, 105; moral, 100, 140; planning, 21, 41, 84, 130; politics of, 33; and women/girls/females, 91, 112, 140, 144. *See also* degree titles; evangelism; theology; universities by name; UNESCO
Edwards, Rev. Seth C., 22, 30–35, 41, 80, 90, 101, 165

Eiwuley, Anthony, 137n10, 173
Ellis, Robert, 15, 49, 63
Episcopal Community in the United States (LECUSA), 26, 128–29, 133–35; service of Liberian priests, 26
The Episcopal Church (USA) (TEC), xi, xviii, 1, 3, 10–11, 85, 94–95, 108, 136; Archives of, xiv–xv, 55; budget/funding, 15–17, 27–29, 91, *92*, 93, 103–5, 109, 125–28; Covenant Agreement, 13, *92*, 108, 131, 135; external ties, 107–10; headquarters of, xiv, 9, 89, 118; identity/autonomy, 3–4; History Society of, xv; organizations of, 101; "triple ministry" (evangelism, education and healing), 26, 44, 143. *See also* Episcopal Church of the United States (USA)
Episcopal Church Drums, 90
Episcopal Church of Liberia (ECL), xi, xiii–xiv, 1, 26, 85, 117, 136, 139–43, 145, 147; Archbishops of, 5, 49, 51, 62, 71, 75, 81, 108, 122–23; Bishops of, xv, 49, 68, 73, 122, 126, 139, 151; clergy (Liberian-born in Diaspora), 160–62; clergy (since 1980), 154–60; displacement of, 19, 46, 63–65, 88; and education/schools, 37; external ties, 107–10; funding, *17*, 127–28; history of, 4, 23, 34, 79, 93–96, 143, 149; identity crisis, 141; leadership, 67; place of, 5; roles of, 95–96; women priests, 23–24. *See also* politics; religion; theology
Episcopal Church of the United States (USA), xiii, 50, 69, 108, 118, 148. *See also* Anglican Church of the Province of West Africa
evangelism (-ists), xi, 3–5, 14, 18–25, 50, 54–55, 63, 90, 112, 125, 130, 145, 148; and education, 27–28, 41, 84, 86–87, 111, 126, 140–41, 143; and faith healing, 20; and language,

54; lay, 18–19; ministry of, 26, 88, 93–99, 134, 137, 141, 143; missions, 18, 26, 29–30, 99, 127; programs, 15; and rural areas, 19, 41. See also Browne, Bishop George Daniel; Neufville II, Bishop Edward Wea

Fageol, Rev. Suzanne, xvi, 24–25, 173
Faith Healing Temple of Jesus Christ, 20–21, 55
Findley, Joseph P. H., 72–73, 163, 170
Flemister, Rev. Abeoseh Bowen, 22, 97–98, 112, 161, 173
Flemister, Clifton, 173
Francis, Bishop Michael Kpakala, 25, 81, 97, 144
Freeman, John Edgar, 161, 173

Gardiner, Bishop Theophilus Momolu Fikah, 81–82, 143, 151
Gay, John, xvi, 31–33
Gbarnga School of Theology (GST), 22, 24–25, 41, 53, 139, 153
Gibson, Deacon Rosetta D., 23, 144
Gibson, Rev. R. H., 23
Gibson, Pres. G. W., 143
Good Shepherd Episcopal Church: Paynesville, xv, 129, 97, 154, 176; Sumter, SC, 80, 113, 176
God, 8, 14–15, 20, 62, 75, 77n10, 80, 82, 85–87, 96, 98–99, 101, 113, 117, 121–23; and baptism, 3; belief in, 44; call of, 95, 110; and Christ, 88, 95; and fear, 87; glory of, 15, 87; and grace, 82–83; and intermediaries/spirit, 2; kingdom on earth, 81, 129, 137; loyalty to, 82; as man, 54; praise of, 120–21; and sin, 20; views about, 2; will, 53. See also baptism; religion
Government of Liberia (GOL), 27, 29, 34, 37, 94, 104, 129, 169. See also Liberia
Gray, Fr. William Vanii, 10, 40

Grimes, J. Rudolph, 48, 50, 53, 70–71, 76, 77nn15–16, 134, 163

Harding, Christian C., 171, 173
Harmon, Deacon Annie E., 144
Harris, Bishop Bravid W., 12, 21, 23, 27–28, 30, 33–35, 47, 51–52, 76, 80, 100, 140, 151, 169–70
Harris, Elijah, 52, 97, 118, 156, 173
Harris, Prophet William Wade, 19, 21, 50, 55
Hart, Bishop Donald, 75, 84–85
Hart, Bishop Jonathan B. B., xi, xiv–xv, 5, 52, 72, 97, 139, 141, 147, 151, 173; and education revival, 102–3; episcopacy of, 117–37; promotion of spirituality, 99
Hines, Deborah Harmon, 173
Hodges, Rev. Emmanuel Douglas, 9, 52, 63, 66, 69–73, 75, 85, 97–98, 101, 119, 156
Horton, Romelle A., 115n32, 173
Howe, Emmanuel, 138n21, 173

Interim Government of National Unity (IGNU), 65, 69, 103
Interfaith Mediation Committee (IMC), 46
Internal Province of West Africa (IPWA), 118, 124–25, 135–36

Jayjay, Roosevelt G., 128, 173
Johnson, Rev. Emmanuel W., 22, 34–35, 80, 134, 146, 165
Jones, G. Alvin, 15, 57n39, 173

Kandakai, Rev. Christopher K., 10, 25, 40, 69
Kandakai, D. Evelyn, 5, 165
King, Fr. Victor, 97, 118, 161, 171, 173
Kpartor, Rev. Momo B., 49, 52, 72, 74, 157, 171
Kulah, Bishop Arthur F., 46, 144–46

Lawrence, Brother OHC, 96, 173
Liberia (-n), xi, 1, 9–10, 45, 86; character, 1–4, 148; church attendance, 4; civil war, xiii, 2–3, 5, 17–18, 25–26, 39–46, 51, 54, 61–67, 76, 79, 84, 87–89, 96, 100, 102–3, 109, 112, 124–25, 134, 136, 140; clergy, 9–10, 13, 18, 24, 26, 41, 51, 53, 132, 134, 160–62; counties of, xi, xiii, 7, 9, 13, 24, 27, 30, 36, 42, 54, 64, 79–81, 83, 89, 92, 94, 96–101, 104, 106–7, 123–24, 144–45, 167–71; culture, 3–4, 48, 108, 136–37, 143, 147; faculty, 33–34, 38, 106; and folk religions/wisdom, 6n5, 14; indigenous population, 110, 119, 139, 143–44; interfaith movement, 8, 25, 42, 46, 63, 149; leadership, 33; learning methods, 32; literature of, 3, 32; "Little Liberia," 19; and national identity, 2–4, 9; non-European domination, 3; prejudices, 44, 82; religious identity, 2–3, 7, 18; rural areas of, 4, 19, 22, 26, 34, 36, 41, 52–53, 54, 80, 83, 96, 106, 119, 132, 144, 153–54; Sierra Leone, 20, 32, 44, 47, 59n70, 107, 124, 147; society, xiv, 1–2, 7–8, 25, 42–44, 54, 85–86, 139, 148; and True Whig Party (*Liberian Age*), 7, 29, 49. *See also* diaspora; Government of; National Democratic Party; National Patriotic Front; University of; Liberia Action Party (LAP), 37
Liberia Council of Churches (LCC), 8, 42, 44–46, 54, 65, 88, 145, 148
Liberia Institute of Statistics and Geo-Information Services (LISGIS), 6n4
Liberian Episcopal Community in the United States (LECUSA), xv, 26, 109, 128–29, 133–35

Mano River Union (MRU), 48, 51
Mason, Jonathan, 173

Mason, Melvin J., 29, 31, 33–34, 38–40, 58n58, 102–7, 158, 165
Masons (-ic), 42–42, 44, 55; Craft of Liberia, 43–44
Masters of Divinity (MDiv), 21, 24, 53, 119, 139, 153
Masters of Sacred Theology (STM), 10, 154
Mbalotahun Leprosy Rehabilitation Program (MLRP), 97
Memorandum of Understanding (MOU), 133–35
missionary (-ies), 4, 10, 15, 25, 75–76, 79, 95, 109, 139, 153, 167; in Africa (continent of), 1, 50, 59n70, 96, 100, 135, 167–68; and the early Episcopal Church, 23, 26, 32, 134; and education, 30–32, 126, 169; and evangelism, 18–26, 93–94; and leadership, 79–82; in Liberia, xiii, 11–12, 18, 33–34, 47, 130, 134, 139, 169; mindset, 11; outreach, 10; and race, 14; and self-reliance, 11–12; and subsidies, 13; Western, 147–48. *See also* Community of the Love of Jesus Christ; Domestic and Foreign Missionary Society; Liberia
Mulbah, Charles K., 106, 173
Mulbah, Elizabeth S., 87, 96, 173

National Democratic Party of Liberia (NDPL), 37
National Patriotic Front of Liberia (NPFL), 8, 65
National Patriotic Reconstruction Assembly Government (NPRAG), 103
Neal, Juanita, xv, 115n36, 132
Neufville, Mrs. Louise Morais, xiv–xv, 81, 97, 111–12, 174, 176
Neufville II, Bishop Edward Wea, xiv, 4–8, 24, 61, 65, 73, 75, 118, 123, 147, 151, 160; draft manuscript, 76n3; episcopate of, 79–113

Neufville III, Edward W., xv, 176

Okine, Archbishop Robert G. A., 73–75, 81, 108
Order of the Holy Cross (OHC), xiv–xv, 25, 30, 40, 94, 96–99, 104, 140, 143, 151, 173
Organization of African Unity (OAU), 51

pension. *See* clergy
politics, 8, 10–11, 29, 34–37, 55, 73, 83, 103; and decolonization, 47; of education, 33; effects on the Church, 37, 46, 109–10; and instability, 50–51, 76, 109, 136; and oppression, 88; and radicalism, 35; and violence, 42–44, 89, 140; and war, 7–8, 17, 42, 51, 76, 89, 109, 136

Quoi, Augustus, 158, 171, 174

RAFIKI Foundation, 101
Reed, Rev. Samuel Y., 38, 52, 102, 165
religion, 43, 141; African tradition, 2, 9, 25, 59n70, 145; in Africa, 3, 6n5, 144–45; Articles of, 123; and ethnic conflict, 148–49; and faith healing, 21; and fear, 2; identity, 2–3; inter-, 8; leadership, 53, 55, 88, 141; Liberian approach to, 2, 43; organizations, 26; persecution, 58n56; pluralism, 59n70; syncretism, 1–2; and tolerance, 149
Roberts, Jr. H. Augustus, 137n4, 138n28, 174
Robertson, Rev. E. Bolling, 34, 40, 126, 165
Rural Development Institute (RDI), 36

Salmon, Bishop Edward, 68, 76n4
Sarfo, Archbishop Daniel Y., 117–18, 125, 174
Schori, Presiding Bishop Katherine Jefferts, 128, 136

Scruton, Bishop Gordon, 132–33
Seaman Church Institute Outreach Ministry, 94, 98
Sellee, Rev. James B., 49, 52–53, 97, 119–23, 139, 146, 159
Sherman, Charles D., 15, 33, 42, 48
Sherman, Mary Antoinette Brown, 29
Sherman, Rev. Philip Kpah, 80, 171
Sierra Leone. *See* Liberia
Simpson, Alpha, xvi, 174
Simpson Jr., C. L., xv, 163
Sirleaf, Pres. Ellen Johnson, 123
stewardship, 4–5, 63, 83, 110, 125, 127, 145; in the 1980s, 16–18; ministry of, 88–93; patterns, 48; and self-support, 10–18
Strategic Plan of 2019, 129–36, 141, 145
St. John's Episcopal Church, Grand Bassa County, v, 89, 167–71, 173–74
St. Martin-on-the Mount Episcopal Church, 80, 93
St. Stephen's Episcopal Church, Sinkor, 16, 126, 154
St. Thomas Episcopal Church, Camp Johnson Road, 97, 119, 126, 134
St. Thomas Episcopal Church, New Kru Town, 94, 97, 121
Suffragan Bishop, 8, 26, 61–67, 79, 89, 93, 109, 147; and growth of the church, 81–82; responsibilities of, 70–72

Taylor, Pres. Charles. G. M., 8, 64–65, 103, 105
Team Ministry, 66–72
theology, 25, 91; adaptation, 11; Africanized, 147; education/training, 15, 21–22, 31, 34, 40–41, 46, 53, 63, 80–81, 101, 106; mindset of the Liberian people, 1–4; and "philosophy of development," 88; spirituality and schizophrenia, 2; terms, 69

Thompson, Rev. Edward, 87, 101, 112, 114, 162, 174
Tokpa, Henrique F., 39, 102–7, 111, 165
Tolbert Jr., Pres. William R., 7, 35, 42–43, 46, 58n58, 146; assassination of, 44
Trinity Cathedral, 7, 16
True Whig Party, 7, 29, 42
Tubman, Pres. William V. S., xiii, 10–11, 23, 32–34, 42–43, 46, 58n56
Tulay, Jeremiah, 15

United Nations Educational, Scientific and Cultural Organization (UNESCO), 39
United States Agency for International Development (USAID), 36–37

United Thank Offering (UTO), 16, 132
University of Liberia (UL), 30, 34–35, 39, 45, 105, 144, 154, 183
Urey, Clemenceau B., 118, 127–29, 174

Vicar General, 9, 65–66, 69–75, 110, 119, 121–22
Virginia Theological Seminary (VTS), 10, 24, 81, 84, 135, 154

Ward, Amelia H., 174
Williams, Rev. A-Too, xvi, 87, 121–22, 159, 174

Yarseah, James, 174
Yekeson, Stephen M., 35–39, 45, 102, 165

# About the Author

**D. Elwood Dunn** (BA, Cuttington College & Divinity School; MA, PhD, The American University) is the Alfred Walter Negley Professor of Political Science Emeritus, Sewanee, The University of the South. He has taught at Seton Hall University, Fordham University at Lincoln Center, Cuttington University, and the University of Liberia. He served in the government of his native Liberia (1974–1980), becoming Minister of State for Presidential Affairs (Chief of Staff, Office of the President of Liberia). As a scholar, Dunn has authored, co-authored, and edited several books and articles. He was editor of the *Liberian Studies Journal* (1985–1995). Dunn is a prolific orator and public speaker, having been called upon twice to provide national orations of Liberia by two Liberian presidents; just as he was once often called upon to chair special Presidential Commissions to investigate matters of state. He was interviewed on public television in the United States during Liberia's civil crises in 1990 and again in 2003, and interviewed as well on a number of radio stations in the United States, Canada, and Jamaica. He is married to the Rev. Dr. Matilda E. G. Dunn and they have four adult children and two infant grandsons

www.ingramcontent.com/pod-product-compliance
Lightning Source LLC
Chambersburg PA
CBHW052039300426
44117CB00012B/1894